Believing in Britain

The Spiritual Identity of 'Britishness'

Ian Bradley

LION

A Lion Book
an imprint of
Lion Hudson plc
Wilkinson House, Jordan Hill Road
Oxford OX2 8DR, England
www.lionhudson.com
ISBN 978-0-7459-5300-7

Hardback edition published by I.B. Tauris & Co Ltd 2007
This edition 2008
10 9 8 7 6 5 4 3 2 1 0

A catalogue record for this book is available
from the British Library

Typeset in 9.5/15pt Adobe Caslon Pro
Printed and bound in Malta

BELIEVING IN BRITAIN

Contents

Acknowledgements

I have derived considerable benefit from Tariq Modood, who has shared much of his own thinking on Britishness with me and kindly read and commented on several draft chapters of this book. I have also benefited from conversations with Ray Simpson, Jeffrey Richards, Robert Beckford, Dilwar Hussain, Steven Sutcliffe, Cheryl Malcolm, Jamie Walker and Alex Wright, my editor. Stephen Bates has been kind enough to give me a regular platform in *The Guardian*'s 'Face to Faith' column to air my views on this and other subjects. Readers of this volume will quickly discover how much I owe to *The Guardian* in more general terms. It has been a continual source of hugely useful information on British identity and has helped to shape the argument of this book at a number of points. It cannot, however, be held responsible for my obsession with perichoresis.

Ian Bradley
The feast day of St Mungo (a thoroughly British saint)

1 Believing in Britain

Disappearing and Reappearing Identities

Britain is in danger of disappearing. I am not thinking here of the threat of long-term flooding and coastal erosion posed by global warming but rather of the demise of Britishness as a concept, an idea and an identity. When the Dublin-based publishers of a well-known and much used school atlas announced in 2006 that they would no longer use the term 'British Isles' they were not simply reflecting Irish unease about the colonialist implications of this description but also echoing what opinion polls and census returns increasingly show about how the inhabitants of all parts of the United Kingdom now regard themselves. The 2005 Social Attitudes Survey, published in 2007, found that just forty-four per cent of the population said that 'British' was the best or only way of describing their national identity, as against fifty-two per cent ten years earlier. Among those living in Scotland, only fourteen per cent described themselves as feeling in any way British, compared with seventy-nine per cent who defined themselves simply as Scottish. For those living in Wales the figure was thirty-five per cent and even in England just forty-eight per cent of the population identified themselves as British, fifteen per cent fewer than in 1992. Other recent studies confirm a waning sense of Britishness among the long-term inhabitants of the United Kingdom. The 2001 census was the first in which a majority of those living in England marked their nationality as English rather than British.[1]

The word 'British' has disappeared from a number of major national institutions in recent years, thanks largely to the effects of privatization, the driving political ideology of the 1980s and 1990s. British Rail disappeared in 1993 to be replaced by more than thirty different train-operating companies. British Steel merged with a Dutch rival, Koninklijke Hoogovens, in 1999 to become Corus. British Telecom has become simply BT and British Gas has transmogrified into BG plc, Transco, Centrica and House.co.uk. British Leyland and British Road Services are more distant memories. Other icons of Britishness have gone – the Royal Yacht *Britannia*, which perpetuated the Roman name for Britain and the female figure who long personified the nation, was decommissioned in 1997. Britannia herself, who once appeared wearing her helmet and carrying her Trident on several coins of the realm, was demoted with the decimalization of the currency in 1971 and banished from her last resting place on the fifty pence piece in 2008. Mainstream political parties increasingly adopt a narrower national rather than UK-wide identity, presenting themselves as Scottish Labour or Welsh Liberal Democrats. Even the Conservatives have dropped their Unionist tag and followed suit.

Britain has largely disappeared from school history lessons. When I was at school in the 1960s, history involved a chronological progression from the Normans to the Victorians, fortified by a little red book entitled *Outlines of British History*. In their history lessons through the 1990s and early 2000s, my children have studied virtually no British history but rather endured a somewhat repetitive diet of twentieth-century world history focusing primarily on the USA in the 1920s and 1930s, the Russian revolution, Germany under Hitler and South Africa during apartheid.

The extent to which Britishness is disappearing as both a concept and a category came home to me when I reached the end of one of those interminable questionnaires which are among the hazards of modern working life, especially in the public sector. The last question in this particular university staff survey was on ethnic origin and provided boxes to tick for Scottish, English, Welsh, Irish, Caribbean, African or mixed race but none for British. This reflects how many young people feel now. When I asked those students in my 'Monarchy, Church and State' class who were born in the United Kingdom how they would describe their national identity, just thirty per cent identified themselves as British against seventy per cent who identified themselves as English, Scottish or Northern Irish (there was no one from Wales in the class). When I asked a further question as to which term best represented the country they felt that they belonged to, seventy per cent again responded England, Scotland or Northern Ireland, twenty per cent the United Kingdom, five per cent Britain and another five per cent gave a dual answer (UK and England or UK and Scotland). A more general survey of young people in Britain carried out by *The Face* magazine in 2002 revealed that most subscribed to the view that 'We don't know what British means and we don't care,' and sixty-five per cent said that they felt ashamed of being British.

Commentators have been chronicling the disappearance of Britain for some time. Much has been made of the effects of the erosion of the four historic pillars of British identity – the Empire, the monarchy, Protestantism and the parliamentary union of England, Wales and Scotland. Tom Nairn's *The Break-up of Britain* appeared in 1977, with the author subsequently writing a book entitled *After Britain* in 2000, the same year that saw the publication of Andrew Marr's *The Day Britain Died*. These authors have had in mind especially the growth of nationalist sentiment and the constitutional changes that have come in its wake, especially in Scotland. The Scottish Parliament which first met in Edinburgh in 1999 effectively ended the constitutional settlement of the United Kingdom set in train by the 1707 Act of Union.

The disappearance of Britain has been accompanied by the growth of separatist feeling on the part of the four nations that make up the United Kingdom. Partly thanks to the re-establishment of the Edinburgh Parliament, there has been a distinct flowering of Scottish identity and self-confidence, manifested as much in economic performance and cultural vitality as in the political sphere. Although Wales is notably less self-confident and buoyant, Welsh identity is also becoming more marked. After a long period of decline, the number of people speaking the Welsh language increased from 18.7 per cent to twenty per cent of the population between 1991 and 2001, thanks partly to the 1994 Welsh Language Act which gave Welsh and English equal status wherever appropriate and reasonably practical. Even in Northern Ireland, home of the most conspicuously pro-British and Unionist-inclined inhabitants of the United Kingdom, relative peace in the last few years has brought a growing sense of Irishness and a waning of Unionist sympathies. Official moves to appease nationalist sentiment and make the province less 'British' have included the renaming of the Royal Ulster Constabulary as the Police Service of Northern Ireland.

England remains in many ways the nation with the least clearly defined identity in the United Kingdom but this too is changing. Leading Conservative politicians have floated the idea of establishing an English Parliament and of having an English rather than a UK passport. St George's Day, which for long had little appeal or impact, is gaining in public profile and observance. Clinton Cards, the greetings card retailers ever on the look-out for new marketing opportunities, introduced St George's Day cards in 1995 and within two years were selling more than 50,000 each April. During the European football championships in 1996 several English fans began painting their faces with a red cross rather than the traditional Union Jack. By the time of the World Cup matches in 1998 those adorned with the English national emblem outnumbered those with the British one. Perhaps the clearest sign of a growing English consciousness is the appearance of St George's flags not just on church towers but on pubs, and on flagpoles in front of houses and lorries and cars. Indeed, the increasing presence of the St George's flag, the Scottish Saltire and the Red Dragon of Wales is one of the most visible indicators of the rise of more distinctive English, Scottish and Welsh identities. It is not so much that they are replacing the Union Jack, although that is happening, as that their appearance in so many places and situations betokens a whole new enthusiasm for flying flags which has not, except in Northern Ireland, been a noticeably British trait.

It is interesting and ironic that these trends coincide with a growing interest in the concept of Britishness on the part of academics, journalists and politicians. A whole new school of history has arisen in the last thirty years to examine the 'British question' and the formation of the United Kingdom out of its long-existent component parts. It has spawned a number of important books, notably Linda Colley's *Britons: Forging the Nation 1707-1837* (1992), Steven Ellis and Sarah Barber's *Conquest and Union: Fashioning a British State, 1485-1725* (1995), Alexander Grant and Keith Stringer's *Uniting the Kingdom? The Making of British History* (1995) and Keith Robbins' *Great Britain: Identities, Institutions and the Idea of Britishness* (1997). In some ways, this 'British project' reached its culmination in Norman Davies' massive work *The Isles: A History* (1999).

British history is also appealing at a more popular level. *The Pocket Book of Patriotism*, a slim book published at the expense of its author, George Courtauld, proved an unexpected bestseller in the run-up to Christmas 2004. It begins with a forty-page chronology outlining the major events in British history, includes a series of 'speeches, commandments and charters' drawing on Shakespeare, Elizabeth I and Churchill, and a selection of songs and hymns including the National Anthem, 'Rule

Britannia', 'Jerusalem' and the metrical version of the 23rd Psalm, and concludes with a list of Britain's colonies and dominions in 1920 and a guide to imperial weights and measures. The author, a City headhunter, wrote the book for the benefit of his own children and out of a more general concern at the level of ignorance about British history among the young, prompted by overhearing a boy on his commuter train to Essex who clearly thought Lord Nelson was a character in *Star Trek*. Rejected by publishers as being old-fashioned and inappropriate for today's market, it sold 26,000 in its first week of publication. Perhaps because it has been so neglected in schools, there does, in fact, seem to be a huge popular appetite for British history and a pride in British achievements, as suggested by the considerable success of recent television series like Simon Schama's *A History of Britain*, broadcast at the turn of the millennium, David Starkey's detailed portrayal of the lives of British monarchs and Niall Ferguson's revisionist and highly sympathetic treatment of the British Empire. Programmes celebrating the British landscape, wildlife and coastline have also drawn large audiences.

It is not just right-wing historians and nostalgic traditionalists who have become excited about Britishness. The topic has engaged and enthused many on the left. This is clear from the most cursory perusal of *The Guardian*, the Bible of the liberal chattering classes, which has devoted pages and pages in the last two or three years to discussing and defining British identity. The Fabian Society devoted its New Year conference in 2006 to the topic 'Who do we want to be? The future of Britishness' and subsequently ran a national competition in conjunction with *The Guardian* for an essay on the theme of Britishness. Left-leaning academics are rallying to the British flag. In *Britishness since 1870* (2004), Paul Ward, a former member of the Socialist Workers' Party, while conceding that 'since the 1970s there has been a sense of crisis about what it means to be British', celebrates the continuing strength of Britishness and argues that, decoupled from whiteness and embracing diversity and the potential for multiple simultaneous identities, it offers a much more open and inclusive future than a radicalized Englishness.[2]

No one has sought to promote and redefine Britain and Britishness with more alacrity than senior members of the Labour Government first elected in 1997. It could be argued that, in implementing the programme of devolution which gave Scotland its Parliament and Wales its assembly and dismembering classic British institutions like the House of Lords and the office of Lord Chancellor, this administration has done more to break up the United Kingdom than any previous British Government. There is, however, a counter-argument that the policy of devolution was essential to save the United Kingdom, taking the sting out of the nationalist threat and promoting a more equal feeling among the different constituent nations. It is too early to say whether the constitutional reforms unleashed by the Blair Government will have the long-term effect of weakening or strengthening the United Kingdom. It may well be that they ultimately prove less inimical to fostering a sense of shared British identity than the privatization agenda promoted so vigorously in the Thatcher and Major years. What is certain is that no previous government has made a more concerted and self-conscious effort to define, promote and redefine the concepts of Britain and Britishness than those elected in 1997, 2001 and 2005.

Notions of national identity played a key part of Tony Blair's New Labour project from its inception. Among his first priorities on becoming Prime Minister in 1997 was a personal crusade to re-brand Britain as a new, modern, forward-looking and self-consciously young country. This project, which gained the soubriquet of 'Cool Britannia', involved, among other things, a close flirtation with the short-lived Britpop movement, epitomized by Blur, Oasis and the Spice Girls, a somewhat ill-judged engagement with Formula One racing cars and the building of the Millennium Dome. This rather frenetic and overly cosmetic exercise has been followed by a more carefully thought-out and historically rooted attempt to define and promote British identity in the interests of social cohesion, inspired partly by evidence of deep-seated social alienation and fragmentation manifested in 2001 when riots broke out in Oldham, Bradford and Burnley. The Nationality, Asylum and Immigration Act 2002 required that UK residents seeking British citizenship be tested to show sufficient knowledge of English, Welsh or Gaelic and of life in the United Kingdom. As part of its aim to raise the status of becoming a British citizen, it also provided for the taking of an oath and pledge of allegiance at official civic ceremonies bestowing citizenship. A 'Life in the United Kingdom' advisory group under the chairmanship of Professor Sir Bernard Crick was appointed to deliberate on the appropriate curriculum, tests and ceremony for those seeking British citizenship.

At the same time as initiating a public debate on the nature of Britishness and the extent to which it should be explicitly taught to immigrants, the Government introduced compulsory citizenship classes in schools. Following the report of the Crick working party in 2003, it announced that those seeking British nationality would face tests in the English language and in British history, institutions and values. The first of the new civic ceremonies to bestow British citizenship took place in Brent Town Hall in North London in February 2004 with an oath of allegiance to the Queen and both the Union Jack and the National Anthem figuring prominently. In the summer of 2004, the Government launched a strategy to reclaim the Union Jack from extremists, encourage its flying from public buildings, make more use of it on official documents and generally promote it as a branding symbol.

In a significant shift from the emphasis on multiculturalism and diversity that had hitherto been New Labour talismans, community cohesion and pride in being British became the Government's new watchwords. The Home Office consultation paper, *Strength in Diversity*, which launched the Union Jack initiative, proclaimed:

> *We need to ensure that all citizens feel a sense of pride in being British and a sense of belonging to this country and to each other, and to ensure that our national symbols, like the Union flag and the flags of the four nations, are not the tools of extremists, but visibly demonstrate our unity, as we saw through the Golden Jubilee celebrations.*[3]

In November 2004, the Labour Party screened a party political broadcast under the title 'Proud of Britain'. A website subsequently launched with the same title made much use of Union Jack imagery and urged those who logged on to it to talk up Britain. The Home Office then issued a 145-page *Journey to Citizenship* in December 2004, hailed as 'the first ever official government history of Britain' and covering a huge range of topics ranging from an explanation of Christmas festivities such as kissing under the mistletoe to strictures on the importance of cleaning up dog mess and keeping front doorsteps rubbish free. In August 2005, a Home Office minister, Hazel Blears, told *The Times* that the Government was proposing to rename ethnic minority groups in an attempt to strengthen and highlight their British roots, so that they would be described as 'British Asian' or 'Muslim British' rather than 'Asian' or 'Muslim'. In January 2007, acting on recommendations by Sir Keith Ajegbo, a former London head teacher, the Education Secretary, Alan Johnson, announced that all secondary schools in the UK should teach 'Britishness' as part of the national curriculum. Specifically, he called for more focus on modern British history and the introduction of a new identity and diversity strand exploring the shared values and communal life of the United Kingdom in the citizenship component of the national curriculum at key stages three and four.

A key role in this reassertion of British patriotism and pride has been played by leading ministers in the Labour Government. Responding to the report of the Commission on Multi-Ethnic Britain in 2000, Jack Straw, then Home Secretary, said, 'Everyone should stand up for Britain and for British values and celebrate the nation's diversity. I do not accept the arguments of those on the nationalist right or the liberal left that Britain as a cohesive whole is dead.'[4] His successor as Home Secretary, David Blunkett, argued in a series of significant academic lectures that, in an age of migration, it is essential for a society to debate and define its foundation values and to inculcate them in its own citizens and newcomers. Like other senior Labour politicians, he sought to articulate distinctive British values and to argue that the time had come to make much more of these in preparing immigrants for naturalization and UK citizenship, a process which in the past had gone by default. As well as putting much more emphasis on shared citizenship and on markers of national identity and social cohesion such as a command of the English language and a commitment to British values, Blunkett also made a more emotional and visceral appeal to patriotism. In a fascinating lecture to the Institute of Public Policy Research in 2005 entitled 'A New England: An English Identity within Britain', he grasped the specific nettle of English identity and encouraged its reassertion within the context of an overarching British identity. Calling for the greater celebration of St George's Day, he produced a list of what made him proud to be English which included the urban landscape of his home town Sheffield, English poetry, the music of Vaughan Williams and Delius, Fabianism and the National Trust and a pantheon of radicals from the Levellers through Tom Paine to the Chartists. He also made clear his conviction that a sense of Englishness can thrive within an overarching British identity. Indeed, for him this overall British identity is strengthened by the celebration of the national identities within the United Kingdom: 'I would like to be English and British, just as the Scots are Scottish and British'.[5]

Tony Blair emphasized the theme of Britishness in several of his major speeches as Prime Minister, most notably in an address on integration in December 2006 in which he said that 'no distinctive culture or religion supercedes our duty to be part of an integrated United Kingdom'. Reflecting on the terrorist attacks in London on 7th July that year, he emphasized the extent to which most Muslims are proud to be

British and the need to balance multiculturalism and diversity with integration into the key values – belief in democracy, the rule of law, tolerance, equal treatment for all, respect for this country and its shared heritage – that 'define us as a people and give us the right to call ourselves British'.

No politician or public figure has thought and spoken more about Britishness, nor defended it so passionately and eloquently over the last ten years, than Gordon Brown, the proudly Scottish Chancellor of the Exchequer in Tony Blair's three governments, who took over as Prime Minister in June 2007. In his youth a strong and fiery advocate of devolution, Brown is now regularly castigated by Scottish Nationalists for ignoring the country of his birth. His budget speech in 2005 was attacked by Alex Salmond, leader of the Scottish National Party, for mentioning Britain forty-four times and Scotland twice. Britishness is the central and recurrent theme of a series of major speeches delivered by Brown since 2004 which exhibit a level of detailed argument, scholarship and passion rare in the utterances of modern politicians. Starting from the premise that 'We have not been explicit enough about what we mean by Britishness for far too long,' he calls for a 'recognition of the importance of and the need to celebrate and entrench a Britishness defined by shared values strong enough to overcome discordant claims of separatism and disintegration'. Like Blunkett, Brown emphasizes the shared values that shape British identity. In contrast to Blair's 'Cool Britannia' project, his vision of Britain is much more rooted in history – in the words of the perceptive political journalist Matthew d' Ancona, 'The Prime Minister posed with Oasis; the Chancellor quotes Cobden and Bright.' Brown has called for the establishment of a new Institute and Forum for Britishness bringing together politicians, academics and journalists to look in depth at 'how the ideas that shape our history should shape our institutions in the future and what effect that might have on policy' and set his Treasury aides and advisers on the task of assembling a database of quotes on British identity, characteristics and values culled from a wide range of literary and historical sources. In a widely reported speech to the Fabian Society conference on Britishness in January 2006, he floated the idea of Remembrance Sunday being turned into a day to celebrate Britain and even suggested that the British should emulate the practice of the North Americans and fly the Union Jack in their front gardens. He has returned to these themes in several speeches since becoming Prime Minister. Indeed, his first speech as Prime Minister to the Labour Party Conference in September 2007 made 80 mentions of

Britain or Britishness, as against only two of Scotland.

At times, Gordon Brown has come close to suggesting that Britishness provides the key to unravelling virtually every contemporary political and social problem:

> *I believe that just about every central question about our national future –*
> *from the constitution to our role in Europe, from citizenship to the challenges*
> *of multiculturalism – even the questions of how and why we deliver public*
> *services in the manner we do – can only be fully answered if we are clear*
> *about what we value in being British and what gives us purpose and*
> *direction as a country.*
>
> *Our ability to meet and master not just the challenges of a global*
> *marketplace but also the international, demographic, constitutional and*
> *social challenges ahead – and even the security challenges facing a terrorist*
> *threat that has never been more challenging – depends on us rediscovering*
> *from our history the shared values that bind us together and on us becoming*
> *more explicit about what we stand for as a nation.*[6]

Why is interest in Britain so high on the academic and political agenda when it seems to be waning among the populace as a whole? Is it simply nostalgia for an idea that is on its way out, or could it in fact be that Blunkett and Brown are right and that the whole concept of Britishness and what it uniquely encapsulates is highly relevant to many of the key questions faced today not just in the United Kingdom but throughout the western world? Can a clearer assertion of and greater faith in British identity help us better to face our insecurity and instability in the face of globalization and the terrorist threat, the rising importance of ethnic, cultural and religious identities at a time of mass migration, the challenge posed by fundamentalism to liberal, secular, democracy and the growing tensions between diversity, multiculturalism and pluralism on the one hand and social cohesion, a welfare state and society and shared values on the other?

This book will argue that the concept of Britishness does have something distinct, positive and helpful to offer as a working model of unity through diversity, overlapping multiple identities and the idea that the whole is greater than the sum of its parts. It is offered as a contribution to the current debate on the importance and nature of British identity and the need to reframe it in the light of contemporary trends and movements. A lively academic discourse on the whole subject of identity is increasingly engaging those from the disciplines of cultural studies, sociology, literature, anthropology, history and religious studies. Postmodernism has raised the profile of identity in all sorts of areas – personal, group, national, tribal and spiritual. For these reasons alone it is timely to focus on the fascinating if hugely fluid and slippery subject of British identity. Taken as a whole, however, that is too vast a subject for a single book and the focus of this one is narrower and more specific. It is particularly concerned with exploring the spiritual aspects of Britishness as they have been imagined and constructed in the past and as they are being re-imagined and reconstructed today. Its central theme and subject matter are the shifting and overlapping spiritual and religious identities, drawing heavily on myths, metaphysical and ethical values and religious principles and interpenetrating each other to create a unity through diversity which have gone into making up Britishness.

This is not to say that these are the only ways in which British identity has been imagined and constructed. But these particular elements have been somewhat neglected, particularly in the recent debate. It is true that academics working in the field of national identity are increasingly inclined to recognize the importance of the religious and spiritual dimension. Harry Goulbourne notes, 'The definition of "the nation" in terms of religion is of as much importance in our contemporary world as it ever was in the less "enlightened" days of yesteryear.'[7] Anthony Smith, Professor of Ethnicity and Nationalism at the London School of Economics, has pointed increasingly in his recent work to the seminal influence of religion and the sense of the sacred on national identity, which he usefully defines as 'the maintenance and continual reinterpretation of the pattern of values, symbols, memories, myths and traditions that form the distinctive heritage of the nation, and the identification of individuals with that heritage and its pattern'.[8] But too often, when academics study the national identity of supposedly secular, modern countries like the United Kingdom, as distinct from more 'primitive' societies in the Middle East or Africa, they give very little if any attention to spiritual or religious elements. As Clifford Longley observes in his recent study of British and American identity:

We are never going to reach the bottom of these issues of national identity until we delve into the religious dimension and give it its proper weight. It has not been given its proper weight in the past – for a long time it was

given too much, more recently (in reaction, no doubt), too little … Religion
is a weightier ingredient in these national stories than most modern English
people or Americans would expect it to be.[9]

Some of the politicians engaged in the current debate about Britishness do acknowledge its spiritual and religious aspects, at least in passing. Gordon Brown notes that the call to civic duty and public services that he sees as fundamental to Britishness is 'often impelled by religious conviction'. Arguing that political independence for Scotland would not necessarily spell the end of Britishness, the committed Scottish nationalist Margo Macdonald has said, 'There's enough Britishness to keep the people in these islands together because I think Britishness should be a thing of the spirit,' an intriguing recognition of the spiritual essence or zeitgeist of Britishness from an unusual source.[10] But on the whole, in the recent discussion of the topic, contemporary Britain is depicted as a wholly secular country, especially in relation to the challenge posed by the strong religious identity found among many Muslims, and therefore as badly placed to deal with the new world which is emerging where religious and cultural factors are taking over from ethnic and political considerations as the key determinants of group identity.

It will be my argument in this book that Britain is not a secular state or entity but rather an embodiment of unity through diversity with spiritual roots and foundations. I shall also argue that the extent to which Britishness, far from being a secular construct, is a matter of overlapping spiritual identities actually makes it particularly well suited to meet and respond to some of the very difficult challenges posed by the growing importance of religion in determining personal, group and national identity, especially noticeable in, although by no means confined to, Muslim communities. I will also be arguing that as old collective, cohesive, solid loyalties give way to much more complex, fluid and hybrid ones, facilitated by globalization and migration, the overlapping nature of the identities which make up Britishness perhaps point to a possible future based on multiple, hyphenated loyalties predicated on the principle of diversity in unity rather than just a series of atomized, separate parallel lives which never meet or intersect.

At a time of growing nationalism, separatism, sectarianism, tribalism, individualism, niche marketing and ever more narrowly focused identities, Britishness offers a counter-model of unity through diversity, the sum being more than the parts and simultaneously held multiple and hyphenated identities. That is its particular distinctiveness and glory. This has been well articulated in political terms in relation to the unusual constitutional arrangement of the United Kingdom by Michael Wills, writing while a junior minister at the Home Office:

> *I believe Britain has come to be a remarkably successful experiment in multinational and multicultural living. I believe that the union of four nations over hundreds of years has demanded a tolerance and openness to others that is the hallmark of a decent and dynamic society. The Union has accustomed all of us to a plural national identity. It is intrinsic in the nature of the Union that we have multiple political allegiances.*[11]

What I hope to argue in this book is that it is not just political allegiance in Britain that is multiple, but also spiritual and religious allegiance, and that this particular aspect of the shifting, overlapping identities that make up Britishness is especially important to affirm, celebrate and refashion today.

As it is, given the levels of insecurity currently felt in relation to immigration, asylum seekers, terrorism and other perceived threats, there is a real danger that British identity will become increasingly narrow and filled with fear, hate and bigotry, defined in terms of exclusiveness and against the other. The only political party proudly to incorporate the term 'British' in its title is the neo-fascist and racist British National Party. The only political party that espouses the UK label is the narrowly xenophobic United Kingdom Independence Party, committed to bringing Britain out of Europe. They reflect not Britishness but a narrow Little Englander mentality (and it is predominantly from England that their support comes). In Gordon Brown's words:

> *The issue is whether we retreat into more exclusive identities rooted in nineteenth century conceptions of blood, race and territory, or whether we are still able to celebrate a British identity which is bigger than the sum of its parts and a Union that is strong because of the values we share and because of the way these values are expressed through our history and institutions.*[12]

History and institutions are of considerable importance in the task of reconstructing Britishness along the lines which Blunkett, Brown and others have been arguing –

as inclusive rather than exclusive and providing an over-arching framework which allows many different identities to be lived alongside each other and respected while yet providing a common focus and shared loyalty. This book will point to the continuing relevance in this regard of both the established churches and the monarchy and point to the carnival atmosphere of Queen Elizabeth II's jubilee celebrations in July 2002 as a modern and vibrant celebration of Britishness. It will also argue for the importance of myths and legends in creating the 'imagined communities' that the American sociologist Benedict Anderson so rightly sees as lying at the heart of communal and national identity. This point should hardly need to be made in an age which has been so fixed on epic stories like The *Lord of the Rings*, the Narnia chronicles and the adventures of Harry Potter and, indeed, where there has also been a huge revival of interest in the Arthurian myths and Celtic legends which have played so major a part in the imagining of British identity. Icons, symbols and myths are hugely important in postmodernity and in that process of discursive construct which identity theorists, following Foucault, have identified as the performative language which brings into being the thing that it names.

But it is not just to the spiritual identities created in the dim and distant past and woven into our collective national myths and history that we should look to find Britishness today. In a very striking way British identity is now most clearly and strongly felt and expressed by those who have recently arrived in the United Kingdom. Those same surveys mentioned at the beginning of this chapter that point to a weakening sense of Britishness among long-term inhabitants also show a strong and growing sense of Britishness among more recent immigrants. The fourth national survey of ethnic minorities in the United Kingdom, published in 1997, found that over two-thirds of Indians, African Asians, Caribbeans, Pakistanis and Bangladeshis feel themselves to be British. A report published by the Office for National Statistics in 2004 found even higher levels, with eighty-seven per cent of people of mixed race, eighty per cent of African-Caribbeans and seventy-five per cent of Indians, Pakistanis and Bangladeshis saying that they identify themselves as British. The 2001 census revealed that, while those from what it describes as 'the white British group' are more likely to describe their national identity as English, Welsh, Scottish or Irish (fifty-eight per cent) rather than British (thirty-six per cent), the opposite is true of non-white groups who are far more likely to identify themselves as British. For example, sixty-eight per cent of Pakistanis describe themselves as British, as against only ten per cent who identify themselves as English, Welsh, Scottish or Irish. Among Bangladeshis, these proportions are sixty-seven per cent and six per cent, among Indians sixty-four per cent and nine per cent and among African-Caribbeans sixty-four per cent and eighteen per cent respectively. Those least likely to identify themselves as British in any sense are in the group labelled 'other white', predominantly North Americans and Europeans, under forty per cent of whom describe themselves as British, English, Welsh, Irish or Scots.

There may, of course, be all kinds of reasons both negative and positive why members of the ethnic minority communities in Britain prefer to describe themselves as British rather than English, Scottish, Irish or Welsh. But it is clear from these and other surveys that they regard 'British' as an inclusive and generally appealing form of identity. Jeremy Paxman has acknowledged this in his book *The English*: ' "Britain" has the advantage of being inclusive. It seems that you can be Nigerian, Moslem, Jewish, Chinese, Bangladeshi, Indian or Sikh British, a great deal more easily than you can be English and any of those things.'[13] Linda Colley, the historian who has worked so much on the forging of British identity, agrees if with a slightly more cynical sting in the tail: 'Britishness is a synthetic and capacious concept with no necessary ethnic or cultural overtones. Consequently, large numbers of non-whites seem reasonably content to accept the label "British" because it doesn't commit them to much.'[14]

This vote of confidence in Britishness on the part of relatively recent immigrants is manifested in other ways. They are often among the most enthusiastic and proud about being British, aside from members of the British National Party and the UK Independence Party, though theirs is, of course, a hugely different enthusiasm from the beleaguered fortress mentality of the BNP and Ukip. It is a positive attraction to a country which they have come to out of choice, or seeking asylum, and where they have found a freedom and opportunities which they did not find in the countries of their birth. There is nothing new about this – throughout history some of the most moving panegyrics to the British way of life have been written by immigrants. It is also the case that it has often been relative newcomers who have done most to define and redefine Britishness and create its identity, and especially its spiritual identity, whether they be new arrivals to these shores like the Celts, Angles and Saxons in the early centuries AD or the Normans in the aftermath of 1066 or new entrants to the United Kingdom like the Scots after the Act of Union of 1707. This book will, indeed, argue that the future of British identity lies in considerable part with the new Britons, especially those who have come in the last fifty years from Asia and the African-Caribbean and their descendants, whose sense of 'Britishness' is often stronger than that found among many of the much longer settled white inhabitants. Many exemplify and champion traditional British values such as respectability, reserve, restraint and attachment to freedom rather more conspicuously and enthusiastically than a good number of white Britons.

This intriguing aspect to the whole subject of British identity, which has struck me more and more as I have worked on this book, does, of course, have to be set against the evidence of growing alienation from Britain and concepts of Britishness felt by many second- and third-generation immigrants. Much was made of this in the aftermath of July 2005's London bombings, which were carried out by young men who had grown up in Britain. By contrast, not enough has yet been made in current debate and discussion about integrating Britons of Asian and African-Caribbean descent of the fact that, on the whole, they feel more British than the white majority. The one commentator who has highlighted this point is the journalist Yasmin Alibhai-Brown, who herself came to Britain from Uganda. She notes:

> *The irony is that black and Asian Britons today feel more deeply about their British identity than any of the indigenous groups. In the last few years we have embraced and transformed Britishness and by doing so redefined the British identity. Now Scottish, Welsh and English nationalists want to relegate us to those lesser beings who have no ancestral connections to this land.*[5]

She is particularly critical of the rise of English nationalism, which she feels is a negation of the true character of the English, who among all European tribes, 'have been the most adventurous, open and promiscuous, wilfully and joyously appropriating, replicating and incorporating different cultures and ideas and peoples from the world'.[16] The white retreat into Englishness will, she fears, leave Britishness as 'an inner-city area, a dejected, hopeless place for poor blacks left behind with nowhere to go':

> *Just as many black, Asian and progressive white Britons were beginning to*

feel that the idea of Britishness was being broadened in a way that could also include them, we may be left rallying around the reclaimed flag, only to find that there is nobody else there – leaving us as some of the newest and yet also the last Britons left.[17]

There are other ways in which relatively recent immigrants are contributing disproportionately to the maintenance of British identity and institutions. The National Health Service, which as we shall see is regarded as one of the quintessential institutional expressions of Britishness, is kept going very largely by medical and other staff recruited from the ethnic minorities and from other countries. The corner shop, long regarded as another distinctively British institution and cherished as such, has largely survived in urban areas thanks to British Asians. If sport, and especially the track and field sports which dominate the Olympic Games, where the United Kingdom competes as a single nation, represent an abiding passion and talisman of Britishness, then its face is now predominantly and proudly black.

There is another very striking feature about the new Britons who have come to the United Kingdom over last fifty years or who have grown up here as the children or grandchildren of immigrants. As well as apparently feeling markedly more British than the long-term white inhabitants, they are also noticeably more religious and spiritually active. The census data shows that, with the exception of the Chinese, those in ethnic minorities are consistently more likely to say that religion is important to them than whites (see page 184-85). This is especially true of the predominantly Christian African-Caribbean population and the predominantly Muslim population originally from Pakistan and Bangladesh. While white churches are declining, African-Caribbean churches in Britain have doubled in size over the last fifteen years. In London there are now more black than white worshippers in church on a Sunday morning. The extent to which British Muslims put their faith into practice is even more impressive, and in even more contrast to, the indifference of the white majority. Calculations made on the basis of extrapolating past and present patterns of attendance at worship suggest that by 2013 there could be more Muslims worshipping in mosques in England every Friday than worshippers in Church of England parish churches and cathedrals on Sunday mornings and that by 2039 the number of regular Muslim worshippers in the United Kingdom may outnumber the total of Christian worshippers each Sunday (see page 184). These and other developments seem bound to change the spiritual identity of Britain and a lot will depend on how, if at all, they overlap, intermesh with and relate to the other spiritual identities identified and explored in this book as traditionally lying at the heart of imagined Britishness: the Celtic emphasis on myth, heroism, land and prayer, the Anglo-Saxon/Gothic strain of liberal tolerance, openness and stoical pragmatism and the Scottish focus on muscular Christianity, moral uprightness, community and responsibility.

The contribution that the relatively new Britons drawn from ethnic minorities are already making and will make to the reshaping and imagining of British identity is hugely important. They are a significant element in the population and they are growing fast. Minority ethnic communities are projected to account for more than half of the growth of Britain's working-age population over the next decade. But even more important is the contribution which will come from the revival, rediscovery and reconfiguring of those other longer-term constructions and imaginings of Britishness which have been among the most important and distinctive contributions of the Irish, Welsh, English and Scots to their common identity. It is worth remembering that, according to the 2001 census, just eight per cent of the UK population belong to ethnic minorities, the same proportion (though not, of course, always the same people) as were born overseas, and five per cent to minority faiths. Ninety-two per cent of the population of the United Kingdom are white and seventy-two per cent identify themselves as Christians. The complex, overlapping and ever-changing set of myths, stories, values, heroes, customs and beliefs which have built up British identity over the last thousand years or so, and which are analysed in Chapters 3 to 5 of this book, are still going to remain a powerful determinant of Britishness in the future, but so too are the new (or perhaps not so new) set associated with the more recent immigrants of the last fifty years which form the subject of Chapter 6.

Let me now come back to the current debate and flag up three very significant issues, confronting not just Britain but the western world, which this book seeks in some small way to address. First, there is the question as to how basically liberal and pluralistic societies respond to extreme religious conservatism and fundamentalism. It is in some ways an unexpected issue. We thought we were living in a secular age. Yet religion is becoming increasingly important to identity, arguably more so than race and ethnicity, and we are finding it difficult to deal with this, especially in terms of the strong assertion of Muslim identity. When *The Guardian* put fifty people into a room early in 2005 to discuss the whole state of Britain, they agreed that perhaps the most difficult and pressing issue was 'How does secular Britain deal with the reassertion of religion in political life?'[18]

One of the points that I shall be seeking to make in this book is that Britain may, in fact, have something uniquely valuable and positive to offer in what often appears an inevitable head-on clash between religious fundamentalism and modern liberal democracy. This is because, with over three-quarters of its population identifying with a faith tradition, a system of established churches and a public space for and acknowledgement of religion, Britain is not in fact secular, certainly not in the way of its nearest European neighbour, France. Indeed, I would argue that it stands midway between the USA, itself increasingly in the grip of a rising apocalyptic Christian fundamentalism, and the official state secularism of France and several other European countries. Britishness as it has been imagined and constructed is about liberty, tolerance, openness and pluralism but it is also about established churches, sacred monarchy and putting the spiritual and the transcendent at the heart of national life.

The second major issue is about how we square the circle between plurality and commonality and manage to preserve social cohesion, shared values and respect for institutions in an era of globalization, greater immigration, more porous national borders and ever-increasing pressures towards individualization, fragmentation and cultural and ethnic autonomy. Throughout the 1980s and early 1990s, there was a consensus, at least among the progressive left-leaning chattering classes, that, in the words of Lord Parekh, chairman of the Commission on Multi-Ethnic Britain, Britain was a 'community of communities', where discrete groups defined in terms of race, culture and religion could co-exist while having little to do with one another. More recently, however, there has been a growing realization that this approach was leading to the development of separatist identities and a weakening of social cohesion. This concern was expressed as early as 1991 by Harry Goulbourne in his book, *Ethnicity and Nationalism in Post-Imperial Britain*:

> *The new pluralism preaches difference and diversity to the extent that any notion of commonality tends to disappear from view. In this respect, there seem to be two flawed assumptions contained in the new pluralism. It is*

assumed that the social aggregate of the separate ethnic groups amounts to
the whole and this whole is, or will, constitute the full expression of British
society. The new pluralism further assumes that it is possible for groups to live
peacefully together without having anything in common, apart from sharing
the same territory and the simplest of exchange relations regulated solely by
the market.[19]

Since 2000, these sentiments have been echoed by a number of influential commentators and official reports. The review into the civil disorders in Bradford, Burnley and Oldham in 2001 found that, far from being genuinely multicultural, these northern cities had retreated behind ethnic lines with segregated housing and schooling and poor political and community leadership reinforcing polarization between communities leading parallel lives which 'often do not seem to touch at any point, let alone overlap and promote meaningful exchanges'. Ted Cantle, who chaired the review – entitled *The End of Parallel Lives?* – has since called for a much greater emphasis on community cohesion and on British citizenship and nation building.[20] In a much-quoted article, first published in *Prospect* magazine in 2004 and republished in full in *The Guardian*, David Goodhart raised concerns about maintaining an extended welfare state, securing public spaces and effective public discussion and respecting public institutions in a society without a common cultural identity. An overemphasis on multiculturalism and diversity, he argued, was eroding social solidarity in Britain. Like Cantle, he called for a much greater emphasis on citizenship and also advocated strong support for institutions like the BBC which provide 'social glue', more teaching of British history, encouragement of immigrants to 'become part of the British "we"' and the institution of new symbols of British identity such as a British national day and a British state of the union address.[21] Many of those who publicly responded to Goodhart's concerns shared his anxieties and echoed his call for a reinvigorated sense of Britishness. John Denham, a Labour MP and former Home Office minister, castigated the liberal left for failing to engage with the whole concept of Britishness – 'a catastrophic case of filing under "too difficult"' – and highlighted the pressing urgency of 'the challenge of creating a modern British identity for the 21st century'.[22]

This growing criticism of multiculturalism and its effects has come as much from leading figures within the ethnic and immigrant communities in the United

Kingdom as from those within the white majority. In several speeches, Trevor Phillips, chair of the Commission on Racial Equality (CRE), has been highly critical of the multicultural agenda that has dominated British social policy-making and suggested that it has failed to provide social glue and cohesion and rather created an increasingly ghettoized and fragmented society. He has highlighted CRE research showing that younger Britons are less racially integrated than their parents, with ninety-five per cent of whites saying that all or most of their friends are white and the proportion of non-whites saying that all or most of their friends are white going down from forty-seven per cent to thirty-seven per cent between 2003 and 2005. Warning that Britain is 'sleep-walking its way into segregation' and that the ghettoizing of ethnic minorities in Leicester and Bradford has reached levels equivalent to that in Chicago and Miami, he has called for a much greater emphasis on common culture and of the need 'to assert that there is a core of Britishness' in which all can share.[23] Reflecting on the London bombings in July 2005, two prominent Pakistani-born British academics have both pointed to the general lack of belief in Britishness as a significant contributory cause of the alienation of young British Muslims. Interviewing second-generation Pakistani immigrants in the north of England, Aatish Taseer found that they took little pride in their Pakistani background but struggled even more to make any connection with their Britishness, not least because 'Britons themselves were having a hard time believing in Britishness and when you denigrate your own culture you face the risk of newer arrivals looking for one elsewhere, in this case in an Islamic identity'.[24] Tariq Modood, professor of sociology at Bristol University, has similarly suggested that while 'to be Muslim is a very clear identity, to be British is not. We have gone too far in the direction of hollowing out and disparaging the British identity that holds us together.'[25]

This book will argue that we do, indeed, need to make more of Britishness and that British identity as it has been imagined and re-imagined over the centuries does provide a way of holding together diversity and commonality, plurality and social cohesion. It does so through its exceptional respect for difference and diversity, which sometimes seems more like a general indifference, at other times a more conscious and positive tolerance and openness, coupled with its deep sense of shared values and foci of loyalty, which rest on a curious but durable mixture of almost transcendent and metaphysical considerations coupled with a unique sense of humour and a pragmatic, resigned stoicism.

The third major contemporary issue with which this book is particularly concerned is the much-vaunted topic of hybrid, multiple or hyphenated identity. It is something with which many British people have lived more or less comfortably for a long time. I am myself a typical example of the hybrid identity which is so common among those who live in the United Kingdom, being someone who is half English and half Scottish, who has lived half his adult life in England and half in Scotland and whose half-English and half-Irish wife grew up in Wales. I could add other identities – I also feel passionately European and strongly attached to the Commonwealth – but, above all, I feel British more than anything else because Britishness for me is supremely about multiple identity, the sum being greater than its parts. I rejoice in the fact that being a citizen of the United Kingdom links me in a series of overlapping identities and in a common loyalty to the Queen with a huge diversity of peoples, cultures and faiths. Being British gives one freedom to assert other identities as well. I often wear one of those 'hyphenated' badges sold at tourist offices and visitor attractions, in my case one that pairs the Saltire and the Union flag. I would dearly love to wear one that offered even more combinations.

My own commitment both to the identity and idea of Britishness is anchored in a Trinitarian Christian faith. The doctrine of the Trinity proclaims that relationality, community and diversity lie at the very heart of the Godhead and that God does not just exist in one form but in the wonderful plurality of three persons. For me, the United Kingdom as a political entity and Britishness as a concept are embodied paradigms and expressions of this theological doctrine, and especially of that key Trinitarian concept of *perichoresis* (to use the technical Greek term; the Latin is *circumincessio*), which denotes the mutual indwelling and interpenetration of the three persons of the Godhead, the exchange of energies between them and their essential sociality. Central also to the perichoretic understanding of the Trinity is a sense that the whole is greater than the parts yet the parts are all essential and contribute something vital. It is because I feel that these same values of mutual indwelling, interpenetration, relationality and unity expressed through diversity stand at the heart of the idea of Britishness that I will be using the adjective perichoretic to describe it at various points in this book. I am conscious that this will strike some readers as bizarre – indeed my musings on this theme have already got me into 'Pseuds Comer' in *Private Eye*. I am also conscious that, for Muslims in particular, the notion of a Trinitarian God is a scandal, providing the grounds for one of their major objections to Christianity and that, as such, an argument based on the Trinitarian nature of the United Kingdom is not calculated to promote a greater sense of Muslim identification with Britishness. I would, however, suggest that the notion of unity embedded in and to some extent even embodied by diversity which is expressed both in the Christian doctrine of the Trinity and the constitutional and cultural arrangement of the United Kingdom is also found in Islam where there is a deep sense of pluralism running alongside an emphasis on the unity and oneness of God. The Qur'an clearly teaches, just as the Bible does, that while all will ultimately be brought back to and reconciled in God, the diversity and plurality of beliefs held among people are not meant to be resolved in this life but rather to be held together in tension and mutual respect. It also crucially states that, had Allah so willed, he would have united all humankind but, instead, 'We have created you from a male and female and divided you into nations and tribes that you might get to know one another.'[26] A similar sense of the interplay of diversity and unity is clearly found in most of the world's other great faiths, most notably Hinduism.

I am certainly not wishing to suggest that Trinitarianism is necessary for believing in Britain or understanding Britishness but for me it is, at the very least, a highly suggestive and fruitful metaphor and way into the topic. I am encouraged by the fact that this doctrine has been invoked in an attempt to heal the divisions in Northern Ireland. John Dunlop, a prominent peace-maker and former Moderator of the Presbyterian Church of Ireland, has appealed to the shared belief in the Trinity in an effort to persuade those on either side of the Catholic-Protestant sectarian divide to give up notions of identity based on opposition and otherness. He quotes tellingly from the great contemporary reformed theologian Jürgen Moltmann:

The Trinity corresponds to a community in which people are defined in their relations with one another and in their significance for one another, not in opposition to one another in terms of power and possession ... The doctrine of the Trinity constitutes the church as 'a community free of dominion'. The Trinitarian principle replaces the principle of power by the principle of concord ... I am free and feel myself to be truly free when I am respected and recognized by others and when I for my part respect and recognize them ... Then the other person is no longer the limitation of my freedom; he is an expansion of it.[27]

29

The Trinity has long had a particularly strong appeal to Christians in the British Isles. This may well go back to pre-Christian times. Triads and trinities of deities seem to have been central to the faith and worship of the Celtic peoples and it has been suggested that part of the reason Christianity appears to have been accepted reiatively spontaneously and easily in Celtic Britain was because of its emphasis on a God who is both three and one. Trinitarianism runs deep in the Welsh spiritual tradition – the very earliest surviving example of written Welsh is a marginal annotation in a seventh-century manuscript proclaiming, 'It is not too great a toil to praise the Trinity'. The doctrine of the Trinity is also underlined and affirmed again and again in the prayers and poems that have come down to us from the early Irish and Scottish saints. The famous Breastplate prayer attributed to Patrick begins:

> *For my shield this day I call:*
> *A mighty power:*
> *The Holy Trinity!*
> *Affirming threeness,*
> *Confessing oneness,*
> *In the making of all*
> *Through love.*[28]

In his hymn, *Altus Prosator*, Columba writes:

> *We do not confess three gods, but say one God,*
> *Saving our faith in three most glorious Persons.*[29]

The perichoretic and Trinitarian nature of the United Kingdom is supremely represented by the symbol of the Union Jack. Consideration of this flag, what it represents and whether it needs to be adapted and changed will be a recurrent theme in this book. Like the British identity it symbolizes, it has undergone significant shifts and changes. It started life in 1606 as a simple superimposition of the red cross of St George over the diagonal white cross of St Andrew following the union of the crowns of England and Scotland. In 1801, when Ireland was officially brought into the United Kingdom, the narrow red diagonal cross of St Patrick was added.

It was only in the early twentieth century that the Union Jack (or Union flag as it should more properly be called when used other than at sea) really came to replace the Royal Standard, which for much of Victoria's reign had been considered the flag of the United Kingdom and flown on many public buildings.

In its present form, the Union flag is an inadequate symbol of the United Kingdom. It is, indeed, too Trinitarian, failing to acknowledge the existence of Wales, the forgotten fourth partner in the union. Adding the (relatively modern) cross of St David would provide a more complete representation of the United Kingdom and also remedy the defect pointed out by Paul Gilroy in the title of his book *There Ain't No Black in the Union Jack* (see page 224). But the fact is that, even in its present somewhat attenuated Trinitarian from, the Union flag does graphically represent the perichoretic, interpenetrating, overlapping identities that have for long made up Britishness. It also underlines their essentially spiritual basis and foundations, being made up of the overlapping Christian crosses associated with three early saints. For all its inadequacies, and for all the embarrassment and ambiguity that the British feel about it (certainly in comparison with the way in which the inhabitants of most other countries regard their national flags), this makes it a fitting illustration for the central theme of this book.

Bearing in mind, however, that the United Kingdom is a quadrant rather than a trinity, let me leave off theological metaphors and thoughts on the flag, and having sketched out three significant contemporary issues with which this book seeks to engage, conclude this opening chapter by mentioning four specific spurs which have led me into writing it. I do so because I think they will help the reader to see where it is coming from.

I am not sure whether it was what first prompted my determination to engage in some depth with the whole concept of Britishness but I should come clean and admit that one of the main spurs behind this book may well strike some readers as somewhat negative. I have felt increasingly conscious over the last few years of the fundamental differences in the area of national identity and values between Britain and the United States of America. This is obviously a huge generalization, and I am all too conscious of the temptation to swim in the strong currents of anti-Americanism which have swept across Europe in the wake of the Iraq war. I work in a university where there are large numbers of students and faculty from the USA, and I feel increasingly aware of just how different their values are from those that I would want to characterize, and affirm, as British.

I am also, frankly, increasingly worried about the Americanization of British culture and institutions, especially the churches. In many ways, the USA offers a model of multiculturalism and of weaving a national identity from vastly different cultures and traditions. Its citizens include many of the most open, friendly and hospitable people that I have ever met. Yet there is a spirit abroad in the USA today, and especially in its dominant political and religious institutions, which I find both fundamentally alien and also threatening to the open-minded tolerance, the unity through diversity and the overlapping spiritual identities which seem to me to be the essence of Britishness.

I began seriously thinking about and planning this book when President Bush was re-elected for a second term as US President in November 2004. Several commentators sought to argue that his re-election showed the hold of spiritual values on ordinary people and the re-emergence of religious narrative. Mary Kenny, for example, suggested in *The Times*, 'The tired old European political class might even absorb the lesson – if you want to engage the people and halt voter apathy, talk about values, discuss religion and faith.'[30] In many ways, my thesis in this book is that Britishness is at heart about the hold of spiritual values on ordinary people and my call is for the re-emergence of religious narrative. But these values and that narrative are wholly different from those that appear to grip and animate President Bush and the majority of Americans. There may well have been a time in Britain's history when it was closer to the contemporary American identity of the chosen people, impelled by manifest destiny – indeed Clifford Longley's book *Chosen People* traces the similarities and suggests that the British consciously handed this mantle on to the Americans. But he also points out the profound differences, especially in the area of patriotism and national feeling, observing that 'The English can only sing "Land of Hope and Glory" with a blend of sentimentality and irony. Americans would regard the same approach to "God Bless America" as impious and disloyal,' and quoting from the American journalist long resident in Britain, Brenda Maddox, writing shortly after the 9/11 atrocities:

When I came to live in Britain in the Kennedy era, I pontificated freely about the superiority of the American way. 'In my country ...' I began one day, when a well-spoken man interrupted me to say, 'In my country we don't

say "in my country".' The polite rebuke struck me with the force of revelation.
There was an alternative to mindless patriotism. In a tolerant, mature, self-
confident country it was not necessary to put your hand on your heart to say
you loved it, or even to refer to it with possessive adjectives.[31]

This book is not in any way an anti-American diatribe but it does at least partly spring out of an unease that the apologetic, hesitant, ironic, non-judgemental entity that is Britishness is under threat from a creeping Americanization, not least in its spiritual aspects, and that it needs to be protected and defended from that threat, just as it needs to be protected and defended from other forms of fundamentalism and distinguished from Continental secularism.

If President Bush's re-election in November 2004 provided one spur for thinking about British identity, another has come from my encounter with the songs of the contemporary English bard, Billy Bragg. I owe my acquaintance with him, as to much else in the world of contemporary popular culture and music, to my son who became fascinated by Bragg's millennium song, 'Take Down the Union Jack':

Take down the Union Jack, it clashes with the sunset
And put it in the attic with the Emperor's old clothes.

We managed to track down a copy of *England, Half English,* the CD which contains this song and other testimonies to Bragg's own particular brand of hyphenated identity (in his case very distinctly English rather than British) while on the island of Orkney, in itself a tribute to the inclusivity and diversity of the United Kingdom even in its furthest extremities. Bragg sees British identity as very narrow and mono-cultural – 'the Queen, the flag, the British Empire. That whole empire thing stops us from moving forward to a better place. It's people who wrap themselves in the Union Jack, the Eurosceptics, clinging to the past.'[32] In its place, he calls for a renewed focus on Englishness which he sees as an inclusive identity based on who you are rather than where you are from. He is quite right to say that England is far more multicultural than Scotland, Wales or Northern Ireland. Scotland, indeed, comes second only to Iceland as the whitest country in Europe. But I will be engaging with him throughout this book on a number of issues, including the role of the Queen, the flag and the British Empire, or rather its reincarnation as the Commonwealth, institutions which I believe have the capacity to unite through diversity and to forge shared loyalties and values in an inclusive rather than exclusive way. I also question whether England is indeed a more multicultural and diverse concept than Britain, which as David Blunkett rightly observes, is 'evidently mongrel, multi-national and multi-ethnic'. In fact, opinion polls regularly show that Englishness is more associated with ethnic purity than Britishness and that this is a key reason why the latter is a more attractive identity for Asians and African-Caribbeans.

While listening to the recent songs of Billy Bragg has proved one stimulant for exploring what Britishness means in the opening decade of the twenty-first century, another has been re-reading a book published more than thirty years ago in 1975 which has a very similar purpose and perspective to this one. Daniel Jenkins begins his important study *The British: Their Identity and Their Religion* by expressing similar concerns to mine about the fragmentation and break-up of Britain and affirming the importance of what he calls 'the separate strands in the British tradition'. When Jenkins was writing, there was relatively little thought being given to examining or defining Britishness. The reason for this, he suggested, 'has been that it has worked and that, until very recently, people have been content with the way in which it has worked… Self-consciousness about it now becomes necessary because it is no longer working well enough.'[33]

Jenkins' central contention is very similar to mine. Although he does not invoke the doctrine of the Trinity, he argues that there is a definite British identity and that the United Kingdom is greater than the sum of its constituent parts: 'The English, the Scots and the Welsh need the best of each other to bring out the best in themselves.' For him, 'The British way of life is one of balance in tension rather than that of a unified community moving towards a commonly acknowledged goal.'[34] It is this creative tension which he sees as under threat from the rising tide of separatism and narrow nationalism:

> *There is a danger of each of the separate nations turning in upon themselves under the pressure of existence in a world changing rapidly in ways that are not to their advantage. In the process, we may lose our British identity and gain only a querulous and backward-looking Englishness, Scottishness or Welshness, which emphasize the worst and not the best qualities of each people. It is only those who are sure of their identity who have the courage to*

be outgoing, and it is only those who have the courage to be outgoing who can be assured of their own identity. Englishness, Scottishness and Welshness in themselves have never proved enough to enable people to do this. Britishness has, both within these islands and beyond them, because it holds a larger number of differences in creative tension.[35]

Jenkins wrote about British identity solely in terms of the English, Welsh and Scots with no mention of British Asians, African-Caribbeans or other ethnic minorities. He also wrote about Britishness entirely in terms of Christian values. Indeed, his main prescription for revitalizing British identity is a process of church reunion to create a British church and he describes his book as 'a contribution to the restoration of the Christian unity of the people of Britain'.[36] Thirty years on, it is impossible to think simply in these terms. The collapse of churchgoing and institutional Christianity and the rise of non-Christian religious observance have been two of the most striking features of British life in the three decades since Jenkins' book came out. Yet at one level Britain remains an overwhelmingly Christian country, with seventy-two per cent of the population describing themselves as Christian in the 2001 census. This does still make Christianity potentially one of the most unifying factors in British identity. As we shall see, it is also the case that a significant proportion of the population in England and Scotland still identify themselves with the national established church. This raises all sorts of questions about the extent to which the established churches are still bearers of national identity and whether some kind of nominal adherence to the Christian faith is still bound up with the idea of Britishness. I will return to these later. As will also become clear, I have much sympathy with Jenkins' call for a united British church in the context of a new form of establishment which is truly national, open, inclusive and hospitable. But this does not detract from the importance of welcoming and accepting other non-Christian faiths and traditions into the shifting kaleidoscope of overlapping identities that make up the spiritual core of Britishness.

The final and most immediate catalyst for this book was the tricentenary of the 1707 Act of Union between England and Scotland which, perhaps more than any other event, created the United Kingdom and forged the modern notion of British identity. As I will seek to argue in Chapter 6, the idea of Britain and indeed the concept of Britishness as it has been developed over last 300 years have, in many ways, been largely Scottish creations. I do not expect all my fellow Scots to relish this revelation but it is difficult to gainsay and a further reminder of how the different parts of the United Kingdom have made the whole and of how newcomers have particularly contributed to the constantly evolving and expanding concept of Britishness.

I fear that the three hundredth anniversary of the 1707 Act of Union was not celebrated with much enthusiasm either north or south of the English-Scottish border. The four hundredth anniversary of the Union of the Crowns in 2003 was even more of a damp squib. The almost total dearth of events, official or otherwise, to commemorate the accession of James VI of Scotland and James I of England as the first King of Great Britain is a sad commentary on our embarrassment, or indifference, about British identity. The 1603 union was a hugely significant event in the creation of British identity and was largely inspired by religious motives. In the words of Anthony Smith, 'British identity can be dated to the Union of Crowns in 1603, and James I's desire to secure a measure of religious conformity between Scotland and England, rather than to the union of Parliaments in 1707.'[37] It inspired some notably enthusiastic affirmations and one hugely important icon of Britishness, which seem to me well worth recalling and revisiting in the context of the current debates around the topic. As one might expect, those writing in this period especially emphasized its spiritual aspects and also what I have described as the perichoretic sense of interpenetration and the whole being more than the sum of the parts. This was a theme dear to the heart of Francis Bacon, an enthusiastic champion of the newly created nation:

> *When this island shall be made Britain, then Scotland is no more to be considered as Scotland, but as a part of Britain; no more than England is to be considered as England, but as a part likewise of Britain; and consequently neither of these are to be considered as things entire to themselves, but in proportion that they bear to the whole.*[38]

A particularly interesting example of the enthusiasm and expectations that the 1603 Union of the Crowns created can be found in the recently republished tract *De Unione Insulae Britannicae*, written in 1605 by David Hume, a leading humanist scholar in post-Reformation Scotland. He argues for the full union of England and Scotland, drawing inspiration in almost equal measure from the civic values of ancient Rome, the covenant theology of Old Testament Israel and the ideals of commonwealth and nation forged by the Protestant Reformers. For him, a united Britannia, at once stronger and more varied than its component parts, would lead a Europe of small independent states against Iberian imperialism and papal pretension. Hume's eschatological sense of Britain as the chosen people and the New Israel and his anti-Catholic bias are outmoded and unappealing today. Some of his specific proposals now also seem somewhat quaint – in order to foster closer community ties and shared identity in the new United Kingdom, he advocated intermarriage, planting English colonies in Lochaber and the Western Isles to promote ethnic intermingling and levying steep fines on those who continued to describe themselves as Scottish or English. He also proposed a single Parliament for the new United Kingdom with powerful regional assemblies in London, York, Lancaster and Edinburgh drawing at least a fifth of their members from the country on the other side of the old border. He also advocated a single established church. But for all its prescriptiveness and eccentricities, Hume presents an attractive vision of a nation based on intermingling and overlapping identities and shared values and institutions.[39]

James VI and I also had a noble and inspiring vision of his new united kingdom. His overall 'British' project was wildly utopian – he dreamed of a unified peaceful realm, where Catholics and Protestants might be reconciled – but it was at least partially fulfilled in the production of the Authorised Version of the Bible. The making of this hugely important literary and spiritual artefact, so often still referred to as the King James Bible, has been wonderfully chronicled by Adam Nicolson who describes it as 'a window on that moment of optimism, in which the light of understanding and the majesty of God could be united in a text to which the nation as a whole, Puritan and prelate, court and country, simple and educated, could subscribe'. For King James, the Bible was an irenicon, 'an organism that absorbed and integrated difference, that included ambiguity and by doing so established peace'. Nicolson vividly demonstrates how, in translating the text, the compilers embraced diversity and ambiguity and 'a deliberate carrying of multiple meanings beneath the surface of a single text'.[40]

It is highly appropriate that the Authorised or King James version of the Bible should be the great lasting monument to the enthusiasm engendered by the creation of Great Britain through the Union of the Crowns of England and Scotland. In many ways Britain itself at its best has been an irenicon in exactly the terms that Nicolson describes – an organism that absorbs and integrates difference, includes ambiguity and revels in diversity and multiplicity. British identity is muddled, ambiguous, messy even but it is also at root fundamentally eirenic. It is not about blind allegiance to the flag, bowing down before abstract principles or my country, right or wrong. It is rather a broad, capacious, changing identity that rests on myth, symbol and tradition as well as on stoical pragmatism and undogmatic practicality. We are often told that we are moving from an age based on community, authority and tradition to one based on individualism, freedom and change. But it is not as simple as that. These other older values are still there – not least in the newer immigrant communities where they often count for more than they do among many in the longer-established white majority population.

This book has a deliberately ambiguous title, for which I am indebted to the editor who commissioned it, Alex Wright. It is both about believing in Britain as an idea, a concept and an identity and about the nature and extent of religious and spiritual believing in the country. I believe that both of these aspects of belief are interlinked. For a long time, certainly since the 1603 Union of the Crowns and perhaps even more since the 1707 Act of Union, Protestantism has underpinned British identity. This is not to say that it has only been those who have believed in and practised Protestant Christianity who have believed in, or even believed most fervently, in Britain but that the nation's character, values, heroes and most certainly its institutions have been fundamentally marked by Protestantism. Three hundred years on from the Act of Union, Protestantism can no longer remain the main spiritual anchor of British identity, however much it has contributed and added to the rich vein of identities, Celtic, Anglo-Saxon Gothic, Welsh, Irish, English, Scottish, Asian and African-Caribbean, which are explored in the middle chapters of this book. Yet much of its contribution is still relevant and can continue to enrich and nourish us.

There are those who will say that there is no point in redefining Britishness and that, like Protestantism, it should be consigned to history along with the Empire, the Union Jack and the parliamentary union whose three-hundredth anniversary was largely ignored in 2007. I ask them simply to join with me in exploring how Britishness has been defined and located and imagined, and how it goes on being defined and imagined and located today before they dismiss its relevance to some of our most pressing and intractable social, national and global problems. I dare to hope that the broadly historical view this book takes might even make them think about changing their minds. Describing the impact of the recent emphasis on the interrelated history and diversity of the nations and peoples of the British Isles and relating it to the significant immigration that began when the *Empire Windrush* brought the first boatload of West Indians to Tilbury in 1948, Bernard Crick has written, 'If we recognized that we have been both a multinational and a multicultural state since 1707, we would have a firm base for an understanding of multiculturalism that is unthreatening to the pre-Windrush English majority.'[41] I would like further to suggest that if we acknowledge the rich and diverse roots of national identity provided by the essentially spiritual constructions and imaginings of Britishness over the last thousand or more years, we might also begin to find at least some overlapping values and loyalties, if not a shared common view, among Britons old and new and to see that this strange, muddled yet distinctive form of identity perhaps offers some hope in our increasingly insecure, frightened and atomized world.

2 Red, White and Blue – What Does It Mean to You?

Locating and Defining Britishness

Britishness is an extraordinarily difficult entity to define. There are at least three ways of approaching it: in ethnic terms, where the emphasis is on ancestry, birth and bloodline; in terms of civic identity, where the emphasis is on the legal and political construct of British citizenship; and through the more elusive route of myths, values and customs. These different approaches cannot be completely separated. Indeed, they are in many ways more closely intertwined now than they have been for a long time. The concept of British citizenship has moved in the last sixty years or so from embracing everyone born under British rule across the world, with its connotations of imperialism and *Pax Britannica*, to being more tightly defined along ethnic lines. There has also been a parallel shift of emphasis from subject to citizen. The Government's concern with establishing tests and ceremonies for those wishing to become British citizens has raised the profile of British identity and prompted a national debate about what constitutes Britishness in which values, beliefs and culture have featured prominently.

There are those who argue strongly that the debate and discussion of British identity should focus solely on the civic dimension. This is essentially the position of Bernard Crick, the man charged by the Government with the task of defining Britishness in the context of preparing immigrants seeking naturalization for life in the United Kingdom. He has written:

> *Britishness is, to me, an overarching political and legal concept: it signifies allegiance to the laws, government and broad moral and political concepts – like tolerance and freedom of expression – that hold the United Kingdom together. But there is no overall British culture, only a sharing of cultures.*[1]

For Crick, Britishness is essentially a political and legal construct. Englishness, Scottishness and Welshness is what people actually feel. Jeremy Paxman takes broadly the same line in his book *The English*, and the historian Linda Colley has called for an end to 'asking agonized questions about the viability of Britishness, which has historically always been a shifting and uncertain concept … Instead of being so mesmerized by debates over British identity, it would be far more productive to concentrate on renovating British citizenship.'[2]

Citizenship is important, but this book will concern itself largely with those other more abstract and intangible elements of British identity. This is in part because the question of British citizenship and civic identity has been exhaustively dealt with elsewhere, notably in Harry Goulbourne's *Ethnicity and Nationalism in Post-Imperial Britain*, but also because I believe that these other aspects are of fundamental importance to the current debate and to the particular challenges which we face today. Consider, for example, the definition provided by Professor Crick's working party in response to the Government's request for guidance on how to ensure that those becoming British citizens have an understanding of life in the United Kingdom:

> *To be British seems to us to mean that we respect the laws, the elected parliamentary and democratic political structures, traditional values of mutual tolerance, respect for equal rights and mutual concern; that we give our allegiance to the state (as commonly symbolized by the Crown) in return for its protection. To be British is to respect those overarching specific institutions, values, beliefs and traditions that bind us all, the different nations and cultures, together in peace and legal order.*[3]

It is very clear that this definition strays from the purely civic to embrace values, beliefs and traditions. The fact is that they cannot be eliminated from any discussion of British identity, however narrowly it is predicated on formal legal and constitutional definitions. This was clearly demonstrated in an article extolling 'the British dream' written by Michael Howard, when he was leader of the Conservative Party. Howard defined pride in being British as having 'a profound respect for, and allegiance to, the institutions that make Britain what it is' but went on to make clear that it was values, notably 'decency, tolerance and a sense of play' rather than institutions that for him constituted the hallmark of Britishness.[4]

There does, of course, remain the option of defining Britishness in ethnic or territorial terms. These do not mean the same thing. Being British can and has been defined as inhabiting the country known as Great Britain or more narrowly as belonging to the British race. It is worth at least briefly considering these definitions if only to see how problematic they are.

On the face of it the easiest and most obvious way to define Britishness is in territorial terms as the identity of those who inhabit the country known as Britain, so named because the Ancient Greeks called it Pritaniké and the Romans Britannia. It is worth noting that Britain was a name imposed from the outside (although there is some debate as to whether the Greeks and Romans were following local usage as expressed in the Welsh word Prydain or whether this came later). The native inhabitants of these islands during the period of Roman occupation would probably not have thought of themselves as Britons.

In many respects, Britishness has continued to be a quality more readily perceived and identified by outsiders than by the British themselves – witness, for example, the multiplicity of British studies departments in North American universities and their almost complete absence here. The British have often been rather unconscious of their national identity, certainly in comparison with their nearest Continental and transatlantic neighbours. British identity is soft, vague and understated. This is often seen as one of its great virtues. Gordon Brown has reflected that, until recently, Britain 'did not feel that its exceptionalism called for any mission statement, or defining goals, or explicit national ethos. Indeed we made a virtue of understatement or no statement at all.'[5] Brendan Bradshaw and Peter Roberts write in their book on *British Consciousness and Identity* that 'The vagueness of British identity is part of its strength … its genius as an ideological concept is found in its capaciousness: its capacity to seem to buttress the self-esteem of each of the constituent nationalities of the British conglomerate.'[6] It is noticeable that Professor Crick's working party concluded, 'We neither need to define "Britishness" too precisely, nor to redefine it.'

The fact that British identity is soft and vague does not necessarily mean that it is a matter of indifference to those who claim it. A survey by the Pew Research Centre in 2004 found that fifty per cent of those in the United Kingdom felt proud of being British, putting them, as in so many other ways, mid-way between the inhabitants of the United States of America, eighty per cent of whom professed pride in their nationality, and those of Continental Europe – only twenty per cent of Germans said they were proud of their nationality.

As defined in territorial terms, Britishness is complex and ambiguous, as shown by the bewildering variety of geographical and political terms that use the word 'British'. France is France, both a geographical unit and a nation state. In contrast to this unity and simplicity, we have the British Isles as a geographical term (though not one, as I recently discovered, that it is advisable to use in Ireland), Great Britain as a common shorthand phrase (to which, in the words of the closing song in Gilbert and Sullivan's *Utopia Limited*, 'some add, but others do not, Ireland') and the official name for the nation as the United Kingdom of Great Britain and Northern Ireland, usually abbreviated to the United Kingdom. Even this is to simplify. Until the sixteenth century, the term Britain was largely used historically and referred to Ancient Britain. Even after the union of Wales and England in 1534 there was little sense of Britishness, and it was only with the Union of the Crowns of England and Scotland in 1603 that the term 'Great Britain' started to be used, notably by King James VI and I. The phrase 'United Kingdom' came into being following the 1707 Act of Union between England and Scotland. It was extended to 'The United Kingdom of Great Britain and Ireland' following the 1800 Act of Union with Ireland and modified to 'Great Britain and Northern Ireland' following the creation of the Irish Free State in 1922. Meanwhile, the phrase 'Greater Britain' was frequently used from the mid nineteenth century in reference to the colonies and dependencies and later gave way to the 'British Empire'. At least four different collective nouns are used for the inhabitants of this muddled and much manipulated country – Britons (as in 'never, never, never shall be slaves'), Britishers (as in Noel Coward's 'Mad Dogs and Englishmen'), Brits (as often used in the United States and in such modern manifestations as Britpop and Britart) and even Brutes (according to the *Oxford English Dictionary*).

Britain has not even always been an island. Until the seventh or sixth millennium BC, it formed a promontory or peninsula of the Continental landmass. Its insular status since it was cut off from the rest of Europe has often been taken to account for many of the distinctive virtues, vices and eccentricities of its inhabitants, although there have long been conflicting views as to whether it has made them aloof and suspicious of foreigners or tolerant and open to outside influences. Colin Kidd points to contrasting portrayals of Britain in the seventeenth and eighteenth centuries as a great ethnic melting pot and a haven of ethnic purity. A 1706 pamphlet in favour of Anglo-Scottish union rejoiced that the sea had kept Britons 'freer from foreign mixtures than most countries upon the Continent'.[7] Gordon Brown takes the contrary view, arguing in his seminal British Council lecture that it is Britain's island status, with its successive waves of invasion, immigration and assimilation and its maritime tradition, that has made 'us remarkably outward looking and open'.

Whether being an island has isolated Britain or made it different from the rest of Europe in some way, it has not prevented invasion and immigration. Although archaeologists are less enthusiastic than they once were about seeing substantial and successive waves of immigrants from the Continent in prehistoric times, it is clear that Celts, Romans, Picts, Franks, Jutes, Angles, Saxons, Danes, Vikings and Normans came to Britain, as invaders as much as settlers, and have left their imprint on the genetic make-up of its inhabitants today. Since the Norman Conquest other immigrants have come in for more pacific purposes, as refugees from religious and political persecution and as economic migrants seeking jobs. In earlier centuries, they included distinct religious groups like Jews and Huguenots, predominantly from Europe. Over the last sixty years or so, the majority of immigrants have come from the Caribbean, Africa and Asia, providing most of the eight per cent ethnic minority population counted in the 2001 census. More recently there has been significant immigration from the Middle East and Eastern Europe.

As a result of these successive waves of immigration, no other European country has quite such a rich and diverse ethnic mix. Indeed, ethnic diversity and ultimate origin from outside the British Isles could well be taken as a key characteristic, if not even a defining aspect of Britishness. For Trevor Phillips, chairman of the Commission for Racial Equality who was born in London but grew up in Guyana, 'the abiding characteristic of the British people is that most of us, at some point, came from somewhere else. We adopted what was here and we added to it'.[8] The ethnic and cultural diversity of Britain is often presented as one of its most exciting features, not least by the Government in its efforts to attract tourists, though not perhaps asylum seekers and refugees. The official 'Welcome to Britain' tourist website (www.visitbritain.com) proudly boasts:

> *Right now Britain is one of the most exciting places on the planet, a world in one island. You will find here a country of fascinating history and heritage, a country busy reinventing itself with confidence and style, influenced by the hundreds of nationalities who now call Britain home.*

The ethnic diversity of London is especially striking and it is often referred to as the most cosmopolitan city in the world, with 300 languages spoken, fifty non-indigenous communities with populations of 10,000 or more and a third of the city's residents born outside the United Kingdom. The ethnic diversity of Britain as a whole, and of London in particular, was almost certainly a major factor in the decision of the International Olympic Committee to award London the 2012 Olympic Games.

If the ethnic mix that makes up Britishness has always been rich and varied, it has become more markedly and conspicuously so over the last fifty years, thanks largely to the arrival of significant numbers of African-Caribbeans and Asians from Commonwealth countries. There have almost certainly been previous waves of immigration on a comparable scale – it has been calculated, for example, that 200,000 Saxons settled in a population of around two million – but, for the 900 years or so between the arrival of the Normans in the mid eleventh century and the onset of substantial Commonwealth immigration in the 1950s, the numbers of people coming into the country were comparatively small and they were predominantly white and European.

The more recent immigration, which is usually taken to have begun with the arrival of West Indians on the Empire Windrush at Tilbury in 1948, has for the first time brought a significant non-white element into the British population. It is a rapidly growing element – the proportion of the population coming from a non-white ethnic group grew by fifty-three per cent between 1991 and 2001, from three million to 4.6 million and, on current trends, one-fifth of the UK population will come from an ethnic minority by 2050. As yet, however, it is still relatively small, accounting for just under eight per cent of the total UK population according to the 2001 census (four per cent Asians, two per cent blacks, 0.4 per cent Chinese and 1.6 per cent other ethnic groups or mixed). The minority ethnic groups are not, of course, concentrated evenly throughout Britain. In Scotland they make up only 1.3 per cent of the population. In the West of England just one in eighty-five of the population is black, whereas in some London boroughs well over half the populace is non-white.

While successive Immigration and Nationality Acts have made ethnicity an increasingly important determinant for British citizenship in the move from Empire to nation state, there is evidence that it is not seen by most people as a key marker of Britishness. In a recent poll, eighty-six per cent agreed with the proposition 'You don't have to be white to be British'. Although it is probably true to say that before the 1960s it was tacitly assumed that whiteness was a component of British identity, narrow or exclusive ethnic definitions have always been problematic given the extent to which the United Kingdom as it developed was the result of four separate peoples and nations coming together, each of whom kept much of their own sense of ethnic identity. Despite the concerns that have recently been raised about the development of exclusive ethnic ghettoes, Britain has the highest level of mixed-race relationships of any country in the developed world.

The fact and extent of recent non-white immigration have played a major role in raising the whole question of Britishness and what it means. The veteran Conservative politician Lord (Norman) Tebbit, who famously suggested the cricket test – whether immigrant communities supported England even when it was playing their country of origin – as a marker of integration, has commented, 'Nobody used to talk about Britishness in the 1940s and 1950s. It is a phenomenon of large numbers of non-British people coming into the country. The question is about foreigners and how foreigners are persuaded to adopt British customs and lifestyles.'[9] Particularly, although not exclusively, for those on the right, non-white immigration has encouraged a greater emphasis on British values and the British way of life, both seen as being under threat, and led to the fears and resentment which have fuelled the growth of the British National Party and other extremist groups.

The new immigrants themselves have also pushed the subject of Britishness up the agenda, not least because, for many of them, in a way not true for long-term inhabitants, it has been a conscious matter of choice to come to Britain and seek naturalization. David Lammy, MP for Tottenham, one of the London boroughs with the largest population of recent immigrants, has said, 'The people I represent are passionate about Britain. Some of them travelled thousands of miles to get here and try to feel as British as they can'[10] I have already noted that black and Asian Britons are generally much more enthusiastically British than whites. For all of the inhabitants of the United Kingdom, of course, there is a sense in which Britishness is as much a matter of choice as of imposed legal status and civic identity. Another Labour MP, Michael Wills, pointed out while a junior Home Office minister: 'More than any other European country, our national identity is a matter of choice. We are born English or Scottish or Pakistani but together we choose to be British. Being British is not a matter of ethnicity or territory, it is a choice to live together.'[11] As we shall see, there is also a growing call among many immigrants for a clearer articulation of Britishness and a feeling that its understatement has allowed other narrower and more sectional identities to flourish.

There is one further point worth noting in connection with the relatively new non-white British. The great majority of them have either come from or are the descendants of those who came from parts of the world which were once ruled by Britain as part of the British Empire. This fact alone would, fifty or more years ago, have been enough to make them British subjects. For its detractors, like Billy Bragg, Britishness remains an essentially imperial quality, long past its sell-by date. I will be returning to this particular criticism later, but for the moment it is just worth asking whether in fact there are still traces of the 'Britishness' that was once to be found across so much of the world in those countries which were once in the Empire and are now in the Commonwealth. In terms of some of those characteristics, values and customs that are often taken as defining British identity, I think that one can say that there are. It seems to me, for example, that one of the features that most sharply distinguishes Canada from the USA is the Britishness of its humour – self-deprecating, subtle and heavy on irony. The qualities of reserve and politeness that have traditionally been identified as key features of the British character are now more likely to be demonstrated by call-centre operators in Delhi or Dacca than those in Durham or Dunfermline. The 'British' sporting ethic is arguably stronger in Lahore and Karachi than at Headingley or Trent Bridge. Certainly it has been my own experience that the inhabitants of the Indian sub-continent as a whole are more likely to exemplify these traditional and stereotypical British values than many of the indigenous white population of the United Kingdom.

The extent to which these British values still transcend the national and geographical boundaries of the United Kingdom further muddies the waters in terms of efforts to define Britishness in terms of territory or ethnicity. Much the same is true of linguistic definitions. If British identity means speaking English, then much of the world is British. If it involves having an appreciation of English literature, then North Americans and Japanese (especially when it comes to Jane Austen and Thomas Hardy) probably pass muster better than many inhabitants of the United Kingdom. Within Britain itself, Gaelic and Welsh have variously flourished and been suppressed and, while they remain very much minority languages, both now enjoy official status. Although the emphasis in the Government's drive to make those applying for citizenship 'more British' is on immigrants achieving at least a basic grasp of reading, writing and speaking English, it also accepts that they may equally learn Gaelic or Welsh. Welsh is, in historic terms, the true British language, being derived from the Brythonic that was once spoken by the inhabitants of much of the British Isles before, as the authors of *1066 and All That*, put it, 'The brutal Saxon invaders drove the Britons westward into Wales and compelled them to become Welsh.'[12]

Can we get a clearer sense of national identity from the way that Britain presents itself to those who arrive from abroad at its airports and ports? There is certainly not much in terms of an instant impression. In the international arrivals lounges of US airports, it is impossible to miss the Stars and Stripes and large pictures of the President. You have to look hard and long to find a picture of the Queen, let alone an unfurled Union flag, in most UK airports. Once again, the emphasis is on understatement. What you do find in British airports are the Glorious Britain chain of shops dedicated to selling Britain as a marketable commodity. Their merchandise, virtually all of which bears a 'made in China' sticker, gives a fascinating insight into what are seen as the best bits of Britishness for a visitor to the country to buy and take home.

My extensive research at the Gatwick and Heathrow branches while waiting for delayed flights has revealed that, apart from Walkers' Shortbread, Scottish heather honey fudge and Dunoon mugs featuring Tudors, Vikings and Romans, Glorious Britain might be better called 'Glorious England', or, indeed, 'Glorious London'.

Indeed, the manager of the Gatwick branch, Catherine Quarm, told me that she regularly has complaints from customers (both from home and abroad) that the goods on sale are too English and not British enough. The shops are piled high with policemen's helmets and models of London taxis, Routemaster buses, beefeaters and red phone boxes. There are giant postcards of Big Ben, Piccadilly Circus, the Houses of Parliament, Tower Bridge, the Guards band outside Buckingham Palace, the Queen, Prince Charles, a fried breakfast, an Irish guards officer with a bearskin (the only item with any Irish connection that I could find), a cup of tea and a jam biscuit. The emphasis is very much on the past rather than the present: there are models of thatched cottages, village churches, Paddington Bear and Thomas the Tank Engine, but none of the Millennium Dome or the London Eye. You can buy teapots with pictures of Churchill, Shakespeare, Henry VIII, Elizabeth I and a London policeman directing traffic but none showing Tony Blair, Gordon Brown or any other contemporary or recent politician. The few books on offer include an illustrated biography of Jane Austen and volumes on the Celts, Saxons and Vikings. There are a few CDs of military bands but none of Welsh male voice choirs or folk music. Many of the postcards have a distinctly nostalgic theme, featuring Queen Victoria, Bracing Skegness, Meccano models, the Coronation Scot, the Morris Minor, the liner Queen Mary, Colman's Mustard, Rowntree's Pastilles and Black Magic chocolates.

Although St George's flag is stocked, I have never seen any Saltires, Welsh Dragon or St Patrick's flags in any Glorious Britain store. The Union Jack, however, features prominently both as a flag to take away and wave and also on items ranging from boxer shorts, children's socks and bar towels to whisky glasses, watchstraps, notebooks, pens, pencils and mouse mats. It is also emblazoned on many of the T-shirts on sale, along with such symbols as St George and the Dragon, a London bus, the logo of Oxford University and the legends 'BRIT BABE' and 'LITTLE BRIT'. Most popular of all the T-shirt designs, I am told, is a rather menacing bulldog with a sharp studded collar and a Union flag tongue, which strikes an alarmingly aggressive and nationalistic note among so much gentle nostalgic kitsch.

An interesting comparative study as to how Britain is marketed abroad can be gained from a visit to the Scottish Loft in the up-market Canadian resort of Niagara-on-the-Lake. Its title is something of a misnomer – the upper floor of the shop is dedicated to Scottish artefacts with swathes of tartan, Celtic crosses and crystal whisky glasses engraved with the words of Auld Lang Syne – but downstairs the accent is very much British, indeed noticeably more so than in the Glorious Britain shops. Welsh Dragon pens and tea towels and CDs of Harry Secombe and Welsh male voice choirs stand alongside ornamental teapots of the Rovers Return from 'Coronation Street' and the Vic from 'East Enders' and busts of beefeaters, Sherlock Holmes and Dr Watson. There is a huge selection of DVDs and videos, particularly of classic British television comedies like *Black Adder, Mr Bean, Fawlty Towers, Keeping Up Appearances* and *The Vicar of Dibley,* but also of Cliff Richard, *The New Avengers* and the Miss Marple mysteries. There is also an extensive selection of foodstuffs, including cans of Homepride Curry and Coronation Chicken, jars of Horlicks, Ovaltine, Branston Pickle and HP Sauce, marmalades of various kinds and numerous chocolate bars. Significantly, Irish artefacts are sold in a separate shop on the opposite side of the street in which the Celtic theme predominates and the atmosphere is less cosy and cluttered and more edgy and cool.

What is striking about both these attempts to sell Britishness is, apart from the salivating bulldog T-shirt, how understated, benign and non-political and non-nationalistic they are. I can't help comparing the comforting, nostalgic items on sale at Glorious Britain and the Scottish Loft with the tub-thumping CDs of patriotic songs and models and biographies of current and recent presidents and politicians in American airport stores. The merchandise chosen to represent Britain, both at home and abroad, is historical, backward-looking even, reinforcing the notion that the country is a gigantic theme park strong on tradition, pageantry and heritage but without much contemporary relevance or cutting edge.

There was, of course, the attempt in the mid and late 1990s to shed Britain's old-fashioned image and re-brand it as a modern, hip nation. To some extent, this image has existed since the swinging sixties. Since the Beatles, pop music has been one of the United Kingdom's most successful exports and most widely recognized and admired cultural products. The 1990s phenomenon of Britpop, associated especially with the Spice Girls, Damon Albarn of Blur and Noel Gallagher of Oasis, consciously built on this legacy and set out to challenge and avenge the more recent American dominance of the popular music world. As its chronicler, John Harris, shows in his book *The Last Party* (Fourth Estate, 2003), Britpop was both nostalgic and patriotic, with songs celebrating tea, chip shops and Cockney values. Gallagher recurrently strummed a guitar emblazoned with a Union Jack and Geri ('Ginger

Spice') Halliwell appeared at the Brit Awards in 1997 clad in a Union Jack mini-dress. Tony Blair sought to enlist Britpop in his efforts to promote an image of Cool Britannia which also built on the fashion revolution associated with Vivienne Westwood and the superstar celebrity of David Beckham. It was all too frenetic, ephemeral and hyped up to last but if the Britpop bubble did burst, along with its close relative Britart, the whole Cool Britannia project stands as a significant episode in a much longer-term shift which has seen British culture defined less by Shakespeare and more by Lloyd Webber. Tony Blair's re-branding of Britain has perhaps had a more lasting effect on the image of Britain abroad than at home. I saw an early effect of it on a tour of the sumptuous British Embassy buildings in Paris in 1999 where, on the orders of the new Government, the Old Masters had been taken down from the walls and replaced by modem works of art. The 'Welcome to Britain' website presents the country to overseas visitors as a hip, hedonistic destination full of 'cutting edge bars' and 'the world's most acclaimed clubs'. The Government has enthusiastically contributed to this new identity by legislating for large numbers of new casinos and twenty-four-hour sale of alcohol.

The marketing of Britain as the place to come for partying, gambling and binge drinking sits uneasily with its continuing promotion as a tourist destination rich in traditions and institutions, exemplified by solid symbols of parliamentary democracy and the rule of law like Big Ben, the Palace of Westminster, the Law Courts and the Old Bailey. The buildings may remain and continue to figure prominently in the models and postcards sold by Glorious Britain but the values which they represent, like other traditional defining symbols of Britishness, are changing rapidly. The police on duty outside them increasingly wear flak jackets and carry sub-machine guns and the judges who process in and out of the law courts may not be wearing wigs and robes much longer. The office of Lord Chancellor, so wonderfully British in its combination of pageantry, protocol and pantomime, has been abolished and a new Supreme Court will make the dispensing of justice at once more American and more European. With parliamentary democracy frequently and increasingly seen as being challenged by the rise over the last quarter-century or more of what Lord Hailsham called elective dictatorship, by an increasingly presidential style of government and by widespread disillusion with politics reflected in ever-lower levels of turnout at elections, Britain is less and less seen as the exemplar and mother of representative democracy. The public-service ethic, long seen as a distinguishing characteristic of Britishness, has been substantially eroded by privatization and an increasingly politicized civil service. All manner of institutions which were once the pride of Britain, from the railways to public parks and toilets, have suffered over decades dedicated to private affluence and public squalor. Compared to the state of services in most Western European countries, Britishness often seems to stand for the shoddy, the tacky and the second-rate.

Some institutions are in better shape. Asked what most exemplifies Britishness, ninety-one per cent of respondents in one survey in 2004 nominated the National Health Service. Gordon Brown has also singled it out: 'Our British belief in fairness and our commitment to public service makes the NHS founded on health care based on need not ability to pay one of the great British institutions.'[13] If the NHS is, indeed, a reflection of the values of the British people, then it suggests that Britishness is as much about stoical acceptance of the second-rate as about fairness and public service. The British education system presents a similarly mixed picture. We trail behind much of Europe in terms of levels of literacy and numeracy achieved by school leavers. Yet foreigners flock here not just to learn English but also management and business studies, engineering, medicine and other skills. In the highly competitive new learning economy Britishness seems to stand for quality and also cheapness relative to other places. In a survey carried out by the *Times Higher Education Supplement* in 2004, Britain had two of the world's top ten universities and four of the top twenty. There was only one other European university in the top twenty. The country's armed forces, which make much use of both the Union flag and the phrase 'best of British' in their recruiting and publicity campaigns, have a generally positive image throughout the world and contribute significantly to the perception of Britishness as consummate professionalism, scrupulous attention to the rule of law and courage under provocation.

Despite successive batterings from the Hutton inquiry, cost-cutting exercises and pressure to be more commercial, the BBC remains the most widely praised broadcasting organization in the world, trusted for its authority and impartiality and still wedded to the public-service ethic. This is particularly true of the World Service and of the domestic radio channels, listened to by almost 33 million adults each week and accounting for fifty-five per cent of total listening time. More, perhaps, than any other institution they represent Britain to itself. BBC radio offers a rich variety of voices – the Irishness of Terry Wogan, the Scottishness of James Naughtie and Eddie

Mair and the Welshness of John Humphreys and Huw Edwards alongside a variety of English accents, some of the most polished of which turn out to hail from overseas, like the New Zealand born Brian Perkins and the Egypt and Cyprus educated Peter Donaldson. Radio 4 in particular, regularly listened to by over nine million adults each week, at its best wonderfully reflects and celebrates the diversity, eccentricity and vitality of Britain. Until recently it opened transmissions at 5.30 every morning with the 'UK theme', which blends 'Early One Morning', 'Rule Britannia', 'Danny Boy', 'What shall we do with the drunken sailor?', 'Greensleeves' 'Men of Harlech' and 'Scotland the Brave'. This musical journey around the British Isles, arranged by Fritz Speigl, an Austrian-born composer who fled the *Anschluss* and ended up in Liverpool, epitomized the perichoretic quality which I have suggested lies at the heart of Britishness. The decision in 2006 by Mark Damazar, the controller of Radio 4, to axe the theme, which had heralded the early-morning switch from World Service to domestic programmes since 1973, provoked three early day motions in the House of Commons and protests from over 6,000 listeners.

The NHS, the armed forces and the BBC take us firmly into the realm of values and, indeed, into the spiritual dimension of British identity. As Mark Leonard points out:

> *The reason why these institutions stand out is because they remain the living embodiment of transcendental values which are at the heart of British identity: the NHS stands for fairness and solidarity, the armed forces for British internationalism, and the BBC for our creativity.* [14]

There is one institution which supremely represents Britishness and especially its spiritual and religious character but which is curiously little cited in many studies of the topic. The monarchy is still a hugely potent icon of British identity. In a 2004 poll of schoolteachers and pupils, it was rated second only to the Union flag in terms of symbols most associated with Britain. In another recent survey, Germans aged between sixteen and twenty-five singled out the language, the monarchy and multiculturalism as the aspects of Britain that they most admired. I doubt whether the monarchy would get such a high vote of confidence among young Britons. Media-induced sensationalism and focus on scandal have hugely sapped British respect for the royal family. Yet the fact remains that, more than anyone else, the

Queen personifies and exemplifies British identity, something that has indeed been reinforced in the new naturalization ceremonies where the act of swearing eternal loyalty to her officially imparts British citizenship. The new citizenship ceremonies also accord a central place to 'God save the Queen' which is almost unique among national anthems in focusing attention on the ruler of a country rather than its land or people and further underlines the extent to which the person of the monarch embodies and expresses British identity.

For its critics, the monarchy sums up what is worst about Britishness – its stuffiness and rootedness in the past. For Jeremy Paxman, who dismisses it as 'primped, planned and pompous':

> *The supreme embodiment of the idea of Britain is the country's royal family. The ambition of uniting the Kingdom is spelled out in the lumbering list of titles of the heir to the throne: Charles is Prince of Wales, Duke of Cornwall, Duke of Rothesay, Earl of Carrick and Baron Renfrew, Lord of the Isles and Great Steward of Scotland. The institution of monarchy belongs to the world of red tunics and bearskins, the Union flag and the Gatling gun.[15]*

Billy Bragg asks in similar vein in his song 'Take down the Union Jack':

> *Is this the Nineteenth Century that I'm watching on TV?*
> *The dear old Queen of England handing out those MBEs?*

It is significant that Bragg refers to the Queen of England. Polls consistently show that the monarchy is more popular in England than in Scotland or Wales. Unionists within Northern Ireland have their own particular love affair with the Crown but have had to put up with recent efforts to downplay its significance such as the renaming of the Royal Ulster Constabulary as the Police Service of Northern Ireland. The monarchy is undoubtedly equated with Britishness and more specifically with unionism among Scottish, Welsh and Irish nationalists who tend as a result towards Republicanism. It has a higher profile in England than in the other constituent nations of the United Kingdom, if only because three of the sovereign's residences are there, at Buckingham Palace, Windsor and Sandringham (all, like the residences of the Prince of Wales and other leading members of the royal family, in the south of the country). Scotland does have two well-used royal residences in Holyrood and Balmoral, whereas Wales and Northern Ireland have none, somewhat weakening the monarch's ability to represent and reach out to the whole of the United Kingdom. In terms of its historical descent, however, the monarchy does encapsulate the hybrid and perichoretic nature of British identity. The Queen can trace her lineage back through the Germanic/Gothic Windsors and Hanoverians, through the Scottish Stuarts, the Welsh Tudors and the Anglo-Norman Plantagenets to the Saxon Alfred and the British Arthur.

I shall be exploring later the whole question of how far the monarchy can still articulate, represent and embody British identity and values, especially in the areas of faith and belief. It is a subject about which I have recently written an entire book, *God Save the Queen: The Spiritual Dimension of Monarchy* (2002). For the moment, let me just make the point that the fact that the United Kingdom is organized and governed not around ethnicity, nationalism or some abstract political principle but rather around dynasty has a significant bearing on national identity. Allegiance to the monarch may not be a major factor in how the British see themselves nowadays, although, as we have just noted, it is the key to becoming a British citizen, bizarrely perhaps, since it is monarchy that makes the British subjects rather than citizens and in the eyes of some critics weakens the hold of citizenship in the United Kingdom. In all sorts of subtle and subconscious ways, however, monarchy still informs the nature of Britishness. It is so long since there has been a coronation that it is difficult to say how far the next one, when it comes, will provide the same intense experience of national communion that many sociologists and other commentators identified in 1953. What is clear, however, is that the presence of the monarchy is central to those great national occasions which come closest to expressing a shared collective sense of British identity – Remembrance Day celebrations, ceremonies to commemorate significant national anniversaries and events and services following major tragedies involving significant loss of life.

It is surely significant that four of the most watched television programmes over the last forty years have centred on members of the royal family. The funeral of Diana, Princess of Wales, in 1997 attracted over 32 million viewers, the 1969 documentary *The Royal Family* over 30 million, the wedding of Prince Charles and Diana in 1981 over 28 million and the wedding of Princess Anne in 1973 over 27 million. These and other more recent royal events, like the funeral of the Queen Mother and the celebrations marking the Queen's Jubilee in July 2002, have also, in their different ways, I think, been significant expressions of Britishness in its uniquely perichoretic hybridity and diversity in unity. In the case of the Queen Mother's lying-in-state and funeral, it was the traditional, nostalgic, restrained element that was to the fore. With the mourning for Diana, many commentators detected the arrival of a much more feminized and Catholic national mood in the open and ostentatious mourning and the placing of candles, flowers and votive offerings outside Kensington Palace. Yet the funeral service itself, for all the very un-British-like applause that, rippled through Westminster Abbey following the eulogy by Earl Spencer and the mid-Atlantic crooning of Elton John's 'Candle in the Wind', was full of traditional patriotic pageantry, symbolized by the coffin draped with the Royal Standard being carried in by the Welsh Guards and the singing of 'I vow to Thee my country'. In the case of the 2002 Jubilee Celebrations, it was arguably the black-led carnival atmosphere which came closest to producing a sense of national celebration and identity (see pages 189-90).

Other national rituals provide a similar picture of the changing constructions of British identity. The annual Festival of Remembrance in the Albert Hall has been given a makeover in which the Opera Babes have replaced community singing. The Last Night of the Proms in the same venue has also undergone a subtle change of emphasis. 'Rule Britannia', 'Jerusalem' and 'Land of Hope and Glory' are still there, although they nearly disappeared during the reign of the BBC Symphony Orchestra's American conductor, Leonard Slatkin, who expressed concern about their nationalistic overtones yet himself wore a Union Jack bow tie to preside over the festivities. What is striking about the Last Night audiences is the number of St George's crosses, Saltires and Welsh dragons that are now waved alongside the Union Jacks. Since 2003, the BBC has staged parallel outdoor Last Night concerts in Scotland, Wales and Northern Ireland. It is as if they feel that the Albert Hall can no longer quite hold the nation together. In these other locations, apart from Northern Ireland, there is hardly a Union Jack to be seen and the emphasis is very much on national songs – in 2003, 'Danny Boy' in Belfast, 'Charlie Is My Darling' in Glasgow and 'All through the Night' in Swansea. Significantly, no comparable English national song was sung in the other outdoor location, Hyde Park.

Where else might one go other than the Albert Hall on the Last Night of the Proms to experience a particularly British atmosphere? Edinburgh at Festival time, I think. The Scottish capital may have lost one of the most visible icons of its Britishness when the mighty North British Hotel that stands guard over Waverley Station changed its name to the Balmoral in 1991. Its Festival, however, although billed as international, has a very British flavour, especially in the Fringe comedy shows. Now that the Royal Tournament is no more, the Edinburgh Military Tattoo remains the only public celebration of and showcase for the armed forces of the Crown and Commonwealth. Massed pipes and drums playing 'The Barren Rocks of Aden' or 'Flowers of the Forest' may give a Scottish lilt but there is more than a whiff of imperial sunset about the Tattoo, and it is the Union Jack rather than the Saltire that flies high over the castle ramparts. The 2003 Edinburgh Tattoo was the only major national event on either side of the border to celebrate the Union of the Crowns in 1603 and the making of the Union Jack through the fusing of the Saltire and the Cross of St George. Edinburgh also has the former royal yacht *Britannia*, which, even in its reduced status as a floating museum, still speaks eloquently of Britishness in a very royal and traditional way, immaculate, superbly run and understated.

Liverpool seems to me the most British city in the United Kingdom. This is certainly true ethnically, culturally and linguistically. Traditionally the gateway to Ireland and North Wales, its inhabitants have for long, like the members of its leading football team, been 'composed of an assortment of Scots, English, Irish and Welsh'. Scouse is said to be a mixture of English, Welsh, Scottish and Irish accents. The city also has substantial numbers of Asian, black and Chinese inhabitants and the highest level of inter-marriage and largest proportion of those of mixed race in its population of any UK city. Its successful bid to become the European City of Culture was based on its claim to be 'the world in one city'. It has been the home of such quintessentially British idols and icons as Bessie Braddock, Ken Dodd, Meccano, mail order catalogues and football pools. Its most famous sons, the Beatles, who are treated as objects of quasi-religious veneration in statues and monuments around the city, remain among the best-known Britons across the world. Until they were supplanted by City of Culture flags, I have never seen so many Union Jacks flying from public buildings in any UK city. They continue to festoon the museum of Liverpool life and the city's maritime museum where the spirit of the Blitz and the great age of the transatlantic liners are vividly evoked. When I was last there they were also draped around the statue of Billy Fury, described after his first hit in 1959 as 'the greasiest, sexiest, most angst-ridden Brit-rocker of them all'.

The approach to Liverpool by train through deep cuttings hung with ferns provides an atmosphere that is at once Celtic and Gothic in its gloom and mystery. This romantic and mythic character is also present in the Walker Art Gallery in the very centre of the City, part of a complex of solid buildings that speak of imperial elegance and spaciousness. Its galleries are crammed with icons of Britishness like the glowing manly stained glass windows of St George and St Patrick designed by Robert Anning Bell for St Paul's Church in Princes Park in 1925 and part of a quartet of national saints – rather tellingly, Andrew and David are not on display. Patriotic manliness is further depicted in two huge paintings of the death of Nelson and Charles Gere's study of the infant St George being discovered in a field by a ploughman, as described in Spenser's *Faerie Queene*, Arthurian romance is represented by Sophie Anderson's painting of the body of Elaine, dead from heartbreak and clutching a scroll declaring her love for Sir Lancelot, drifting in a boat downstream towards Camelot, and the gloomy romanticism of North Britain by Daguerre's dark etching of the ruins of Holyrood Abbey.

Liverpool is also arguably the most spiritual city in Britain, with one of the highest levels of churchgoing, and is dominated by its great Anglican and Roman Catholic cathedrals. Its vibrant religious life encompasses Unitarians and Welsh Presbyterians, Sikhs and the Maharishi Mahesh Yogi's transcendental meditators, who chose West Kirby for their community of yogic flyers or levitators. The anthem of Liverpool United Football Club, which became the city's lament after the Hillsborough disaster, 'You'll never walk alone' ('When You Walk through a Storm' from Rodgers and Hammerstein's *Carousel*) is well on the way to becoming Britain's new national hymn, having made the transition from stage to sanctuary and being found increasingly in hymnbooks sandwiched between 'What a Friend We Have in Jesus' and 'While Shepherds Watched Their Flocks by Night'.

If Liverpool is perhaps the city which most encapsulates the soul of Britain, is there a rural area which speaks of Britishness as, say, the Malvern Hills do of England, the Kilmartin Valley with its sacred hill of Dunadd of the soul of Scotland, the hidden valley that leads up to the tiny church of Pennant Melangell of Welsh spirituality or the hills of Tara and Slane of Ireland's sacred heart? My nomination would be the rather nondescript hamlet of Eamont Bridge just off the M6 south of Penrith in Cumbria. It was here in AD 927 that the kings of the Scots, the Welsh, the Strathclyde Britons and the Northumbrians came to acknowledge the supremacy of Athelstan, King of Wessex and grandson of Alfred the Great. Because all the rulers agreed to suppress idolatrous pagan practices in their territories, this meeting has been taken as marking the establishment of Christianity as the accepted and official religion of the emerging united kingdom of Britain. Holding together Anglo-Saxon Wessex, Mercia and Northumbria, the Britons of Strathclyde, Wales and Cornwall, the Scots and the Anglo-Scandinavians, Athelstan could reasonably claim to be, as coins issued during his reign proclaimed, 'rex totius Britanniae'. He also took his responsibilities as a Christian ruler very seriously, describing himself as 'supervisor of the Christian household' of his extensive realms.

There is, surprisingly, no mention of or memorial to this particular event in Eamont Bridge today; there are though several other pointers to its distinctively British heritage. The main historic site in the hamlet, in a field across from the Crown Inn, is Arthur's Round Table, a prehistoric monument probably dating from the period between 2000 and 1000 BC which, despite its name, has no apparent connection with King Arthur. A wide ditch encloses a flat area with a low circular platform over which cattle nonchalantly graze. In the corner of the field nearest the road, a war memorial to four local men who died in the Boer War records that they responded to the calls' at that crisis in the History of Empire when volunteers were invited for active service in the South African war'. Patriotism and imperialism were further on display as I walked along the busy road towards the bridge that gives the place its name. Over the door of one cottage the words 'Omne-Solum-Forti-Patria-Est' were engraved in 1671. The house on the other side of the bridge was covered with 'Empire Scaffolding' and in the windows of two houses on a side street there were pairs of Union Jacks.

Just outside Eamont Bridge a fifty-ton block of granite from nearby Shap quarry has been erected by the road and carved with the intertwined symbols of Alpha, Omega and a Cross and the date 2000. It was dedicated by the Bishop of Penrith as the 'Eden Millennium Monument' and represents an imaginative consecration by the modern church of an ancient British sacred site. The location was chosen not for its associations with the gathering in 927 but because of its proximity to the 4,000-year-old Mayburgh Henge, a natural amphitheatre with a great standing stone in the middle. When I last visited it, a small group of mourners were scattering the ashes of a loved one under one of the great oak trees on the side of the Henge. Their simple and dignified ritual spoke of a deep primeval connection with an ancient British spirituality of sacred groves and wide open spaces.

Food and drink vie with landscape and place as totems of Britishness. Fish and chips long held sway as the nation's favourite food and received overwhelming recent endorsement in a poll among fourteen- to sixteen-year-olds, fifty-seven per cent of whom said it was the food they most associated with Britain. However, a combination of declining North Sea cod and haddock stocks and changing tastes have ended its pre-eminence. In terms of eating out and preparing ready-made at home, Britain's favourite food, as revealed officially by Robin Cook when Foreign Secretary, is now chicken tikka masala. Curry is not a new item in the British diet – it first appeared on a London menu in 1773 and the first dedicated Indian restaurant in the capital was opened in 1809 – but it has taken on considerable significance in recent decades as a symbol of the increasingly hybrid and multicultural nature of British identity. There are now over 8,000 curry houses in the United Kingdom. A recent contribution to the Student Room Forum on the web identifies curry as the nearest thing that there is to a British symbol:

> *Britishness doesn't exist any more. What you see on a Saturday or Friday night outside a club is the same as any country. Britishness was washed out long ago ... but if there was anything like Britishness, it would be curry and popadoms, not that tough upper lip cricket-playing git.*[16]

On this reading, Manchester's curry mile, the largest concentration of Indian restaurants in the UK, could be said to be the gastronomic centre of Britain. Yet, rather surprisingly, only one per cent of the youngsters polled in the 2004 survey mentioned curry as the most British food.

It is, of course, not just curry that is transforming British identity from a culinary point of view. Pasta, pizza, Mexican and Chinese food is hugely popular both for eating out and at home and the seemingly unstoppable march of McDonalds, Burger King and Kentucky Fried Chicken has imparted a North American flavour to British eating habits and tastes as it has to much of the rest of the world. (The recent closure of twenty-five McDonalds branches in the UK because of a downturn in sales, however, suggests that this tide may at last be turning.) In terms of drink, Continental influences have been predominant with lager sales outstripping those of bitter, which was never really a truly British tipple anyway, being little favoured in Ireland or Scotland, and wine consumption soaring. The growing popularity of alcopops and combinations such as rum and coke stands in a more obviously British imperial tradition of mixing unlikely combinations like tea with milk and gin with tonic water. Maybe, indeed, the wonderfully mixed diet hymned by Billy Bragg in his song 'Half English' is just the latest incarnation of the great British gift for hybridity and perichoresis:

> *My breakfast was half English and so am I you know*
> *I had a plate of Marmite soldiers washed down with a cappuccino*
> *And I have a veggie curry about once a week*
> *The next day I fry it up with bubble and squeak*
> *'Cos my appetite's half English and I'm half English too.*[17]

Sport is often taken as a defining characteristic of Britishness, not least in the context of the British Empire. For Richard Holt, who has chronicled this national love affair in his book *Sport and the British*, 'Wherever the British went, the gospel of sport went with them.' No other colonial power gave sport the same prominence, nor approached it with the same gentlemanly amateurism and conviction that playing was more important than winning. In Holt's words, 'Gym was for Germans. Britons played rather than exercised.'[18] The gentleman amateur has long disappeared from the ranks of British sporting heroes – one of its last representatives was the Oxford medical student Roger Bannister who broke the four-minute mile in May 1954. The MCC abolished the distinction between gentlemen and players in the early 1960s and Wimbledon has gone professional, although it has provided a classically British underdog and non-winner in the figure of Tim Henman. Gentlemanly amateurism remains in the Boat Race, although an alarmingly high proportion of the Oxbridge crews are now from the USA. In most sports, however, it has long given way to professional superstars, who take their place in the celebrity culture, none more so than David Beckham, thanks to his marriage to Victoria Adams of the Spice Girls, a leading figure in the Britpop and Cool Britannia projects. Despite his emigration to Spain he was recruited as a key player in the British bid to host the 2012 Olympics.

Most sports in fact divide the United Kingdom rather than unite it. Scots complain about the amount of airtime the BBC devotes to cricket. Rugby and football pit the four nations against each other and are hardly conducive to producing a common sense of Britishness. It is really only with the Olympics that the United Kingdom plays as a single nation and perhaps it is significant that so many of the leading British Olympic athletes are black. The victory parade through London by the 2004 Olympic medal winners, described by *The Guardian* as 'a very British affair – warm and restrained' and the more exuberant celebrations in Trafalgar Square the following year when it was announced that London would be hosting the 2012 games were both marked by a good deal of Union Jack waving. It will be interesting to see how far hosting the Olympics does, in fact, engender feelings of shared British identity.

In other aspects of culture and lifestyle, it is increasingly difficult to discern traits that are distinctively British. It is tempting to suggest that the most striking features of Britishness in terms of dress and appearance are dowdiness and slovenliness. Certainly in comparison with the dress and fashion sense of other Europeans, the British appear shabby. Our television and entertainment is very Americanized. When I look back on the programmes which have most gripped and influenced my own children I realize that they are virtually all American, led by *Friends* and *The Simpsons*. Overall, the typical British lifestyle, as defined by Malcolm McLaren, is now very cosmopolitan, at least for the under fifties:

> *It's about singing Karaoke in bars, eating Chinese noodles and Japanese sushi, drinking French wine, wearing Prada and Nike, dancing to Italian house music, listening to Cher, using an Apple Mac, holidaying in Florida and Ibiza and buying a house in Spain. Shepherd's pie and going on holiday to Hastings went out about 50 years ago and the only people you'll see wearing a Union Jack are French movie stars or Kate Moss.*[19]

If it is increasingly difficult to define Britishness in terms of ethnicity, institutions, culture or lifestyle, what of the more intangible area of attitudes and values? For many of its proponents, this is what Britishness has always been about. Gordon Brown insists that 'Britain's identity was never rooted just in imperial success or simply the authority of its institutions, nor in race or ethnicity' but rather in 'shared values that bind us together'.[20] But what are these values? Those most often cited are creativity, adaptability, openness, tolerance, liberty, fairness, decency, fair play, courtesy, civic duty, forbearance and magnanimity. For Gordon Brown, 'being creative, adaptable and outward looking, our belief in liberty, duty and fair play add up to a distinctive Britishness that has been manifest throughout our history and shaped it.' In his book, Daniel Jenkins cites reserve – a respect for privacy, personal space and dignity – and modesty – a distrust of the cult of personality – as the two leading attributes of the British character.

Once again the parameters are changing. Not so long ago, Britishness was equated with the stiff upper lip, politeness and a degree of reticence and respect. Nowadays, North Americans, Continental Europeans and Asians are markedly more polite and respectful than most British people. Britishness has increasingly taken on negative qualities. We may have passed through the era of the British disease, when the country was seen as the sick man of Europe and associated with laziness, poor economic performance and a propensity to strike, but we stand at the top of the European league for teenage pregnancies and football hooliganism. Binge drinking, as Tony Blair warned in 2004, is in danger of becoming the new British disease and the dominant image of the Brit abroad is that of the pot-bellied, skin-headed lager lout, hell-bent on violence. Despite being among the eight richest nations in the world, the United Kingdom continues to have some of the most glaring poverty and social disparity in Europe.

Part of this undoubtedly has to do with a legacy of industrial decline, the transition from Empire and the long period of self-criticism and low esteem that has followed in their wake. Where once British identity was about feeling superior, there is now perhaps something of an inferiority complex, allied to a culture of low expectations, an acceptance of the second-rate and a lack of drive and dynamism. It goes also with a fondness for grumbling and complaining which is a longer-standing aspect of the British character, well captured and pandered to in the hugely successful BBC series *Brassed Off Britain*, which delighted in slagging off favourite targets like the railways, estate agents and package holidays. There is something in the British psyche which actually rather enjoys things being tacky, badly run and a bit of a shambles and giving vent to gripes and complaints. 'Disgusted of Tunbridge Wells' in fact resides throughout the United Kingdom.

The other side of the coin is a patient, resilient stoicism, seen at its best in that characteristically British institution, the queue. In fact, as the word suggests, the habit of queuing started on the other side of the Channel. As Thomas Carlyle observed in 1862, 'that talent of spontaneously standing in a queue distinguishes the French people.' However, it was taken over with particular alacrity by the British, having been apparently introduced in London by Richard D'Oyly Carte, the theatrical impressario, when he opened the Savoy Theatre in 1881 as the home of the operas of Gilbert and Sullivan. The British continue to queue with a greater degree of patience and cheerfulness than anyone else, just as they endure traffic jams and crowded public transport with that mixture of mild grumbling and stoical resignation expressed in the First World War chorus 'We're here because we're here because we're here because we're here.'

This patient stoicism is accompanied by a sense of humour which remains distinctive and baffles many foreigners. At one level, the British sense of humour is very basic and full of innuendo and smutty jokes. More than one commentator has suggested in all seriousness that the best way of inculcating Britishness into those seeking naturalization would be a compulsory viewing of all the *Carry On* films. The designers of the CNN webpage on British citizenship clearly had something of the same idea when they illustrated it with a still of Benny Hill chasing a group of busty girls. The naughty seaside postcard remains a peculiarly British icon. Billy Bragg was right to ask in his song 'Take Down the Union Jack' apropos of the artists Gilbert and George, 'What could be more British than "Here's a picture of my bum"?' Yet the humour that the Americans call Britcom and that fills the screens of their public television channels is anything but vulgar. Rather it is full of irony, understatement and subtle self-deprecation. Programmes with a more narrowly domestic consumption – such as *Bremner, Bird and Fortune* and *Have I Got News for You?* – stand, like the magazine *Private Eye*, in a long British satirical tradition where nothing is sacred and where the establishment takes great delight in sending itself up. Those from overseas find it very hard to understand how the British can be so dismissive about themselves and their most cherished institutions.

Do the British take anything seriously? To Americans, in particular, we display a baffling flippancy and insouciance. It results, I think, from a combination of irony, indifference, irreverence and broad-minded tolerance. It is not a matter of being laid back, because the British aren't particularly laid back. Although there is a prevailing lackadaisical latitudinarianism, which is non-judgemental and is happy for people to do their own thing, there is, too, a more positive espousal of tolerance. For Monica Porter, coming to Britain after growing up in Hungary and then living in America, it is summed up by *the happy fact you are allowed on the grass in public parks. You can sit on it, lie on it, eat your sandwich or kiss your lover on it. This is a nation of glorious parks, but however glorious they are, the grass is never ranked higher than the people. You can judge the whole national mentality by this single detail.*[21]

Is this simply a matter of indifference or a display of the qualities of tolerance and openness that official statements about Britain still make so much of? The Government's guide, *Life in the United Kingdom: A Journey to Citizenship*, comments that 'People are usually very tolerant towards the faiths of others and those who have no religious beliefs.' The Queen made a similar point in her 2004 Christmas broadcast, expressing her belief 'that tolerance and fair play remain strong British values'. This tolerance and respect for diversity are also noted in less official circles. One of the contributors to the Student Room Forum discussion on what constitutes Britishness had no doubt in defining it as 'London – it's so diverse and colourful. So many different people getting on. Where else in the world can you find this?' A study by Richard Florida in 2003 found that tolerance and respect for difference are higher in Britain than in other European countries and in the USA.

This mixture of tolerance, openness and indifference impacts on the spiritual identity of the British, insofar as they have one. Spirituality and religiosity have never been notable British characteristics. In a tradition of pragmatism, anti-enthusiasm and reticence about matters of faith, the phrase 'holier than thou' has been just as much a put down as 'too clever by half'. Britain has not produced very many saints (at least since Celtic times) or systematic theologians, although it has produced a good many pastors, religious poets and hymn writers. Some of its greatest mystics, from the anonymous late-fourteenth-century author of *The Cloud of Unknowing* to R. S. Thomas, the twentieth-century Welsh priest-poet, have been much concerned with the absence and unknowability of God. The British unease about deep and emotional religiosity was well expressed by the respondent who, when asked by a pollster, 'Do you believe in a personal God replied, 'No, just the ordinary one.' It is also manifested in the very different approach towards mixing personal faith and politics taken by Tony Blair and George Bush. Though himself a strong and committed Christian, Blair generally kept his religious beliefs out of his public and political utterances and said, 'I do not want to end up with an American style of politics with us all going out there beating our chest about our faith. Politics and religion – it is not that they do not have a lot in common, but if it ends up being used in the political process, I think that is a bit unhealthy.'[22] His first press secretary, Alistair Campbell, put it even more succinctly: 'We don't do God.' It is almost impossible to conceive of a British premier ending addresses to the nation with the phrase 'God bless Britain.' As Prime Minister, Gordon Brown has spoken of how much he owes to the practical Prebyterian faith of his father, John Ebenezer Brown, a Church of Scotland minister, whom he describes as his 'moral compass', but has displayed a similar reticence to Blair about baring his religious soul and intimate beliefs in public.

In this area, as in so many others, Britain comes midway between the pronounced religiosity of the USA and the secularism of much of the rest of Europe. In a 2002 poll by the Washington-based Pew Research Centre, thirty-three per cent of Britons said that religion played a very important part in their lives, compared to sixty per cent of those living in the USA, twenty-one per cent of Germans and eleven per cent of the French; the figures for those living in Africa and Asia were eighty per cent and ninety per cent respectively. Fundamentalism and secularism are both alien to the British tradition of broad-based established churches and latent low-key folk religion of the kind that surfaces on Remembrance Sunday, the recent resurgence of which has been one of the more intriguing and unchronicled aspects of contemporary British spirituality. It also surfaces at Christmas time, when nearly half the population still finds its way into churches and cathedrals for carol services, even though surveys record that more people now identify Christmas as a time for enjoyment or getting together with family and friends than as a religious festival and that young people know more about the plotlines of *EastEnders* than about the story of the Nativity.

There is much debate as to whether Britain can still really be called a Christian country. In the 2001 census, seventy-two per cent of the population described themselves as Christians. A further fifteen per cent said that they had no religion, eight per cent did not state their religion and just five per cent identified themselves as adhering to non-Christian faiths, 2.8 per cent being Muslims, one per cent Hindus, 0.5 per cent Sikhs, 0.5 per cent Jews and 0.3 per cent Buddhists. These figures suggest that we need to be careful about talking of Britain as a multi-faith society. A very small minority belong to non-Christian faiths and a rather smaller minority claim to have no faith at all but the great majority of the British population regard themselves as Christian, a fact confirmed by other poll findings, which consistently show around seventy per cent saying that they believe in the central tenets of Christian religion. In terms of religious observance, of course, the picture is very different. Adherents to minority faiths, and especially to Islam, are much more devout and much more likely regularly to attend places of worship than the Christian majority. Around eight per cent of the UK population regularly attend church, with blacks being much better attenders than whites, and Scots (10.3 per cent) somewhat better than English (6.7 per cent). The overall religious mood of the majority of the population in Britain has been well encapsulated by Grace Davie in the phrase 'believing without belonging' and by the sociologist Steve Bruce as 'tolerant indifference'.[23] In a survey of social attitudes in Scotland in 2001, Bruce found that while only twelve per cent of respondents claimed regularly to go to church, fifty per cent supported the principle of public prayers in state schools and ninety-four per cent favoured compulsory religious broadcasting by the BBC and ITV.

The idea of the church, and especially the parish church, as a visible embodiment of British identity (and more specifically of English and Scottish identity) lingers on, even as more and more church buildings are declared redundant and turned into bijou residences or second-hand furniture depositories. It is part of the rural idyll, which is still a strong element in the British as well as the English myth. It was no coincidence that John Major, not a noted churchgoer himself, ended his elegiac vision of Britain in the mid twenty-first century with a reference to churchgoing. It would still, he predicted, be 'a country of long shadows on county grounds, warm beer, invincible green suburbs, dog lovers and pools fillers and – as George Orwell said – "old maids cycling to Holy Communion through the morning mists."'[24] This very English picture was already out of date when Major painted it in 1993, with the shadows over county grounds likely to be cast by new speculative developments, beer being chilled as though it were lager, in-fill building making the suburbs less green and the pools about to be eclipsed by the Continental-style national lottery which, like railway privatization, hammered another nail into the coffin of traditional Britishness. Indeed, the elderly ladies cycling to Communion were just about the one part of the picture that had not been airbrushed out by the Thatcher and Major administrations. They may well remain its only surviving feature in fifty years' time.

Although most people have stopped going to church, they have not stopped identifying themselves with a particular Christian denomination. When MORI carried out an extensive representative poll of the inhabitants of the United Kingdom in 1989 for its survey 'Britain under the MORIscope', it found that eighty-eight per cent claimed to belong to a Christian church of some kind, with the great majority (sixty-five per cent) claiming adherence to the Churches of England, Scotland and Ireland and the Church in Wales.[25] This level of identification has slipped over the last decade or so, but the 2001 census revealed that forty-two per cent of Scots still describe themselves as 'Church of Scotland' even though fewer than ten per cent attend its churches. A similar proportion of people in England (forty per cent) describe themselves as 'Church of England' despite fewer than five per cent attending its services. This continuing relatively high level of identification with the two established national churches suggests that these institutions may still play a significant part in defining national identity and raises interesting questions about the actual and potential role of established churches in the changing construction of Britishness which will be discussed later.

Despite this evidence about the continuing hold of established churches, it seems clear that Protestantism has lost much of the force that it once had as a key contributor to British identity. Several historians, most notably Linda Colley, have identified the central role played by Protestantism, or perhaps more accurately anti-Catholicism, in forging a unity between the English, Scots and Irish in the aftermath of the 1707 and 1801 Acts of Union. Other studies reaching further back have pointed to the importance of Bonfire Night and commemorations of the victory over the Spanish Armada in cementing national identity in the seventeenth century. To a considerable extent, Britishness was defined over and against the perceived superstition, tyranny and absolutism of Papal claims and the Popish states of France and Spain. As we shall see in Chapter 4, this somewhat negative construction went alongside other more positive identifications of Britishness with freedom, tolerance and open liberalism. Protestantism is still built into heart of the British state, not least in the overtly Protestant character of the monarchy. The Act of Settlement prohibits a Roman Catholic from succeeding to the throne and the Coronation Oath commits each new sovereign to maintaining the Protestant and reformed religion. But outside Northern Ireland, and the somewhat esoteric realms inhabited by the British Israelites, it is hard to feel that Britain is now a very consciously, let alone militantly, Protestant nation.

It could, indeed, be argued that along with cafe lattes, lager and pasta, the British are now enthusiastically espousing Catholic beliefs and practices. The public reaction to the death of Diana, Princess of Wales, in 1997 was widely taken by commentators to signify the Catholicization of Britain and the waning of the Protestant stiff-upper-lip tradition of restraint and buttoned-up emotions. Certainly it is more common now for emotion to be more openly displayed, especially in the context of grieving, and there are other indicators of a more Mediterranean or Continental mentality like the increasingly widespread practice of establishing shrines of flowers and other offerings at the sites of road accidents, murders and disasters. In terms of levels of church attendance, it is almost certainly true to say that Britain is now more of a Catholic than a Protestant country. A head count of those in church on a Sunday morning reveals more Catholics than Anglicans in England and more Catholics than Presbyterians in Scotland. This remarkable turn in the fortunes of a faith group who were for long seen as a potentially treacherous and seditious fifth column perhaps offers a message of hope for the currently beleaguered Muslim community in the United Kingdom.

This is just one of the spiritual revolutions changing the nature of Britishness. Another, which has recently been investigated by researchers from Lancaster University, is the extent to which people are forsaking patterns of belief and behaviour based on given precepts about how life ought to be lived, categorized as religion, in favour of a much more subjective culture of wellbeing, described as spirituality. A detailed study of the inhabitants of Kendal has identified two constituencies – the congregational domain, made up of the 7.9 per cent of the population who participate regularly in church and chapel life and attend Sunday worship, and the holistic milieu, embracing the 1.6 per cent who engage at least once in a week in activities ranging from acupuncture and yoga to circle dancing, flower essence therapy and tarot card reading. On the face of it, these figures suggest that churchgoing is still a considerably more popular activity in Britain than participation in holistic therapies and alternative spiritualities. However, on the basis of projecting forwards the steep decline in church attendance over the last forty years and the rapid rise in the appeal of alternatives, the Lancaster researchers predict that within the next twenty years or so the congregational domain and the holistic milieu will be of similar size, each engaging around three to four per cent of the population in active participation in a typical week. Indeed, they suggest this may be an optimistic projection on the congregational side. If current trends continue, they predict that just 0.9 per cent of the population of England will be attending church by 2016.[26]

There are, I think, some serious flaws in this thesis, not least in its presentation of the congregational domain and the holistic milieu as if they are two discrete and separate camps when there is, in fact, much overlap between them. The authors of *The Spiritual Revolution* make much of the fact that there are more people involved in a yoga group in Kendal than in any church apart from the Anglican, Roman Catholic or Methodist. Yet surely several of those who take part in yoga classes on a weekday evening are also to be found in church on a Sunday morning. What is wholly missing from their study is any consideration of the 90.5 per cent of the population who are not actively involved in either religious or spiritual activities according to the researchers' definitions. I suspect that the great majority of these people are still very much more touched by the traditional churches, in terms of funerals, weddings, school and hospital contacts, than by alternative spiritualities. For them, indeed, what is described in this study as religion is surely still a more significant force than spirituality, as it manifestly is for the minority ethnic faiths in the UK who are almost entirely unrepresented in the Kendal study.

What this and other recent research projects do show, however, is the increasingly subjective and eclectic nature of beliefs and practices in modern Britain and the extent to which religion, understood in terms of subscription to creeds, obedience to authority and a sense of duty and responsibility is, at least on the part of the white majority, giving way to spirituality, where the most important goal is to fulfil yourself. This undoubtedly has considerable implications in terms of the emerging spiritual identities within our society and it does not bode especially well for a more communal and cohesive sense of identity, British or otherwise. But as well as this individualistic spiritual revolution, we have to bear in mind the very different religious revolutions being wrought by black Christians and Muslims in contemporary Britain. Nor should we forget or underplay those deeply corporate expressions of muddled, inchoate but basically Christian belief which still surface especially at times of national or local tragedy or celebration.

Something of the flavour of popular British spirituality is caught by the BBC television programme *Songs of Praise*, which has been broadcast every Sunday at teatime for more than forty-five years and plays on the British love affair with hymn singing. It is not what it was either in terms of audience or content. In the early 1990s, when *Songs of Praise* went round the country reflecting the faith and lives of communities across the United Kingdom, it shared the protected early

Sunday evening 'God slot' and an audience amounting to a quarter of the entire population with ITV's very similar *Highway*. Now *Songs of Praise* is competing with entertainment shows on numerous other channels, its audience is around three million and it often exemplifies television's general obsession with celebrities, 'specials' and show business schmaltz. At its best, however, it continues to reflect the understated, modest and remarkably buoyant Christian life of contemporary Britain, inner city, suburban and rural, young and old. Its impressively perichoretic team of presenters – ranging from very English (Pam Rhodes), Welsh (Aled Jones) and Scottish (Sally Magnusson) to black (Diane Louise Jordan) – uncovers and celebrates a Britain of strong community ties, voluntary endeavour and quiet unostentatious local heroes.

Occasionally, even the star-studded *Songs of Praise* 'specials' manage to catch something of Britain's elusive spiritual ethos. One such was the programme to mark the start of the new millennium broadcast live from Cardiff Arms Park on the first Sunday of 2000. It featured both classic traditional icons of Britishness – royalty in the persons of the Prince of Wales and his sons in the stands, military bands and the football stadium setting – and modern British idols, with Cliff Richard singing the Lord's Prayer to the tune of 'Auld Lang Syne' and Andrew Lloyd Webber introducing a three-way mix of his setting of a millennium prayer written by an Ipswich school girl and two numbers from his musical *Whistle Down the Wind* sung by a Welsh male voice choir. Daniel O'Donnell, the Irish singer, crooned 'Light a Candle in the Darkness', a black gospel group performed and Bryn Terfel sang a medley of Welsh hymns. There was a wonderful vulgarity to the whole event and also an infectious sense of community. No one talked about their faith but the thousands who filled the stadium sang their hearts out and waved the Welsh Dragon and the Union Jack.

I want to end this chapter by coming back to this most simple and also most spiritual symbol of British identity. The Union flag is on display in the Glorious Britain shops, at the Last Night of the Proms, at Remembrance services, at the Olympic games, on occasions when royalty is present and is back, after a short absence, on the tail fins of British Airways planes. For Gordon Brown, it is 'a flag for all Britain – symbolizing inclusion, tolerance and unity'. It continues to be the symbol most readily associated with Britain both at home and abroad - in the 2004 survey of fourteen- to sixteen-year-olds, fifty-nine per cent identified it as such. It also continues to provoke considerable controversy, as is clear from contributions to a recent debate initiated by *The Times* on how far it presents a rallying point for Britain. The leader of the Conservative Group on Ware Town Council wrote in to say that one of the first things his group did when they came into office was to fly the Union flag over the council offices, 'starting a move to reclaim the flag for everyone in Great Britain'. He went on: 'I have lived abroad for a number of years and I cannot think of any other country where they fly their flag as little as we do here. In fact, I am sure that we are the only country in the world where the act of flying our national flag would cause so much debate.'[27] Others, however, claimed that it was too associated with racialism and imperialism to provide a rallying point for the disparate population of the modern United Kingdom and echoed Billy Bragg's call:

> *Take down the Union Jack, it clashes with the sunset*
> *And put it in the attic with the emperor's old clothes.*

There may be a case for amending the Union Jack, as it has been amended in the past, to make it more inclusive and represent more fully and satisfactorily modern British identity. I shall return to that case in the final chapter of this book. There is an even stronger case for not ditching it but rather keeping it, albeit perhaps in an amended form, as the key symbol and icon of Britishness. It is an amalgamation of essentially spiritual symbols and it proclaims that at the heart of British identity is a series of overlapping spiritual identities.

Let us just remind ourselves of what constitutes the Union flag. It is made up of three overlapping crosses – in all cases modelled on the cross of Christ – which were taken up as the symbols of three of the four patron saints of the countries which make up the United Kingdom. The two most prominent – the red cross of St George and the white diagonal cross of St Andrew – ironically belong to patron saints who were not native to the United Kingdom. George probably hailed from Lebanon and died at Lydda in Palestine around AD 303. He did not become patron saint of England until 1415, having earlier been taken up as a champion by English soldiers fighting in the Crusades during the twelfth century. Andrew, one of Jesus' apostles, who is also patron saint of Russia and Greece, was appropriated for Scotland in the eighth or ninth centuries by the Picts of North East Fife to trump Columba, who was the patron saint of their enemies, the Gaels. There is, in fact, a strong case for making Columba Scotland's patron saint and for finding a native alternative to

George for England, but that might mean too substantial an alteration of the flag and I will leave my further thoughts on this matter to the last chapter.

The only British figure whose cross is represented on the Union Jack, albeit in rather subdued form, is Patrick, and he is not wholly British being at least half Roman. It is ironic that he has ended up as the patron saint of Ireland, a country that he did not much like and in which he spent his formative years as a slave, having been captured by Irish pirates. His autobiographical *Confessio* is the heartfelt account of one who regards himself as a victim of Irish aggression and who equates Ireland with paganism and barbarous practices like slave owning. In many ways he might make a much better patron saint for Britain as a whole. According to a display in the recently opened St Patrick Centre in Downpatrick, possible sites for his birth include Dumbarton in the West of Scotland, Caerwent in South Wales, Ravenglass and Carlisle in Cumbria and various places in Northumberland, Gloucestershire, Somerset, Dorset and Devon. But there is a strong argument for keeping him on as Ireland's patron saint because of his position as a reconciling figure among the divided religious communities there. In the audio-visual presentation at the St Patrick Centre he is endorsed both by the local Roman Catholic bishop and by Ian Paisley, by Orange lodge members and Irish Republicans.

The most genuinely representative British saint is the one who is left off the Union flag. David is the only one of the four patron saints to have been actually born in the country which he represents, and, indeed, the only one to be fully British. He was probably born in the early sixth century, the son of Ceredig, king of Ceredigion. He is arguably the only one who should remain as a patron saint of the United Kingdom, but more of that later. He certainly deserves to be on the Union flag because along with Columba, Patrick, Aidan, Cuthbert and others, he takes us back to the Celtic faith and fire in which we find the soul which is at the heart of British identity.

3 The Celtic Spirit

The Welsh and Irish Contribution

Historically speaking, British identity is Celtic before it is anything else. The people who are, for better or worse, known as the Celts are the first inhabitants of the British Isles about whom we really know very much. They were the founders of Britishness in respect of origin myths and legends, spiritual roots and traditions and language. The Brythonic language, which was once spoken by all those living from southern Scotland to Cornwall, is the ancestor of modem Welsh. The Gaelic still spoken in the Western Highlands and islands of Scotland is a direct descendant of the Irish Gaelic that was another main member of the Celtic linguistic family.

The last thirty or forty years have seen an explosion of interest in Britain's Celtic past. There is huge interest in all things Celtic, whether it be mythology, music, poetry, artwork and artefacts, landscape or belief systems. Although the word Celtic originally applied to most of Europe, it is the British Isles that are now seen as the surviving heartland of Celtic culture and it is to them that seekers now flock from Australasia, North America and Continental Europe in search of the Celtic experience, whether it is crystals and goddesses in Glastonbury or eco- and feminine-friendly Christianity on Iona.

Fascination with the distinctive character and contribution of Britain's Celtic past has, in fact, been a recurring theme in the country's history and has provided one of the richest sources of British identity. From it have come such colourful and stirring figures as Brut, Boudicca, Britannia and King Arthur, the story of

Joseph of Arimathea and the suggestion that Jesus' feet did, 'in ancient time, walk upon England's mountains green', as well as the bevy of Celtic saints, including Patrick, David, Columba, Aidan and Cuthbert, who have contributed so much to the Christian identity of Britain.

Celts have supplied the 'wild side' of the British spirit in contrast to the more prosaic, dull and regulated Anglo-Saxon element. They are often thought of as existing on the edge of Britishness, as epitomized by the phrase 'the Celtic fringe', which suggests an untamed region of noble savages living on the margins of Britain and deserving to be treated as a rare and exotic species. This is, indeed, how many travellers to the Celtic realms of the British Isles have viewed them, from Giraldus Cambrensis, who went off to Ireland in 1183 'to examine the primitive origins of our race', to Samuel Johnson and James Boswell, who embarked on their tour of the Scottish highlands and islands in 1773 hoping 'to find simplicity and wildness, and all the circumstances of remote time and place, so near our native great island'.[1] There has long been a quaintness and even a cachet about Celtic identity which has made it a highly desirable element in the hyphenated and hybrid mix that is Britishness. In the words of Murray Pittock, 'Ethnic Celticism, a touch of the Celt in one's ancestry has, at least since the eighteenth century, been a frequently desirable designer accessory of Britishness'.[2] Celtic influences are credited with contributing the feminine side to Britishness, although it has to be said that most Celtic heroes, and heroines, are decidedly macho and bloodthirsty. They are also often associated with the more intuitive, imaginative and sensitive aspects of the British psyche and with supplying its melancholy side. It is certainly true that the Celtic regions of the British Isles have provided more than their fair share of poets, visionaries, mystics and dreamers as well as of doughty warriors and fighters.

Above all, perhaps, the Celtic strain in Britishness has supplied a strong and distinctive spirituality, stretching from the druids and bards of pre-Christian times through the saints of the sixth and seventh centuries to modern Welsh and Irish poets. It is there in the emotional intensity and spiritual rapture of the *hywl* which grips revivalist preachers and male voice choirs in Wales and in the readiness with which Irish poets from Columba to Patrick Kavanagh have embraced angels as everyday companions. Places even more than people express this Celtic spiritual contribution. Maybe, indeed, it is those ancient pre-Christian Celtic sites of barrows, burial mounds, earthworks, standing stones and stone circles that provide the most truly

British landscape. Kilmartin Valley in mid Argyll, Callanish on Lewis, the Cerne Abbas giant and Eggardon Hill in Dorset, Stonehenge in Wiltshire, Newgrange in the Boyne Valley in Northern Ireland, like the prehistoric sites around Eamont Bridge in Cumbria mentioned in the last chapter, somehow seem more British than distinctively English, Scottish or Irish. This is not just because they date from the period long before the British Isles were divided into separate nations. Is it their primitive spiritual power and their mysterious connections with ancient patterns of belief and ritual which give them their British feel? It is, I think, significant that in a recent poll in which over 30,000 people were asked to name the people, places or institutions which summed up Britishness over the last 1,000 years, both Stonehenge and Glastonbury came high on the list and were, indeed, the only two out of the top hundred nominations which had any religious connection. When BBC Radio 4's Sunday programme asked listeners in 2004 to name their favourite spiritual place in the United Kingdom the winner, with just under twenty per cent of the total vote, was the Marian shrine at Walsingham in Norfolk – a reflection, perhaps, of the fact that Roman Catholics are now the biggest active. Christian community in the United Kingdom and a further indication of how far Britain is shifting from its historic Protestant identity. The next five places, however, making up between them sixty-two per cent of the total vote, all belonged to the British/Celtic past: Iona, Avebury, the shrine of St Alban, Durham and Lindisfarne.

The term 'Celtic' has long had connotations with otherness, exoticism and existing on the fringe. It derives from *keltoi*, a word which the Ancient Greeks used to describe those peoples living north of the Alps and therefore beyond the bounds of civilized Mediterranean society. It has to a considerable extent continued to be a label imposed from outside. There are several anthropologists who argue, as Malcolm Chapman does in his book *The Celts: The Construction of a Myth* (Macmillan, 1992), that the whole concept is a complete fabrication. The word 'Celtic' only came into general use from the sixteenth century onwards, initially to describe a group of languages and then to describe those who spoke them. Although the peoples labelled '*Keltoi*' by the Greeks inhabited most of Western and Central Europe, and possibly had their origins around the Black Sea or in Galatia, the term has come to be used largely to describe the early inhabitants of the British Isles, specifically the Gaels of Scotland, Ireland and the Isle of Man and the Cymri of Wales and Cornwall together with the inhabitants of Brittany and Galicia in northeastern Spain.

The relationship between Celtic and British identity has been ambivalent and fraught. In Ireland, the two have been seen as standing in distinct opposition. Ulster Unionists, those most self-consciously British of all the inhabitants of the United Kingdom, regard 'Celtic' (with a soft rather than a hard C) as standing for Catholicism, Fenianism, Republicanism and hostility to the Union and the Crown. In Glasgow, it is the Catholic (and traditionally Republican and anti-Unionist inclined) football team that is called 'Celtic' and the supporters of the rival Rangers team who wave the Union flag and sing the National Anthem. Several historians, especially those writing from a Scottish, Irish or Welsh perspective, have seen Celtic and British identity as being in opposition to each other. They have also suggested that the dominant English element in the United Kingdom has patronized, colonized and appropriated the Celtic elements. It has, on the whole, been English writers who have identified and emphasized the Celtic contribution to British identity. This is true of the Anglo-Saxon Bede, with his sympathetic portrayals of Irish monks, the Anglo-Norman medieval chroniclers, Victorian enthusiasts like Matthew Arnold who extolled the sensitive, imaginative Celts in contrast to the dull and leaden Anglo-Saxons and many of the enthusiasts for Celtic Christianity today.

In one of the most powerful recent treatments of this vexed relationship, *Celtic Identity and the British Image*, Murray Pittock argues forcefully that what is generally taken to be Britishness is in reality Englishness and that Scotland, Ireland and Wales have been essentially treated like colonies. For him, Celtic identity is in reality a significant challenge to Britishness, in terms of both nationalist and linguistic aspiration and autonomy. He quotes approvingly the words of the prominent Welsh Nationalist, Gwynfor Evans:

> *What is Britishness? The first thing to realize is that it is another word*
> *for Englishness: it is a political word which arose from the existence of the*
> *British state and which extends Englishness over the lives of the Welsh, the*
> *Scots and the Irish. If one asks what the difference is between English culture*
> *and British culture one realizes that there is no difference. They are the same.*
> *The British language is the English language. British education is English*
> *education. British television is English television. The British press is the*
> *English press. The British Crown is the English Crown, and the Queen of*
> *Britain is the Queen of England. The British Constitution is called by Dicey,*

the main authority on the subject, 'the English Constitution' ... Britishness is Englishness.[3]

It is certainly true that the terms 'England' and 'Britain' are often used interchangeably (perhaps most often by North Americans) and that the English have dominated constructions of Britishness. This in many ways is inevitable, given their numerical dominance. England has a population of 49.1 million, Scotland of 5 million, Wales of 2.9 million and Northern Ireland of 1.6 million. English imperialism has undoubtedly played a major part in the construction and reconstruction of the 'imagined community' that is Britain as the pages that follow clearly show. But it is erroneous to suggest that the Celtic dimension of British identity is simply the result of English colonization, appropriation and romantic patronizing. For a start, those who have been at the forefront of emphasizing this element and inventing and reinventing the myths that have sustained it have often themselves, like so many inhabitants of the British Isles, been of hybrid descent with Celtic genes alongside others in their make-up. Furthermore, the Celtic element in and contribution to Britishness has been supplied voluntarily and even enthusiastically by the Welsh, Irish and Scots themselves and not just from what the English have forced, or romanticized them into being.

This Celtic strain has come largely from the Irish and the Welsh. The Irish have provided a double contribution, also being responsible for the Celtic element in Scottish identity. Scotland is, after all, the land of the Irish, *Scoti* being the name that the Romans gave to the inhabitants of Ireland, substantial numbers of whom later crossed over from Ulster to colonize Dal Riata, the modern Argyll, and gradually spread westwards, either subduing or establishing harmony with the elusive Picts who occupied most of the country and the Brythonic peoples of south and west Scotland. Ireland has, of course, had a more complex and troubled relationship with Britain and Britishness than any other part of the United Kingdom. It has produced both the most fervent Britons in the shape of the Ulster Unionists, essentially lowland Scottish Presbyterian in origin rather than Gaelic or Celtic Irish, and also some of the greatest critics of and fighters against the British state in the shape of Republicans and Fenians. But it has, too, produced those of hyphenated identity, the Anglo-Irish who have operated on a British as much as an Irish stage, sometimes literally so, as in the case of the dramatists George Bernard Shaw and Oscar Wilde.

The Welsh are, in ethnic and linguistic terms, the most direct descendants of the ancient Britons who once occupied much of the British mainland. The old name for Wales, before *Cymru*, was *Brython*, reflecting the fact that it was the final home of the Britons, squeezed westwards by the advancing Angles and Saxons, and that the Welsh or Brythonic language was once spoken from Penzance to Glasgow. The first known British patriot, Boudicca, or Boadicea in her less appropriate but better-known Roman name, comes of this Brythonic stock. The warrior queen of the Iceni who fought the Romans after her husband's death in AD 61, burning Colchester, London and St Albans, stands as the first in a long line of queens who have shaped British national identity. A prototype for both Elizabeth I and Victoria, she is appropriately immortalized in a statue designed by Thomas Thornycroft in 1856 and sited on the Thames Embankment near the approach to Westminster Bridge. There she stands defiantly in a chariot with spear up-raised, offering in the words of one recent commentator, 'the British Empire in touch with its feminine side'.[4]

Several of the most distinctive contributions that the Irish and Welsh have made to British identity are reflected in the personalities and achievements of their patron saints. Patrick, as already noted, was himself not Irish but a Romano-Briton and as such a wonderful representative of the hyphenated and hybrid identity that has been so central a feature of Britishness. If anyone can claim him, it is probably the Welsh – the language that he spoke was certainly Brythonic. Patrick Thomas, who has written much about Celtic and more specifically Welsh Christianity, describes him as 'the last of the Britons and the first of the Welsh' and the Welsh scholar Ifor Williams noted that he swore in Welsh and is the first recorded speaker of the language.[5] Although there was not a drop of Irish blood in him, Patrick does epitomize two qualities which came to be associated especially with the Irish and Gaelic temperament. His autobiographical *Confessio* shows him to be both a dreamer and a somewhat wily and skilful demagogue and politician. The same qualities were combined in the genuinely Irish Columba, whose nicknames, *Crimthann* (the fox) and *Columcille* (the dove), sum up the two contrasting sides of his personality. Even more than Patrick, Columba demonstrates two very Irish attributes which have fed into Britishness – the deeply spiritual and mystical poetic qualities so evident in the work of contemporary Northern Irish poet, Seamus Heaney, and the resolute courage and manliness of the Irish warrior aristocracy which found perhaps its supreme embodiment in that very British hero, the Duke of Wellington. Irascible, ascetic, awkward and autocratic and at the same time gentle, humble and a born pastor and healer, Columba epitomizes much of what the Irish have given to Britishness, a complex and often uncomfortable contribution whose intense spirituality sits uneasily with the tolerant indifference of the dominant Anglo-Saxon strain.

David similarly epitomizes what has been perhaps the most distinctive Welsh contribution, a concern and sympathy for the underdog and the marginalized. His last words to his followers are said to have been a call to remember especially the little things and the little people, *isselder* in Welsh. For Daniel Jenkins, himself a Welshman who felt that 'Welsh identity needs to be more sharply stated in the British context today', this is one of the key elements that the Welsh give to Britishness: 'It is a Welsh virtue to be able vividly to enter into the pity of the human condition without self-pity, so that they can be genuinely sympathetic.' He points out that 'The Welsh word for small, *bach*, is also the diminutive of affection' and suggests that 'If the Welsh could do with a little more of the English upper-class "stiff upper lip", the latter's reserve needs no less to be tempered with that warm and ready identification with human need that the Welsh can offer.' It is surely no coincidence that the chief political architects of the twentieth-century welfare state and the National Health Service, David Lloyd George and Aneurin Bevan, were both Welsh. Indignant radicalism and strong concern for the weak and dispossessed have been abiding Welsh contributions to British politics. So, too, has been a passionate and poetic style of oratory which is part of a broader contribution, acknowledged by Jenkins in his observation that 'the Welsh lyrical gift helps to give colour and imaginative power to the British ideal.'[6]

Both Ireland and Wales have contributed disproportionately to what might be called the spiritual treasury of Britishness, especially in respect of religious writings, hymns and church music. C. S. Lewis, the creator of Narnia and an influential Christian apologist who wrestled in a very honest and very British way with the problems of pain and grief, was an Ulsterman. C. V. Stanford and Ralph Vaughan Williams, whose compositions, especially in the field of church music, seem quintessentially British, were respectively Irish and Welsh. In terms of both usage and tone, there are few more 'British' hymns than 'All Things Bright and Beautiful', 'There Is a Green Hill Far Away' and 'Once in Royal David's City', all the work of Cecil Frances Humphreys, who spent her entire life in Ireland and also provided the most popular and widely used translation of St Patrick's Breastplate, 'I bind unto myself today'. More distinctively Celtic in tone, but equally British in terms of their adoption and appeal, are the great Welsh hymn tunes *Cwm Rhonnda*, *Hyfrydol*, *Blaenwern* and *Aberystwyth*.

The Irish and Welsh contribution to Britishness goes back to pre-Christian times. It is about much more than druids and daffodils, shamrocks and shillelaghs. Rather it has supplied many of the origin myths and foundation legends which helped to establish the roots of British identity. Folk tales and epic sagas have always been of central importance in giving identity to nations, peoples, tribes and cultures. They answer the question 'where do we come from?' and also bind people together, providing collective folk memories and common points of reference. Certain peoples, like those of Scandinavia, seem to have held on to their national folk tales and sagas more enthusiastically than others, like the British. But of recent years there has been an explosion of interest in the myths and legends of the British Isles. Books, television programmes and tourist attractions are retelling the stories of Arthur, Merlin, Taliesin, Finn MacCool and Ossian. The reasons for this resurgence of interest in Britain's mythic origins and Celtic past are not hard to find. It is in part an aspect of the enthusiasm for all things Celtic and the stirring national consciousness of Ireland, Wales and Scotland. But it is also very clearly a manifestation of the postmodern mindset. Myths appeal to the subconscious and to the spiritual and emotional rather than the rational part of the human psyche. The growing fascination with them is an aspect of the spiritual revolution noted in the last chapter. They work through narratives and archetypes, by re-presenting the reality expressed through human experience as distinct from the *logos* approach, which is open to critical analysis and can be codified to produce empirical truth. Postmodernism, we are often told, has destroyed meta-narratives and overarching metaphysical ideas which bind people together and produce coherent communities. But it also favours imagination, intuition, feeling and fantasy over rational and empirical analysis. A generation hooked on *Harry Potter*, *The Lord of the Rings* and computer games based on Arthurian romances and medieval fantasy worlds is avid to rediscover the Celtic myths and legends which were foundational in the construction of the idea of Britishness.

Both the new postmodern fascination with Celtic myth and the distinct ambivalence in the relationship between Celtic and British identity are clearly displayed at Celtica, the tourist attraction opened in 1995 in Machynlleth in mid

Wales which aims to let visitors 'experience the world of the Celts'. Its predominant tone is one of defiant Celticism with an undercurrent of pre-Christian paganism. One of the first announcements made through the audio headsets to visitors sitting in the swirling mist around the reproduction cauldron at the start of their journey through 'the Celtic experience' is a reminder that Celtic people still occupy the western extremities of Europe and that 'in Wales, Cornwall, Ireland and Scotland, the Celtic spirit lives on in a lineage that goes back to before the time of Christ.' Myth, magic and macho heroes loom large in the audio-visual displays which follow. The longest sequence features a young Welsh boy, Gwydion, who is plunged into a whirlpool at the behest of an ailing druid and metamorphoses into an eagle, a horse, a mouse and a wolf so that he can journey into the future, revealed as a grim mixture of oppressive Christianity, polluting motor cars and baton-wielding English riot police attacking miners during the miners' strike of 1984-1985. In the last scene witnessed by Gwydion, druids are being hunted down and killed on Anglesey – whether by Romans or Christians is left ambiguous. At the end of the presentation, visitors are herded into a small room to watch a video of a Welsh choir singing *Yma O Hyd*, a pounding nationalist anthem written in 1983 by Dafydd Iwan, a leading figure in the Welsh Revival and also joint president of Plaid Cymru. No translation is offered to English visitors other than of the defiant last words of the song: 'We are still here.'

Celtica presents a distinctly ambiguous view of the relationship between Celts and Britishness. Its promotional leaflet bears the statement, 'The Ancient Britons have never gone away.' Yet Britons, and Britain, are never once referred to in the exhibition, nor the fact that the whole of Britain could lay claim to being Celtic. There are three timelines in the souvenir booklet and on the wall charts in the upstairs galleries headed 'Wales', 'The Celtic World' and 'The World'. In fact, 'The Celtic World' turns out in reality to be Britain and encompasses such Anglo-Saxon figures and events as Alfred, Isaac Newton, the Tolpuddle Martyrs and the Glorious Revolution of 1688. Aside from this, the emphasis is purely on the seven Celtic lands of Wales, Scotland, Ireland, Cornwall, the Isle of Man, Brittanny and Galicia. T-shirts with their symbols entwined in the form of a Celtic knot are on prominent display in the shop along with the ubiquitous CDs of Celtic mood music and more defiantly political albums mixing traditional Welsh songs with the *Internationale* and African freedom songs.

Visitors making their way from the ground-floor audio-visual show to the more traditional interpretive galleries upstairs are confronted halfway up the stairs with the striking incongruity of a display of the flags of the seven Celtic lands next to a huge portrait of the 5th Marquess of Londonderry, dressed in his scarlet British Army uniform as Colonel of the Durham Light Infantry and looking every inch the imperial pro-consul. Of Anglo-Irish stock, he married a Welsh girl and spent much time in Machynlleth, staying in the house where Celtica is now located. The juxtaposition of fierce Celticism and British unionism is continued at the top of the stairs where an exhibition on 'The Royal Connection' celebrates royal visits to Machynlleth in 1896 and 1911. The town itself also manages to combine a proud Welshness with a strangely and nostalgically British feel. It has more than a whiff of Glastonbury and boasts the only surviving national milk bar that I have seen in recent years (very British and very 1950s) which stands next door to the Taj Mahal Indian and Bangladeshi Restaurant. Of such delightful and incongruous pairings is Britishness made up.

Celtica is somewhat unusual in projecting the Celtic theme forwards as much as backwards in time and it testifies to the rising consciousness and confidence of the Celtic nations and regions at a time when the United Kingdom looks as though it may be in danger of breaking up. The more usual pattern over the last 2,000 years has been for the construction and reconstruction of myths around the Celtic spirit at the heart of British identity by nostalgic chroniclers and commentators bemoaning the state of the country in their own day and looking fondly back to a golden age in the past. Indeed, they have perhaps contributed as much as anyone to what is often seen as the particularly British disease of nostalgia for the good old days. More often than not, these myths have been made by non-Celts, with Romans, Anglo-Saxons and Anglo-Normans starting the process but Celts themselves have also been involved in the construction of British identity and especially its spiritual and religious dimension on the basis of its Celtic heart and soul.

The Romans were the first to appropriate ancient Celtic religion and mythology to give an identity and a name to the islands that they occupied with their creation of the figure of Britannia. There has been much speculation about the origin of the female goddess who came to personify Britain, and still does so on the fifty pence coin and at the Last Night of the Proms. It seems most likely that she was based on Brigantia, a Celtic fertility goddess. Brigantia was also the name of a large Celtic tribe. The first known appearance of Britannia is on a rock relief carved in south-west Turkey in the middle of the first century AD, apparently illustrating the conquest of

Britain. A figure excavated in Dumfriesshire and dated around 210 bears the wings of victory, wears Minerva's Aegis and holds a shield and spear. The original Celtic deity seems to have been associated with orgiastic cults and an earth mother figure. The orgiastic connotations disappeared but the earth mother survived. For the Romans, Britannia symbolized the land they had conquered. Although she disappeared after the Romans left Britain, Britannia resurfaced, along with other symbols of Britishness, in the reign of James VI and I and his 'Great Britain' project. She took on attributes of the Virgin Mary and, by the early nineteenth century, when the Britannia cult reached its height, was seen as a *mater dolorosa* weeping over the death of Nelson and other heroes. Along with Boudicca/Boadicea, Britannia became the maternal, somewhat Amazonian embodiment of the steady and stolid British character.[7]

The Romans also bequeathed the name of Britannia to the island which they occupied. One of the first native Britons to use it was a monk who probably lived in Wales in the early sixth. century, a hundred years or so after the Romans had departed. Gildas' *De Excidio Britanniae* begins with a description of the country which manages to suggest that it is both on the very edge of and at the centre of the world: 'The island of Britain, situated on almost the utmost border of the earth ... and poised in the divine balance which supports the whole world'. It continues in a less enthusiastic tone: 'This island, stiff-necked and stubborn-minded, from the time of its being first inhabited, ungratefully rebels, sometimes against God, sometimes against her own citizens, and frequently, also, against foreign kings and their subjects.' For Gildas, indeed, the greatest disaster that befell Britain was the departure of the Romans from the country: 'No sooner had they gone, than the Picts and Scots, like worms which in the heat of mid-day come forth from their holes, hastily land again from their canoes.'[8]

Gildas' words serve as a reminder that not all those of Celtic or British stock were implacably opposed to the Roman occupation, just as not all were later to be opposed to the Anglo-Saxon invasions. He makes clear that tensions within the native Brythonic, Irish, Scotic and Pictish communities could be greater than those between these 'Celtic' peoples collectively and invaders from the Continent. His reference to the stubbornness and belligerence of the British provides an interesting early testimony to the stiff upper lip of the 'bulldog breed'. He is also important in being the first writer to compare Britain to Ancient Israel. For Gildas, God was punishing the British for their obduracy with the Saxon invasions just as he had unleashed the

Assyrians on the disobedient Israelites. Later propagandists gave a more positive spin to this parallel and suggested that Britain, like Israel, was a chosen nation with a special divine mandate and destiny.

Two hundred years or so after Gildas, in the 720s, another monk, this time Anglo-Saxon, produced one of the most important and most quoted works on the origins of Britain, its mongrel identity and Celtic soul. As a Northumbrian writing from his monastery at Monkwearmouth, the Venerable Bede saw himself as English rather than British and carefully distinguished between the two. His *Ecclesiastical History of the English Speaking People*s is, however, about Britain as a whole, which extended well beyond those like him in the *gens Anglorum* who had achieved a dominant position over much of what was later to be called England and southern Scotland. *Britannia* is indeed the opening word of his history, which begins with a lengthy geographical and topical description of the British Isles, the home of four separate peoples speaking five languages: English, British, Scottish (i.e. Irish) and Pictish, with the fifth language being Latin. It goes on to provide a chronology of the successive waves of immigration which had contributed to the hybrid and pluralistic population of Britannia in his own day. The earliest inhabitants Bede identifies are the Britons who crossed over from Armorica (Brittany), occupying first the southern parts of Britain and later spreading northwards. They were followed by the Picts who came to the north coast of Ireland from Scythia (probably Scandinavia). There they found the Scots, who did not want them, so they moved over to the north part of the British mainland and settled there. Much later, the Scots started moving from Ireland to the north part of Britain. Nearer to Bede's own time, the Angles, Saxons and Jutes had arrived from northern Europe. From the Jutes were descended the people of Kent and the Isle of Wight, from the Saxons, the East, South and West Saxons, and from the Angles, the East and Middle Angles, Mercians and Northumbrians, whose kingdom extended from the Forth southwards to the Humber. At the time of writing his history, Bede considered the island to be in a state of relative harmony. The Picts had a treaty of peace with the English, the Scots were content with their own territories and not contemplating 'any raids or stratagems against the English' and the only awkward element were the Britons 'who for the most part have an inbred hatred for the English'.[9]

Bede's description of the various peoples of the British Isles and their origins was to be very influential on subsequent historical treatments of British identity.

So, too, was his emphasis on what Britannia had in common despite its very diverse ethnic mix. He ended his book with a description of Britannia as it was in his own day, united by the Christian faith, loyal to Rome and yet also deeply affected by the early Irish monastic Christianity of Columba and Aidan. Bede is often regarded as one of the founding fathers of English nationalism and of English dominance over the rest of Britain. Yet although he undoubtedly writes from an Anglo-Saxon perspective, he is extremely sympathetic to the earlier Irish and British strains of Christianity, especially in respect of their primitive simplicity and purity which he contrasts with the worldliness and compromise of the ecclesiastical structures and leaders of his own time. He is, indeed, the first of many chroniclers who cast longing glances back at what later came to be seen as the golden age of 'Celtic Christianity'. Although he himself never used the term 'Celtic', which was not taken up until the time of the Reformation, he was in many ways the originator of the myth of a pure and primitive Celtic Church, springing from Irish and Welsh roots, which was to be hugely influential in shaping the idea of a distinctive British Christianity and, indeed, of a wider British spiritual identity.[10]

Bede did much to build up the significance of both Iona and Lindisfarne as cradles of British Christianity. He had a huge admiration for the Iona-trained founders of his own Northumbrian Church, especially Aidan, its first great apostle and bishop. He contrasted the simple austerity of the monastic life at Lindisfarne under its first three Scottish-trained abbots, Aidan, Finan and Colman, with the more extravagant and ostentatious ways introduced by the Anglo-Saxon abbot Eadfrith. He also greatly enhanced the reputation of Cuthbert, the monk from Melrose who became the best-known abbot of Lindisfarne and whose relics were eventually housed in the great Norman cathedral at Durham. Indeed, Bede effectively set out the stall for the British Cuthbert to be patron saint of the English, which he perhaps would have done had the Crusaders not returned from Palestine full of stories of St George and had Edward III not decided to found the Order of the Garter under his patronage.

Bede makes one particularly interesting comment about the beliefs of the British. He says that they were especially affected by Pelagianism, the heresy associated with and named after Pelagius, who was born in either Britain or Ireland around 350, became a monk, spent some time in Rome, where he was scandalized by the louche behaviour and indulgent living of the churchmen, and died around

418 probably in Egypt. While in Rome, Pelagius fell foul of Augustine of Hippo, the leading theologian of the day and strong advocate of the doctrines of original sin and predestination. Augustine accused Pelagius of overvaluing human effort and undervaluing God's grace in the attainment of salvation. Whether Pelagius was, in fact, guilty of the heresy with which his name has been associated is debatable. It may well be that he antagonized Augustine and other church leaders because of his emphasis on high standards of personal morality and behaviour, which came from his monastic background and training, and which he perhaps saw as more important than subscription to particular doctrines and theological tenets. He does seem to have had a sense of the innate goodness of humanity, and indeed of all creation, in contrast to Augustine's emphatic assertion that even the tiniest baby is fundamentally tainted by original sin. As it developed, Pelagianism came to be associated with an emphasis on free will and choice and on the ability of individuals to help themselves against the Augustinian doctrine of predestination. It also stressed practical good works as much as assent to doctrines and creeds.

Pelagianism has long been seen as a particularly British heresy. The great Swiss theologian, Karl Barth, described British Christianity as 'incurably Pelagian'. Robert Van de Weyer reflects in his book *Celtic Fire*, itself an impassioned testament to the importance of the Pelagian strain in the spiritual identity of the British:

> *The rugged individualism of the Celtic monk, his conviction that each person is free to choose between good and evil, and his insistence that faith must be practical as well as spiritual, remain hallmarks of Christians in Britain. And the British imagination has remained rooted in nature, witnessed by the pastoral poetry and landscape painting in which Britain excels; indeed, that peculiar British obsession with gardening is Celtic in origin. Visitors to the British Isles are often shocked by how few people attend church each Sunday. Yet to the Britons, church-goers as well as absentees, the primary test of faith is not religious observance, but daily behaviour towards our neighbours – and towards our pets, livestock and plants![11]*

Whether or not the British love of gardening can really be put down to Pelagianism, it is certainly true that other values associated with this obscure fourth-century monk have lingered long in the national psyche. There is, for example, the concern about good behaviour and individual morality which can at times be taken to excessive lengths, as Lord Macaulay observed in his celebrated dictum, 'We know of no spectacle so ridiculous as the British public in one of its periodical fits of morality.' This is why so many British politicians get hounded out of office for relatively minor peccadilloes that would hardly cause a stir in the rest of Europe. There is, too, a more positive side to the Pelagianism of the British, manifested in the view that practical good works and charity are at least as important an aspect of living the Christian life as going to church and believing in the creeds. This is evident in the Church of England's attachment to the Epistle of St James with its emphasis on the practical work and effects of love, in the Church of Scotland's commitment to practical Christianity and social action, reflected in the title of its monthly magazine, *Life and Work*, and in the Methodist doctrine of perfectionism, developed by Charles Wesley and expressed in the hymn 'Love Divine, All Loves Excelling' with its line 'changed from glory into glory'. It is also, perhaps, why the British give so much to charity and regularly top the international league of donors to the relief effort after major disasters.

Bede's description of the origin of Britain was fleshed out and embellished by later chroniclers. Nennius, writing his *Historia Brittonum* in the ninth century, pointed out that Britain had first been called Albion, possibly because of its white cliffs (*alba* being the Latin word for white) or possibly from Albion, the son of Neptune, and introduced the legendary figure of Brut, or Brutus, who had given the country its name. The story of Brut continued to provide an origin legend for Britain until at least the late sixteenth century. It reached its fullest expression in the writings of the twelfth-century chronicler, Geoffrey of Monmouth, born and raised in the Welsh borders, whose *Historia Regum Britanniae*, which first appeared around 1138, was highly influential in creating a British identity on the basis of a Celtic past. It begins with a splendidly up-beat picture of the richness and variety of the landscape:

> *Britain, the best of islands, is situated in the Western Ocean, between France and Ireland. It stretches for eight hundred miles in length and for two hundred miles in breadth. It provides in unfailing plenty everything that is suited to the use of human beings. It abounds in every kind of mineral. It has broad fields and hillsides which are suitable for the most intensive farming*

and in which, because of the richness of the soil, all kinds of crops are grown
in their seasons. It also has open woodlands which are filled with every kind
of game. Through its forest glades stretch pasturelands which provide the
various feeding-stuffs needed by cattle, and there too grow flowers of every
hue which offer their honey to the flitting bees. At the foot of its windswept
mountains it has meadows green with grass, beauty-spots where clear springs
flow into shining streams which ripple gently and murmur an assurance of
deep sleep to those lying on their banks.[12]

Geoffrey of Monmouth provided a detailed account of the origins of Britain, taking it back into the romantic realms of ancient history and Greek mythology. Following the Trojan War, Aeneas, the hero of Virgil's *Aeneid*, fled to Italy where he founded Rome. Brutus was his great-grandson who was himself expelled from Italy and went to Greece. Following the fall of Troy, he sailed with a group of Trojans westwards, seeking the Promised Land. After visiting Africa, Mauritania and Aquitaine, he eventually reached the island known as Albion and came ashore at Tomes in what is now Devon. Brutus achieved supremacy over the whole island, defeating the giants who ruled it, renamed it Britain and called his Trojan companions Britons. The language of the people, which had up to then been known as Trojan or Crooked Greek, henceforth became known as British. Brutus established his capital at a place on the Thames called Troia Nova (New Troy), later known as London. After his death, the kingdom of Britain was divided up by his three. sons, Locrinus, the eldest, ruling what was to become England (called Loegria), Kamber ruling Wales (called Kambria) and Albanactus taking Scotland (called Albany). Later kings, who included Lear, Cole and Lud, styled themselves *Rex Brittanniae* and ruled the whole mainland.

Geoffrey of Monmouth followed Gildas and Bede in emphasizing both the primacy of the Britons, as the original inhabitants of the country, and their arrogance, which God punished by subjecting them to invasion and occupation. He identified five distinct races living in the British Isles: the Norman French, the Britons, the Saxons, the Picts and the Scots. 'Of these the Britons once occupied the land from sea to sea, before the others came. Then the vengeance of God overtook them because of their arrogance and they submitted to the Picts and the Saxons.'[13] Like Bede, he identified Pelagianism as the besetting sin of the Britons and the cause of their divine punishment with the Anglo-Saxon invasions. Despite the efforts of the British king, Arthur, the Saxon invaders proved impossible to resist and the Britons were pushed back into Wales as the Anglo-Saxons effectively took over England and southern Scotland. Cadwallader, the last British king, failed in his efforts to resist them and fled to Britanny. An angelic voice told him that God no longer wished the Britons to rule their land any more but prophesied that they would one day return to rule it. Cadwallader went as a penitent to Rome and died there in 689.

Geoffrey of Monmouth's work was foundational in establishing a sense of British identity in at least three respects. First, it promoted the notion of Britain as a particularly blessed and beautiful place, the 'fairest isle, all isles excelling' of Dryden's poem. Secondly, it reinforced the close association between religious belief and practice and the fortunes of the British. God had punished the British and inflicted the Anglo-Saxons upon them because of their apostasy. If Pelagianism remained the besetting sin of the British, it was accompanied by an Old Testament sense that they were a chosen people and that, though they had fallen from grace, they would rise again and achieve their destiny. This went along with a view of the surviving Britons, which meant essentially the Welsh, as a faithful remnant. Thirdly, Geoffrey's emphasis on the monarchy, evident from the very title of his work, helped considerably to establish the sense that Britishness, past, present and future, was indissolubly bound up with its monarchs. Britain as a whole was, indeed, what Shakespeare defined England as 'this royal throne of kings, this scepter'd isle'. The monarchy became central to the creation and recreation of British identity.

This, of course, hugely suited the personal agendas of those monarchs who sought to extend their domains and forge a united kingdom out of the disparate lands of the Anglo-Saxons, British/Welsh, Scots and Picts. The Norman and Plantagenet kings enthusiastically invoked and espoused Britishness as they sought to conquer Celtic regions, as did Edward I when he effectively annexed Wales to the English crown in 1282. It helped that the two monarchs who did most to create a united British kingdom both themselves had strong Celtic blood. Henry VIII, conscious and proud of his Welsh descent, saw himself very much as the heir of Cadwallader in restoring a British monarchy when he formally united Wales with England in 1536. James VI of Scotland was widely hailed as a second Brut when he united Scotland with England and Wales through the Union of the Crowns in 1603.

Far more important than either Brut or Cadwallader, both as a model for later rulers of the United Kingdom and as an icon of Britishness, was another figure whom Geoffrey of Monmouth launched on the road to fame and fortune. Arthur Pendragon had received earlier mentions in Welsh chronicles and poems but it was Geoffrey's *Historia Regum Britanniae* that established him as a major player in the story of Britain. Geoffrey presented Arthur as the man who restored the British royal line following the period of Roman rule, made a heroic stand against the Saxons, subdued the Scots and Picts, conquered Ireland and became the first king to rule over Great Britain and Ireland. Geoffrey also managed to link him with prehistoric Britain's most important sacred site, suggesting that his father, Uther Pendragon, having come over from Brittany to take on the sinister usurper Vortigern and his allies the pagan Saxons Hengist and Horsa, had transported the Giants' Ring from Ireland to build Stonehenge as a monument to the massacred Britons. Arthur himself, according to Geoffrey's account, went on after his triumphs in the British Isles to conquer Iceland, the Orkneys, Norway, Gaul and Burgundy and was about to march on Rome when news reached him that his nephew Mordred had seized the British throne and taken his queen, Guinevere, adulterously. Arthur returned to Britain, drove Mordred into Cornwall and killed him in a battle on the River Camlann but was himself mortally wounded and carried off to the isle of Avalon. The wizard Merlin announced that he was only sleeping and prophesied that the once and future king would one day awake and return to reunite Britain and rule it again.

Later chroniclers expanded and elaborated the story of Arthur. He was linked with the quest for the Holy Grail and with the notion that it had been brought to Britain and was to be found perhaps in the Cistercian abbey of Strata Florida in mid Wales, perhaps in Rosslyn Chapel near Edinburgh or maybe in Glastonbury where Joseph of Arimathea had brought it after Jesus' death. Arthur became a prototype of Christian kingship, seen as defender of the faith as well as of British values against the pagan Saxons and as the epitome of chivalry and muscular Christianity. He was enlisted in what has been called England's 'British project', whereby the dominant Anglo-Normans sought to expand their hold over the whole of the British Isles. Ironically, the man remembered for driving the English out of Britain was adopted by the country's new Norman rulers in order to help establish the legitimacy of the expansion of England into the Celtic realms of Wales, Scotland and Ireland. In 1187, Henry II named his grandson after the Celtic hero in the hope that he would one day rule as King Arthur II. Edward I's identification with Arthur was a vital part of his attempt to portray himself as the King of Britain and to justify his efforts to stamp out what was left of Welsh independence and claim overlordship of Scotland. The romance of Arthur continued to exert a powerful hold on the imaginations of later British monarchs. Henry VII chose to call his first son Arthur to emphasize the British lineage of the Tudors. Victoria also chose Arthur as the name of her third son, who became Duke of Connaught, and it was also Prince Charles's choice for the son born to him and Diana, Princess of Wales in 1982. His mother's preference for William prevailed but Arthur is his second name.

Retold by Thomas Malory, Edmund Spenser and others, the Arthurian legend continued its appeal as a vision of Britishness through the Reformation and the Enlightenment. His cult was eclipsed by that of Alfred during the Hanoverian period but revived again in the Victorian era when it was taken up by both moralists and romantics. Alfred Tennyson produced a considerable corpus of poems about Arthur, notably *Idylls of the King* (1857-1875), in which he turned the British king and his knights of the Round Table into patterns of Victorian gentlemen, selfless pillars of moral order and exemplars of the values of duty, bravery, loyalty, courtesy, generosity and faithful love which coalesced in the particularly British virtue of chivalry. Pre-Raphaelite paintings confirmed his standing as the archetype of muscular Christianity and romantic heroism. In the words of Anthony Smith:

> It is not difficult to see how the holy 'mission' of the Arthurian knights was so well suited to the imperial mission of Victorian Britain and to a sense of its costs and sacrifices. The very adaptability of the Arthurian epic made it so easily assimilable to current needs and interests. Yet, an original ethno-religious core remained, even if it had been overlaid by romance and legend, which served both Welsh and English ethnic pride, and ultimately a modern British imperial nationalism.[14]

Arthur's appeal has continued through recent times, with T. H. White, Rosemary Sutcliffe, Stephen Lawhead and many others retelling his story, and both British and American films portraying him as a heroic figure with a relevant message for the modern age. Jeffrey Richards, who has made a special study of Arthur's cinematographic image, has shown how he was portrayed in 1950s films as a cold war warrior combating Communist totalitarianism, atheism and juvenile delinquency. In MGM's *Knights of the Round Table* (1954), the first feature film to seek to dramatize the Arthurian epic of Thomas Malory, the King and his Knights of the Round Table were held up as exemplars of constitutional monarchy and chivalry. Two other Arthurian films of the same year, *Prince Valiant* and *The Black Knight*, portrayed Arthur as a Christian king dealing with the external threat from barbarian and pagan invaders and the internal threat from subversion. Arthur came to stand as much for a shared Anglo-American as much as a British national identity 'based on chivalry, Christianity and constitutional government'.[15] In the 1995 film *First Knight* a British (actually Scottish) Arthur, Sean Connery, symbolically handed over the Camelot project to an American Lancelot, Richard Gere, confirming the USA's assumption of Britain's role as the divinely appointed bringer of civilization and democracy to the world. More recent films with an Arthurian theme, like *Prince Valiant* (1997) and *Merlin* (1998), have had a greater emphasis on mystical and esoteric aspects, reflecting the waning hold of traditional Christianity and the rise of New Age spiritualities. In the latest, *King Arthur* (2004), set at the tail end of Roman rule in Britain, Arthur is a tolerant, outward-looking, syncretistic Roman-British king based on Hadrian's Wall who forms an alliance with the Picts against the Nazi-like Saxons.

If the image of Arthur has been adapted and manipulated to suit the changing self-image of Britain and the United States of America, that of Merlin, the wizard, prophet and seer who figures so prominently in Arthurian myth, has remained more constant. Merlin represents the overlapping of the old primal religions and the new faith of Christianity which has long been a key feature of British spiritual identity. He is at once the Welsh druid, magic man and Celtic shaman and also the Christian priest and mystic. Geoffrey of Monmouth initiated this overlapping double identity by turning Myrddin, the legendary Welsh seer and wild man of the woods, into Merlin the druidic prophet and shaman at the royal court and writing a life of him in the style of the *Vita* of a Celtic saint. There is a wonderful blending of pagan and Christian identity in the story of Arthur plucking the sword out of the stone and being crowned at a ceremony where Merlin is portrayed as standing alongside Dubricius, the Archbishop of the Britons. As the story of his life and deeds was developed and embellished by subsequent chroniclers, Merlin came to stand for elements of the old pre-Christian rituals and beliefs which have long been an important theme in popular British spirituality, as displayed in such pagan survivals as the Green Man, mistletoe, well dressings and maypoles. In his most recent incarnation, in the 2004 *King Arthur* film, Merlin appears as a Pictish New Age wizard practising nature religion. He has also stood for the figure of the Welsh wizard, supremely brought to life in the highly charismatic, radical and mercurial figure of David Lloyd George, and the druidic bard full of wisdom and prophetic truth, as represented by the poet R. S. Thomas. The present Archbishop of Canterbury, Rowan Williams, the first holder of the office to be a member of the order of bards and portrayed in cartoons as a bearded druid, is to some extent a modern Merlin, representing Welsh wisdom and spirituality. His Nonconformist upbringing in Swansea still shows through his Oxford education and role at heart of the English and Anglican establishment and his intellectual and spiritual authority attests to the continuing power and influence of the Celtic spirit in British identity.

More than any other figure from Britain's mythical past, Arthur has links with virtually all parts of the United Kingdom and is claimed alike by Welsh, English and Scots, although not by the Irish whom he is said to have brought into Great Britain. Wales has several Arthurian sites, including the modern tourist attraction, Arthur's Labyrinth, which is just a few miles from the Celtica centre at Machynlleth and offers visitors a subterranean boat journey to learn about the enduring tales of Arthur and other Welsh legends. Among the places in Scotland with Arthurian connections are the Eildon Hills near Melrose, under which he is supposed to be buried, and Arthur's Seat, which dominates the city of Edinburgh. There are numerous Arthurian sites in Cumbria and in the south west of England, notably Tintagel in Cornwall. Of all the places associated with Arthur, the most important by far is Glastonbury, which since the twelfth century has been widely seen as the site of his Avalon. It also acquired other significant claims to fame. Around 1130, William of Malmesbury identified Glastonbury as the site of the first Christian church in Britain, set up by Joseph of Arimathea in AD 63 on the express orders of the apostle Philip. According to William, Patrick came over from Ireland via Cornwall to serve as the first abbot of Glastonbury and the church there became a resting place of Irish saints and haven for wandering Celtic monks, being visited, among others, by Brigit, David and Aidan, whose relics, along with those of Patrick, rested in its grounds. At a time of increasingly strained relations with Rome, the story of Joseph of Arimathea provided the English church with a native non-Roman foundation legend. The links invented by William of Malmesbury between Glastonbury and the leading saints of Ireland, Northumbria and Wales also helped to support the idea of a native British Christian tradition. In 1191, the bodies of Arthur and Guinevere were 'discovered' lying in a tomb under the abbey floor, showing that the great Celtic king had been buried in English soil. Now firmly linked with Arthur, the Grail, Joseph of Arimathea (whose body was later discovered in the abbey grounds and placed in a silver casket) and the golden age of Celtic Christianity, Glastonbury became, in the words of the Arthurian expert, Geoffrey Ashe, 'the pre-eminent shrine of knighthood, the holy place of the monarchy, and the accredited apostolic fountain-head of the British Church'.[16]

Glastonbury continues to play a significant if somewhat esoteric role in defining British spiritual identity. Each year, shortly before Christmas, sprigs from the thorn bush on Weary All Hill that supposedly sprouted from Joseph of Arimathea's staff are cut at a special ceremony and sent to the Queen so that she may have a spray from the thorn which traditionally flowers on Christmas morning. This ceremony, which was revived in 1929 after falling into abeyance after the Reformation, preserves a link between Arthurian legend and the modern British monarchy. The slightly surreal and somewhat shabby Somerset town is now the centre of New Age Britain, its long main street full of mind, body and spirit shops stocked with crystals, tarot cards and goddess books and its pavements crowded by ageing hippies with dogs. It provides a point of overlap between the worlds of Celtic Christian revival and New Age spirituality, being home to the Wessex Research Group, committed to awakening the ancient religions of the east and west and reviving the 'active mystical, Arthurian and Christian heritage' of Wessex, and the Quest Community which seeks to bridge Christianity and the New Age and 'take up the unfinished work of the Synod of Whitby' by bringing long-lost Celtic values of holism, eco- and feminine friendliness back into the mainstream British churches. Glastonbury is also the headquarters of the Church of the Holy Grail, also known as *Ecclesia Apostolica Jesus Christi*, the Grail Church, the Celtic Church and the British Church. Claiming foundation by Joseph of Arimathea at Glastonbury in AD 39, it presents itself as being older, purer and closer to Christ than the Roman Catholic Church or any other branch of the Christian church. Sidelined by Augustine's mission of 597 and defeated at the Synod of Whitby in 664, it had disappeared by the early eighth century, only to be wonderfully resurrected in 1973. Together with the

Celtic Orthodox Church, another relatively new creation which has an outpost in Glastonbury, it testifies to one of the more recondite aspects of the recent revival of interest in Celtic Christianity.

Several of the themes that are central to the Arthurian cult – the uniting of Britain, the appropriation of a Celtic past for an English-dominated present, the importance of monarchy and the intermeshing of Christianity with older more primal beliefs and rituals – also cluster around the Stone of Destiny, for the last 700 years a central prop in the coronation rite which, in the absence of a written constitution, arguably stands as the defining expression of British identity. This piece of cracked sandstone on which every English sovereign since 1307, apart from Mary I and Mary II, has been crowned, represents the fusing of Irish and Scottish mythology with English imperialism and underlines the sacred basis of British monarchy. Legend has it that the stone started life as the pillow on which Joseph slept when he had his dream of a ladder leading up to heaven. The next chapter in its history provides an origin legend for the Scots and forges a link between Old Testament kingship, the pharaohs of Egypt and the kings of Ireland. There are various versions of the story. One recounts that around 580 BC, when the Babylonians under King Nebuchadnezzar were invading Israel, the prophet Jeremiah and King Zedekiah's daughter, Tea, the last survivor of the Davidic line, smuggled the sacred stone out of Israel so that it would not fall into the hands of the Babylonian invaders. They went first to Egypt as guests of the Pharaoh and then via Spain to Ireland where Tea married Eochaid, king of Ireland, and took the name Scota. According to another version, the stone remained in Egypt for some time where it became the property of the country's rulers before being taken to Spain by Scota, Pharaoh's daughter, and subsequently to Ireland by one of her descendants, Simon Brek. This links up with the wider origin legend for the Celtic peoples of the British Isles as the descendants of the lost tribe of Dan.

In its 'Irish period', the stone acquired the name *Lia Fail*, or Stone of Destiny, and is said to have been sited at Tara, the holy hill on which Ireland's high kings were crowned. A piece was apparently broken off and taken to the Irish colony of Dal Riata in Argyllshire, possibly even by Columba who, according to some stories, used it as his pillow or his altar. After residing at Iona for a time, and possibly being used at Dunadd for the crowning of Dal Riatan kings, it was taken to Dunstaffnage Castle near Oban. Then, around 840, it was moved to Scone in Perthshire, the capital of the new united kingdom of Picts and Scots established by Kenneth MacAlpin. Kings of Scotland were enthroned sitting on the stone at Scone until it was removed to London in 1296 on the orders of Edward I as part of his bid to annex the Scottish crown to that of England.

The Stone of Destiny symbolizes the sacred character and history of monarchy in the British Isles and illustrates the considerable efforts which have been made to connect it with Old Testament kingship and Biblical narratives. For British Israelites, it is an important part of the evidence showing a direct descent of the British royal house from the throne of David. Symbolically and spiritually, the stone links the crowns of Ireland, Scotland and England. In the words of Arthur Stanley, Dean of Westminster from 1863 to 1881, it 'carries back our thoughts to races and customs now almost extinct, a link which unites the throne of England to the traditions of Tara and Iona, and connects the charm of our complex civilization with the forces of our mother earth – the sticks and stones of savage nature'[17] Its recent history illustrates both the tensions between Celtic and British identity and the way that they can be reconciled. Stolen from Westminster Abbey in 1950 by Scottish nationalists, it was subsequently recovered and officially returned to Scotland in 1996, with an understanding that it will be brought back to London for future coronations.

The idea of the Celtic spirit at the heart of Britishness, which had been built up by medieval chroniclers, supported by the Arthurian romances and the legend of the Stone of Destiny, was given a huge boost by the Reformation. Protestants in England, Scotland, Wales and Ireland united in a new shared sense of spiritual identity and heritage as they affirmed the rebirth of the original 'Celtic' church which had existed in the British Isles before the coming of the alien Roman mission of St Augustine of Canterbury. Protestant propagandists were, indeed, the first to use the word 'Celtic'. The earliest use of the term that I have been able to find is in the writings of John Bale in the 1540s. He was one of the first to posit a distinct Celtic-British Christian identity defined over and against Roman-Continental Christianity and suggested that Merlin's prophecy that the descendants of the ancient Britons would one day be restored to their primeval and rightful position in the island had been fulfilled by the ending of Roman domination brought about by the Reformation. Emphasizing the British character of the Church of England created as a result of Henry VIII's break with Rome, Bale portrayed the native Celtic people, Irish, Scottish and British, as heroes and the Saxons, Angles and Normans as 'baddies'. The Britishness of the early

English church was a major theme of *De Antiquitate Britannicae Ecclesiae*, written in 1572 by Matthew Parker while Archbishop of Canterbury.

It was not just the English who felt more British as a result of the Reformation. Several recent studies have demonstrated how Protestantism produced a dual, overlapping loyalty in Wales both to the Tudor monarchy and to the Welsh, Cymric tradition. The Welsh celebrated their distinctive British inheritance and their special relationship with the ruling dynasty. For the most part, the Welsh were happy to be incorporated in a British state and ruled by a British monarchy, as formally happened with the Act of Union with England in 1536. In the words of Peter Roberts, 'Welsh identity emerged from the imperial programme of the Tudors strengthened rather than undermined'.[18] While English was used as the official language for law and government, Welsh was officially recognized as the language of worship. Richard Davies, the Bishop of St David's from 1561 to 1581 and one of those responsible for translating both the Bible and Book of Common Prayer into Welsh, published an 'Address to the Welsh Nation' (*Epistol at y Cembru*) in 1567 as a preface to his Welsh translation of the New Testament in which he set out to show that Anglican Protestantism, far from being the religion of the Angles and Saxons, in fact represented the restoration of the faith of the ancient British (and, therefore, of the modern Welsh) people. Roberts has observed that 'The Tudor Protestant commitment to the principle of vernacular Scriptures revivified the ethos of a distinctive nationality despite, even perhaps because of, the closer ties with England' and remarks on the 'British consciousness of the Welsh Elizabethans' and the influence of the self-styled 'Cambro-Britons' in creating a new concept of British identity from a Welsh perspective.[19] John Owen of Pembrokeshire celebrated James I's accession as a fulfilment of Merlin's prophecy, hailed him as first king of the whole island of Britain since Brutus and rejoiced that the name Briton would henceforth be shared by Welsh, English and Scottish, the triple kingdom having been restored to British blood. Sir William Maurice of Clenennan was also convinced that James's accession was providentially ordained to fulfil the prophecy 'that out of the Bryttishe line should desende one that sholde restore the kingdom of Brittaine to the pristine state' and is said to have been the first subject to address him as 'King of Great Britain'. William Herbert of Glamorgan in *A Prophesie of Cadwallader* (1604) hailed James as 'our second Brute' who 'shall three in one, and one in three unite', using appropriately Trinitarian language to describe the restoration of the long lost British kingdom.[20]

The Reformation also encouraged feelings of Britishness among the Scots. We have already noted (page 37) David Hume's spirited advocacy of 'The British Union' published in 1605. Sixty years earlier, James Harrison had exhorted his fellow countrymen 'to conform themselfes to the union between England and Scotland' and advocated 'ye names of both subjectes and realms ceasing, and to be changed into ye name of Britain and Britons, as it was at first, and yet ought to be'. Struck by the similarity of place names in Scotland, Ireland, southern Britain, Gaul and Spain, George Buchanan, a leading humanist scholar and lay moderator of the General Assembly of the Church of Scotland, posited the notion of a common descent from a people whom he named Celts. His *Rerum Scotiarum Historia*, published in 1582, is generally taken to be a pioneering work in the identification of the Celtic origins of the peoples of the British Isles. A hundred years or so later, Edward Lhuyd, keeper of the Ashmolean Museum, Oxford, and a strong Welsh patriot who described himself as 'an old Briton', developed Buchanan's theories about the common basis of the native languages of the British Isles, demonstrating in his *Archaeologia Britannica* of 1707 that Welsh, Cornish, Breton, Scottish and Irish Gaelic all belonged to the same linguistic family. Lhuyd probably did more than anyone to promote the term 'Celtic' and to give it specifically British associations. Hitherto, the Celts had been thought of as a European people who belonged to Gaul, Spain and regions further afield. From the beginning of the eighteenth century, they came to be thought of primarily as the original indigenous inhabitants of the British Isles, there before the Romans, Saxons, Angles, Vikings and Normans.

While the Welsh and the Scots were generally happy to be incorporated within an overarching British identity in the aftermath of the Reformation, the Irish were more ambivalent. For the Catholic majority, Gaelic and Celtic consciousness asserted itself against what was seen as alien English Protestantism and led to the growth of Irish nationalism in the sixteenth and seventeenth centuries. Anglo-Irish Protestants, on the other hand, enthusiastically adopted Ireland's Celtic past. The new cathedral built in the colonial city of Londonderry between 1628 and 1633 was dedicated not to St Paul or St George, as its London patrons might have been expected to favour, but to Columba. James Ussher, Archbishop of Armagh from 1625 to 1641, sought to prove that the Anglican Church of Ireland was the natural heir and successor to the Celtic church founded by Patrick in the fifth century which, he argued, had been Protestant (and British) in all but name.[21]

This greater consciousness of the Celtic element in Britishness as a consequence of the Reformation in England, Wales, Scotland and among the Protestant population of Ireland was accompanied by a virulent anti-Catholicism which, as Linda Colley and others have pointed out, was one of the key factors in forging a common British identity across the United Kingdom. It had other less negative effects, leading in the eighteenth century to a growing appreciation of Britain's pre-Christian heritage and a sense that Celtic Christianity had drawn on and taken over some of the values of pagan and primal religions.

This syncretist agenda, which fitted with the broad, deist outlook of much of the church in eighteenth-century Britain, was initially put forward on the basis of the similarities between Druidism and early British Christianity. In one of the first studies of the ancient stones of Britain, *Stonehenge, a Temple restor'd to the British Druids* (1740), William Stukeley, a Lincolnshire clergyman, argued that the Druids, who had come over to Britain soon after the Flood, had a religion 'extremely like Christianity'. His book presented an attractive vision of a broad and non-dogmatic patriarchal religion, practised in both pre- and early Christian Britain, which appealed to many of his fellow clerics. Stukeley, who called the Britons Celts, also argued that the doctrine of the Trinity was a Celtic (and therefore British) invention. In 1766, John Cleland argued that Druidism so successfully permeated early Christianity with its doctrines that the Mass took its name not from the phrase *Missa est* but from mistletoe. Edward Williams, a Glamorgan stonemason who moved to London and adopted the pen name Iolo of Glamorgan, claimed in 1794 that the Welsh medieval poems of Taliesin 'exhibit a complete system of DRUIDISM' and that 'by these writings it will appear that the Ancient British CHRISTIANITY was strongly tinctured with DRUIDISM.'[22]

The Celtic soul at the heart of Britishness was a major theme of several leading Victorian writers. Matthew Arnold was disappointed to find on a visit to an *eisteddfod* at Llandudno in the 1860s that the 'spell of the Celtic genius' had been destroyed by the triumph of 'the prosaic, practical Saxon'. The speeches had been in English, the proceedings dull and lifeless and the atmosphere ruined by the 'miserable looking Saxons' who arrived on the Liverpool steamer. In short, the philistinism of the English had been allowed to prevail over the poetic sensitivity of the Welsh. So it was in Britain as a whole, which Arnold characterized as a country having 'a vast obscure Cymric base with a vast visible Teutonic superstructure'.

His experience at Llandudno led him to write his *Study of Celtic Literature* (1867), which extolled the Celtic temperament as sensitive, visionary, poetic, spiritual, mercurial and given to melancholy and contrasted it with the more steady-going, prosaic, plodding and materialistic Saxon temperament. Drawing on early Irish, Scottish and Welsh religious poetry, he saw no great discontinuity between pagan and Christian Celtic religion and found that pre-Christian themes and images permeated Celtic Christianity. Although he portrayed the Celts in some sense as outsiders, standing at the edge and defined in terms of their 'otherness', he was also struck by their essential Britishness: 'Of the shrunken and diminished remains of this great primitive race, all, with one insignificant exception, belongs to the English empire; only Brittany is not ours; we have Ireland, the Scotch Highlands, Wales, the Isle of Man, Cornwall.' The note of English imperialism here is unmistakable but Arnold was genuinely concerned at his countrymen's lack of awareness of this part of their national heritage. The Celts, he wrote,

> *are a part of ourselves, we are deeply interested in knowing them, they*
> *are deeply interested in being known by us; and yet in the great and rich*
> *universities of this great and rich country there is no chair of Celtic, there is*
> *no study or teaching of Celtic matters; those who want them must go abroad*
> *for them.*[23]

Nineteenth-century churchmen also vigorously pursued the theme of the common Britishness of their Protestant heritage. Thomas Burgess, Bishop of St David's and later of Salisbury, in 1815 gloried in the knowledge that 'the Church of Britain was a Protestant church nine centuries before the days of Luther.'[24] G. T. Stokes, Vicar of All Saints, Blackrock in Dublin, wrote in his *Ireland and the Celtic Church* (1886):

> *English Christianity, the Christianity of the Angles and of the Saxons, dates*
> *from Augustine and was derived from Rome. British Christianity was the*
> *Christianity of the Britons; it existed here before Augustine, and must have*
> *been derived immediately from Gaul.*[25]

As the Roman Catholic Church in Ireland looked increasingly to Rome and Continental influences, the Anglican Church of Ireland affirmed its Celtic roots, incorporating early Irish hymns into its worship and dedicating its new parish churches and cathedrals to Irish saints. James Cooper, Church of Scotland minister and Professor of Ecclesiastical History in the University of Glasgow, called on his own church to draw much more on its Celtic inheritance, especially in the area of liturgy, suggesting that contemporary use should be made in both public and private worship of Patrick's *Confessio*, Columba's hymns and the Antiphonary of Bangor. He argued that the Celts had been founders not just of Scottish but of British Christianity and campaigned for what he called 'imperial reunion', in which all the Protestant churches of Great Britain and the Empire would join together on the basis of their common Celtic heritage.

The Britishness of the Church of England was championed with particular enthusiasm by Samuel Stone, rector of the City of London church of All Hallows' On the Wall, who fell under the spell of Iona after visiting it while on holiday in Scotland in 1872. He argued that the Church of England owed far more to Columba of Iona and Aidan of Lindisfarne than it did to Augustine of Canterbury and that 'the chief debt of Anglo-Saxon Christianity is due to the Celtic Church and its Fathers.'[26] Stone felt that the *via media* between the extremes of Protestantism and Catholicism pursued by the Church of England and its resistance to authoritarianism were enduring testimonies to 'the pure Celtic blood in our spiritual ancestry'. In a stream of highly romantic poems, like 'The Spirit of the Church From Iona, Or the Union of the Celtic, British and Gregorian Churches in the Anglican Church', he sought to show that Celtic Christianity was not dead but remained alive as a living spiritual force:

> *Say not the Celtic Church is gone,*
> *Like sunset beam from mountain brow;*
> *The Celtic soul lives on, lives on,*
> *The old pure heart is beating now!*
> *Nor say the British Church is gone,*
> *As dies some legendary lay;*
> *The British Church lives on, lives on,*
> *Saint David's Church is here today!*[27]

There was less emphasis on both Britishness and Christianity in the predominantly

Irish 'Celtic Twilight' movement at the tail end of the nineteenth century. Although most of its leading protagonists came of Anglo-Irish Protestant stock, several of the most prominent Celtic revivalists eschewed orthodox Christian belief in favour of various forms of mysticism, occultism and nature worship. Their main focus was on recovering pre-Christian and pagan folklore. Indeed, it was a collection of such material, culled from old peasant tales and published in 1893 by W. B. Yeats, that gave the movement its name. His latest biographer has encapsulated Yeats's conception of the Celtic tradition as 'non-English, anti-materialistic, anti-bourgeois and connected to Theosophical and Rosicurian symbolism, via Blake and Swedenborg'.[28] Druidism, fairy lore and pre-Christian heroes loomed much larger in this scheme of things than monasteries, hymns and saints. The Order of the Golden Dawn, which Yeats set up, was primarily focused on the esoteric and mystical elements of Celticism. One of its most enthusiastic Welsh members, Arthur Machen, the son of an Anglican clergyman, became fascinated by the pagan aspects of Welsh folklore and the Quest for the Holy Grail, and espoused a religion of nature. Other romantic Celticists, however, adopted a more Christian and a more British perspective, like the Church in Wales clergyman who adopted the name Brother Ignatius, styled himself 'a monk of the British church' and established a monastery at Llanthony in the Black Mountains.

The recent revival of Celtic consciousness has similarly encompassed romantic, esoteric, neo-pagan, Christian, nationalistic and British elements. Undoubtedly, it has in considerable part been fuelled by the rise in nationalist sentiment that has led to the establishment of the Scottish Parliament, the Welsh Assembly and various experiments in devolved government in Northern Ireland. But there is also a strong British emphasis in many of the manifestations of the current Celtic revival. This is evident, for example, on the web pages of the Britannia Historical Re-enactment group, dedicated to recreating the experience of 'living in the Dark Ages' which focus on the topic of 'Arthur's Britain' as well as on Bardic workshops and drumming (www. durolitum.co.uk). The extent to which a reinvigorated and re-spiritualized Britain features in the dreams of New Age and neo-pagan Celtic revivalists is evident from this comment by Sir George Trevelyan in the preface to one of the many recent books which trace an unbroken thread from pagan, druidic roots through Celtic and Gnostic Christianity into the Grail legends and beyond into the present age:

Many people share the irrepressible hope that Arthur, the Once and
Future King, is coming again and that he represents a kingdom which
will reanimate the dying Earth's existence, and bring a flood of divine
warmth and light into our darkened and embattled world. And Merlin, his
magician, is the power which oversees and inspires the 'Matter of Britain',
for it seems that this beloved land of ours carries a spiritual destiny and task,
the fulfilling of which is to be realized in our generation.[29]

It is interesting that this same book quotes the Prince of Wales commending 'an awareness of what lies beneath the surface of the visible world and of those ancient, unconscious forces which still help to shape the psychological attitudes of modern man'. Prince Charles's personal crusade to return to deep primal values and re-emphasize the spiritual dimension in life could, indeed, be seen as part of the revival of the Celtic spirit in Britishness. It also has considerable potential to engage and enthuse those of other faiths and cultures in a new British spiritual identity which builds on native traditions of organic agriculture and vernacular architecture while also drawing on eastern traditions of holistic medicine and Islamic approaches to art and design. [30]

At a more popular and commercial level, Rheged, the 'village in the hill' created just off the M6 motorway near Penrith in Cumbria in 2000 as a major tourist attraction to tell the story of Celtic Britain, presents a fascinating mixture of history, myth, postmodern romanticism and British patriotism. The name was chosen after extensive canvassing of focus groups in Newcastle, Glasgow, Birmingham, Manchester and Penrith. 'Rheged' was the largest native Celtic kingdom that emerged at the end of the period of Roman occupation of the British Isles and flourished through the Dark Ages from AD 450 to 700, stretching from southern Scotland to Cheshire and at the height of its power from Stranraer in the west to Catterick in the east. The large format film which is the centrepiece of the Rheged experience tells the story of a young American, Luke, coming to Cumbria to retrace the steps of his grandfather, who had emigrated from there in the early twentieth century. He meets a sultry and seductive gypsy girl who, as well as providing sex interest, wonderfully blends the pagan and Christian aspects of the British Celtic past by wearing a Celtic cross round her neck while dealing out tarot cards. The film focuses on the legend of Urien, Rheged's most famous king who was said to have worn the symbol of a raven round his chest. Luke has inherited this symbol from his grandfather and his quest is to hurl this talisman off a Cumbrian mountain to release Urien's imprisoned spirit. Arthur also features prominently in the film and much is made of the fact that Cumbria has more sites with Arthurian associations than anywhere else in Britain. The film mixes primal and Christian symbols with the raven talisman, the Celtic cross, monks, frenzied pagan dancers and gypsies all being given equal prominence. William Wordsworth also makes a cameo appearance to give a touch of English romanticism. There is a distinctly postmodern message in the narrator's final words as the helicopter-borne camera swoops over the Cumbrian fells: 'For those who look, it is not just the mountains they can find, it is themselves.' Rediscovering the Celtic heart and soul of Britain is, it seems, as much an inner journey as an outer one.

It is certainly about retail therapy. Visitors leave the multiplex cinema at Rheged to stroll down 'Retail Street', Europe's largest grass-covered shopping mall where CDs entitled *Dalriada – Sophistry and Illusion, Celtic Mist, Celtic Embrace, Celtic Blessing, Celtic Legend* and *Stone of Destiny* are piled high next to Celtic crosses and talismans. A special collection of bronze figurines, produced by a local Cumbrian firm and marketed under the collective label *Avalon – The Magic of King Arthur*, include 'Sir Kay', 'Questing Beast', 'Lancelot's Lost Love' and 'The Last Embrace'. There are also numerous eating outlets on Retail Street, including a food bar entitled '100% British' which describes itself as 'an entirely British food hall, proudly supporting more than forty Cumbrian producers and promoting over 500 products from Northern England'. This description of geographical origin is generously interpreted – there are shelves of wines from southern England, Scottish whiskies and tea and coffee with an imperial rather than a northern English provenance. But there is undoubtedly an overarching sense at Rheged of celebrating Britishness, reinforced by the fact that the other main film shown on the giant screen features the triumphant coronation-year conquest of Everest. In that respect, it contrasts strongly with the downplaying of Britishness at Celtica.

There is much hype and hyperbole in the current enthusiasm for all things Celtic, but there is also much that is genuine and positively helpful in paving the way for a new more grounded and also more spiritual British identity. This is especially true of the revival of Celtic Christianity, which has perhaps been the most substantial and enduring element in this whole fascinating and continuing phenomenon. The recovery of the Celtic spirit at the heart of British Christianity, and the creative and imaginative invention and re-invention of ' Celtic' elements which may not have actually existed at the time of Patrick, Columba, David and Aidan, but which certainly speak to our needs and concerns now, has been a truly ecumenical enterprise which has engaged Christians across denominations and theological divides and brought them closer together in shared witness, worship and pilgrimage. It has hugely enriched the worship of many churches, making it less prose-bound and long-winded and more mystical and poetical. It has fostered a growing interest in living in community, going on pilgrimages and celebrating and affirming the sacred places of Britain. New pilgrim routes have opened up like St Cuthbert's Way from Melrose to Lindisfarne, which straddles Scotland and England, and the walk to Bardsey through the Lleyn peninsula in north-west Wales. Iona has become a mecca for tens of thousands of pilgrims each year as well as being the base of a community committed to a gritty, inclusive, incarnational faith predicated on the principles of peace and justice. Celtic Chistianity in its modern incarnation is both deeply British and yet also outward-looking and internationalist, orthodox and Trinitarian yet syncretistic at its edges and offering real possibility for inter-faith dialogue and engagement with contemporary concerns and New Age spirituality. It has put passion and mystical experience back into the rather insouciant and lukewarm world of British Christianity but not narrowness and fundamentalism.

One of the most striking features of the revival of interest in Celtic Christianity is that it has been a truly British project, linking church people, academics and enthusiasts from all parts of the United Kingdom and, indeed, from the Republic of Ireland. It has demonstrated the Trinitarian perichoresis which I have suggested is a central feature of Britishness, bringing ancient Irish prayers into English parish churches and Welsh praise poems into the Scottish Kirk. It has led many people living in Britain to make journeys within their own country, taking some on significant and permanent pilgrimages, like those made by Donald Allchin from Oxford to North Wales and by Ray Simpson from Norfolk to Lindisfarne. These two southern Englishmen have respectively opened up the riches of the Welsh spiritual tradition and established a community to live out and explore the principles of Celtic Christianity on the model established by Aidan. In his recent book, *Church of the Isles: A Prophetic Strategy for Renewal*, Ray Simpson reflects on what a renewed Celtic spirit might do to make Britain a more coherent society:

The British are a mongrel people – Roman, Saxon, Scandinavian, Norman, Jewish, Afro-Caribbean, Asian – but before all of these we are Celtic. Christians in Celtic times united peoples from four hostile ethnic groups: the Gaels (mostly from Ireland), the Picts (mostly from Scotland), the Anglo-Saxons (mostly from England) and the ancient British (many from Wales). This offers hope to our multi-ethnic society.[31]

There are, of course, parts of the British Isles where the faith of the people has always been Celtic, defined in the strictest sense as practised in a Celtic language and culture. This is most clearly the case among the inhabitants of the Outer Hebrides off the north-west coast of Scotland. This remote region has the highest levels of churchgoing in the United Kingdom outside Northern Ireland. In some ways, its Christianity seems very polarized and old fashioned: an austere, very Biblical Protestantism in the northern isles of Lewis and Harris and a Catholicism rich in folklore and imagery in the southern isles of Barra and South Uist. Yet the fact is that there is no bigotry or sectarianism between the Protestant and Catholic communities of the Western Isles. It is also striking that the island of Lewis, which usually only finds its way into the national news for some example of religious extremism, like padlocking swings in public paths on the Sabbath, has proved one of the most welcoming places for Muslims settling in Britain.

Whether in its original state in the windswept Outer Isles, or reconstituted and reconstructed at Celtica, Rheged, Iona or Lindisfarne, the Celtic spirit undoubtedly remains a key element in British identity, real and imagined. It does, indeed, perhaps represent the closest that Britain gets to an ethno-cultural identity, providing shared myths of descent, origin legends and founding mother and father figures and archetypes. In the next chapter we move to an identity that is more about ideas and principles.

4 Liberty, Tolerance and Indifference

The Anglo-Saxon and Gothic Contribution

In considering the second great element in British identity, the deep-seated attachment to freedom and tolerance, we move from myths, legends and archetypes to traditions and principles. We also shift geographically from the Celtic fringes to England. Myth is not absent from the creation of the British love affair with liberty – it is at least partially behind such key constructs as the sturdy, independent Saxon yeoman and the oppressive Norman yoke. The Scots, and to a lesser extent the Irish and Welsh, have also played a part in planting a love of freedom at the heart of British identity but it is pre-eminently the contribution of the English, framed and developed in terms of ideals and principles.

The equation of Britishness with freedom is made very explicitly in the patriotic songs belted out with such enthusiasm each year at the Last Night of the Proms, which provides the nation with one of its few occasions for unembarrassed flag waving. 'Rule Britannia', written by a Scotsman in 1740, is a sustained paean to Britain's special and even God-given role in the world as a beacon and defender of freedom, a land which will not, like those benighted nations on the Continent in the thrall of absolutism and Catholicism, 'to tyrants fall' and whose inhabitants 'never, never, never shall be slaves'. A. C. Benson's 1902 Coronation Ode, better known as 'Land of Hope and Glory', refers to Britain as the 'Mother of the Free', lists the nation's virtues as 'Truth and Right and Freedom' and affirms the British as being 'strong in faith and freedom'. A more recent popular song, Ross Parker and Hughie Charles' 'There'll Always be an England', written in 1939, proclaims that 'Freedom remains, these are the chains, nothing can break'. It is significant and appropriate that this song, while containing the line 'Red, white, and blue – what does it mean to you' used in the heading for Chapter 2, is essentially focused on England rather than the United Kingdom as a whole and makes Britishness and Englishness largely indistinguishable.

So they seem in many ways to the Scot, Gordon Brown, for whom commitment to individual liberty stands as the heart of the Britishness that he wishes to promote:

There is a golden thread which runs through British history of the individual standing firm for freedom and liberty against tyranny and the arbitrary use of power. It runs from that long ago day in Runnymede in 1215 to the Bill of Rights in 1689 to not just one but four Great Reform Acts within less than a hundred years. And the great tradition of British liberty has, first and foremost, been rooted in the protection of the individual against the arbitrary power of first the monarch and then the state.

It was Montesquieu who wrote in the 18th century that ours was 'the freest country in the world'. I would suggest that it is because several different ethnic groups came to live together in one small island that we first made a virtue of tolerance, welcoming and including successive waves of immigrants – from Saxons and Normans to Huguenots and Jews and Asians and Afro-Caribbeans and recognizing plural identities. Today eighty-five per cent believe a strong sense of tolerance is important to our country's success. And I would suggest that out of that toleration came a belief in religious and political freedom – illustrated best by Adam Nicolson's story of the creation of the King James Bible: different denominations coming together in committee to create what was called 'irenicon' which means a symbol of unity for the whole nation.

Liberty meant just not tolerance for minorities but a deeply rooted belief – illustrated early in our history by trial by jury – in the freedom of the individual under the law and in the liberty of the common people rooted in

constantly evolving English common law. When Henry Grattan – the 18th
century Irish politician – attempted to sum up our unique characteristics,
he said that you can get a Parliament from anywhere but you can only get
liberty from England. Indeed, so powerful were the ideas contained in the
1689 Bill of Rights which led to liberty associations all over Britain that
both sides in the American War of Independence fought in the name of
British liberty and before America took the world to be its own, liberty was,
in fact, identified with Britain.[1]

I have quoted this stirring paean of praise to British liberty at some length because, as well as being very inspiring, it is also gives a fascinating insight into a leading twenty-first-century Labour politician's understanding of the essence of Britishness. It is in many ways very old-fashioned, a classic statement of the Whig view of history as formulated by Lord Macaulay and mid-nineteenth-century historians. The icons of British liberty cited by Brown are located far in the past - Magna Carta, the Glorious Revolution and the Reform Acts of the nineteenth century. It gives a distinctly rosy impression of the way that successive waves of immigrants were welcomed by the British that is at odds with the historical evidence. To quote from another popular patriotic song, the Men of Harlech were hardly extending the hand of friendship to their Anglo-Saxon invaders when they sang

Now, avenging Briton,
Smite as he has smitten!
Let your rage on history's page
In Saxon blood be written!

There is a deep vein of romantic nostalgia evident here. Gordon Brown spoke earlier in this same speech in fond terms of the days of his early childhood – the world of Winston Churchill, a coronation that was reported with almost religious enthusiasm, an unquestionably United Kingdom and around us symbols of an imperial Britain'. He pointed out that this was a country 'whose confidence was built – unlike the USA – not on aspirations about the future but on real achievements of the past' and that could legitimately claim to be the first country in the world to reject the arbitrary rule of monarchy and to make a virtue of tolerance and liberty.

Brown's speech reflects a key aspect of British self-identity in locating the attachment to liberty not in terms of abstract demands and rights (the French way) but rather in precedents and traditions built up and preserved over a long period and in a fundamental belief in the rule of law. The British, indeed, dislike abstract theories almost as much as they dislike absolutist powers. Unlike those living in or governing the USA, they do not feel the need to trumpet their belief in liberty and express it in some kind of mission statement or explicit national ethos. The anti-Americanism implicit, and indeed, explicit, in Brown's definition of Britishness is matched by a strong Anglophilia. When this very Scottish politician, who chose to make his career at Westminster rather than in Edinburgh, speaks of British liberty, it is an essentially English quality he is thinking of, as indicated by his reference to English common law and quotation of Grattan talking about English liberty. Montesquieu was also specifically referring to England when he made his remark about it being the freest country in the world. So, much later, was Joseph Conrad when he wrote in 1899 to a fellow Pole that liberty 'can only be found under the English flag all over the world'.[2] The fact is that it is largely the English who have given the British their characteristic love of liberty and their profound tolerance, so rightly highlighted by the Queen in her address to both Houses of Parliament during her jubilee celebrations in 2002 and in her 2004 Christmas broadcast, which was a powerful plea for greater understanding and respect between those of different faiths and cultures. Significantly, in her broadcast, the Queen cited the example of London and the experience of a visitor from abroad landing at Heathrow and impressed on his tube journey into the city centre by the way children from diverse ethnic and religious backgrounds were at ease and trusted one another.

We might want to ask whether what this visitor witnessed was, indeed, respect, tolerance and commitment to freedom and diversity or rather the reserve, concern with privacy and indifference that makes the British so reluctant to engage with one another in any conversation or even make eye contact in public spaces, or to intervene if someone is being harassed or attacked. There is a thin dividing line between tolerance and indifference and this needs to be borne in mind in any discussion of the much-vaunted British attachment to individual freedom. Nonetheless, it is undoubtedly true that liberty, both as an ideal and a principle, has been a defining British characteristic and in some ways the most enduring British export. Elliott Dodds, crusading liberal journalist and president of the Liberal Party in the mid-twentieth century, certainly thought so: 'The argument of liberty from Locke to Mill, and on through Green and Hobhouse to Ramsay Muir, has been the characteristic gift of Britain to the world.'[3] It is, of course, not just the intellectual idea of liberty that Britain has exported but also liberal institutions as diverse as the rule of law, parliamentary democracy, an impartial civil service and public service broadcasting. We have also given refuge to those fleeing discrimination and persecution in lands where the lamp of liberty no longer burned, from the Huguenot weavers who set up their looms in Kent in the sixteenth century to the East African Asians who brought their business skills to our cities in the 1960s and 1970s.

It is significant that it is to England more than to other parts of the United Kingdom that political and religious refugees across the centuries have come. The English have long been notably more tolerant than the Scots, Northern Irish or Welsh. It was this quality that most struck and endeared my Scottish mother to them when she came south to London in the late 1920s and that she missed most when she returned to Scotland in the mid 1980s. It was also the quality that endeared King James VI and I to his English subjects who proved more amenable than his fellow Scots to his project to establish the new kingdom of Great Britain on the principle of religious tolerance that he hoped the new Authorised Version of the Bible would promote. 'Liberty is the English ideology,' the Australian-born literary scholar, George Watson, wrote in his book celebrating *The English Ideology*, 'and its achievement within parliamentary institutions dignified by traditional and ceremonial forms – sometimes called "the Westminster model" – is still the first image that springs to mind when most men hear the name of England.'[4] I am not at all sure that would be true today, a little over thirty years since Watson wrote it. But he is right to argue that, at least in historical terms, it has been the dominant English ideology, fostered on a historic appeal to Anglo-Saxon freedoms and reaching its apogee in the Victorian era when, as he so lovingly celebrates, it took on a wonderful literary richness, being championed by Dickens, Thackeray, Trollope, Browning, George Eliot, Mill, Acton and Gladstone. As he rightly observes, it was not merely a political ideology predicated on a penchant for free institutions but a moral creed: 'The English ideology is a moral system. It is not ultimately based on practical considerations … but on a perceived difference between right and wrong. Its hallmark is a zeal for righteousness.'[5]

Much of this English, and British, attachment to liberty and toleration, and perhaps some of the indifference or relativism that goes with it, springs from

Protestantism. The argument that Protestantism was the single most important factor in the making of Britishness has been stated perhaps most emphatically by Linda Colley in her book, *Britons: Forging the Nations* (1992). In her words, 'It was their common investment in Protestantism that first allowed the English, the Welsh and the Scots to become fused together, and to remain so, despite their many cultural divergences.'[6] Religion, for Colley, was the key matrix of British identity in the period between 1707 and 1837, when the separate parliaments, and identities, of England, Scotland and Ireland were fused to create the United Kingdom. Her thesis has been criticized, notably by Jonathan Clark who points to the diffuse nature of Protestantism and suggests that she overstates 'the simple dualism of Protestant versus Catholic as an explanation for a putative consensual national identity'[7]. It is undoubtedly true, however, that Protestantism was hugely important in defining British self-identity over and against the superstitious, despotic, priest-ridden Catholicism perceived to pervade most of Continental Europe. It was against caricatures of Popish absolutism arid tyranny that the sturdy British love of liberty and personal freedom was championed and promoted.

Protestantism also helped to contribute to the arrogance, imperialism and insularity of the British character. In particular, it played a major role in encouraging the idea of the British as a chosen people, a second Israel even, called by God to lead the crusade against Catholic Europe and then to spread civilization across the globe through the British Empire. This sense of election, which has more recently been taken over by the USA, is well explored by Clifford Longley in his recent book *Chosen People* (2002). More positively, the influence of Protestantism has been felt historically in the British love of liberty, commitment to toleration, respect for the rule of law and peaceable, orderly behaviour. It was not, however, the earliest influence promoting love of liberty; hatred of oppression and arbitrary authority and commitment to ordered government and society based on the rule of law at the heart of British self-identity. For this we need to go back to the Anglo-Saxon invaders and their descendants, so hated and despised by the Celts who were the subject of the last chapter. It was these Germanic Gothic people, the ancestors of the English, who brought a passion for individual liberty and its protection in law to these shores, just as they later initiated the Protestant Reformation in Europe.

We have already encountered one of the earliest and most important Anglo-Saxon contributors to the emergence of British identity in the figure of the

Venerable Bede, chronicling the history of Christianity in the island of Britannia from his perspective as a Northumbrian monk in the early eighth century. He was one of the first to conflate Englishness with Britishness, the *Gens Anglorum* with *Britannia*, and he has been hailed by many historians, notably Patrick Wormald, as the founding father of English identity.[8] Yet, as we have seen, he also did much to promote the Celtic strain in Britishness, especially in its spiritual aspects and was instrumental in laying the foundations of the idea of an independent (and proto-Protestant) British church exhibiting a gentler and less oppressive Christianity than that found in Rome and on the Continent.

The key figure in establishing the Anglo-Saxon commitment to individual liberty, expressed through the institution of the common law, was Alfred, ruler of Wessex from 871 to 899 and the first man to be thought of as King of the English people. Having secured the safety of his kingdom by beating back the invading Danes, he devoted most of his reign to administrative and ecclesiastical reforms and to promoting the advancement of learning. He promulgated the first systematic set of laws in England, drawing heavily on the law codes of the Old Testament, and sought to promote the principles of justice and equity. He single-handedly launched a crusade to improve the pastoral, intellectual and liturgical standards of the clergy, and he led by example, being a man of regular prayer and deep faith, as well as exhibiting what were to become the characteristic British virtues of reserve and restraint. Thanks in large part to his own personal example, and also to the hagiographical biography of him written by Asser, Alfred came to assume a similar heroic role among the English to that of Arthur among the Celtic people of the British Isles. Although rooted in Anglo-Saxon Wessex and lacking the association that Arthur had with places in Wales, Scotland and Ireland, he came after his death to be taken up as a symbol of Britishness as much as of Englishness, nowhere more so than in Thomas Arne's masque, *Alfred* (1740), the climax of which is the song which we know as 'Rule Britannia' in which this Saxon king and his people are celebrated as Britons and their nation as 'Britannia'. Although lacking the romance of Arthur, the Excalibur-wielding Celt, Alfred, a much more solidly historical figure, came to embody several key British virtues, including the stability and impartiality of the rule of law and benevolent Christian monarchy. The heyday of his reputation was in the Hanoverian-dominated eighteenth and early nineteenth centuries. In the twentieth century he was rather eclipsed by Arthur. Two world wars against a

Germanic nation made Saxon heroes less acceptable in Britain and just one film has been made about him in the last fifty years (*Alfred the Great* in 1969) in contrast to the whole clutch devoted to Arthurian themes. Yet the king whose imposing statue with sword defiantly held erect still stands in the centre of Winchester is now being rehabilitated, as exemplified by Bernard Cornwell's trilogy on Alfred, the first volume of which, *The Last Kingdom*, was published in 2005.

The Anglo-Saxon commitment to freedom is invariably seen as having been consolidated and cemented in Magna Carta, the famous charter wrested out of 'bad' King John by the barons at Runnymede in 1215, which established the principle that no free man can be imprisoned or punished without prior judgment by the law of the land and that justice will never be denied, delayed or sold. This is often taken as the origin of the key English common law principle of *habeas corpus*, although the writ enshrining this principle did not acquire its main purpose of freeing those unjustly imprisoned until the reign of Henry VII. The huge importance of *habeas corpus*, and its guarantee of individual liberty against arbitrary and authoritarian government, as a defining hallmark of the unwritten British constitution and the British way of doing things is shown by the extent to which it was cited in 2005 by both Conservative and Liberal Democrat opponents of the Labour Government's anti-terrorist legislation, which involved house arrest and detention without trial. Significantly, the motivating force behind the drawing up of Magna Carta was spiritual as much as political. Stephen Langton, the Archbishop of Canterbury, had a crucial role in encouraging the barons to set down their demands, almost certainly had a major hand in drafting the charter and was instrumental in persuading Henry III to reissue it when he came of age in its definitive version of 1225. It was no coincidence that some of the most powerful speeches made against the Government's assumption of arbitrary powers in 2005 came from the bishops' benches in the House of Lords.

Magna Carta undoubtedly played a key part in the development of England as a nation state. The great constitutional historian William Stubbs observed, 'The Great Charter is the first great public act of the nation, after it has realized its own identity.'[9] It stands, too, as a foundational document for the British tradition of constitutional monarchy and Parliamentary sovereignty. Its emphasis on the liberty of free men is unparalleled in contemporary Continental documents although somewhat similar language is to be found in the Scottish Declaration of Arbroath in 1320. This defiant call on the English to leave the Scots alone and not make war on their 'smaller neighbours' justifies their struggle against their more powerful southern oppressors 'for we fight not for glory, nor riches, nor honours, but for freedom alone, which no good man gives up except with his life'. The Declaration of Arbroath also forcefully expresses other themes often more associated with English, and later with British identity, notably the notion of a chosen people. Starting from the origin legend that the Scots are descendants of one of the lost tribes of Israel, it builds on Andrew's role as their patron saint to suggest that 'Our Lord Jesus Christ called them, even though settled in the uttermost ends of the earth, almost the first to his most holy faith.'[10] It is not the only important medieval Scottish document to emphasize the theme of individual freedom. An epic poem on the wars of independence against the English, *The Bruce*, written in the 1370s by John Barbour, constitutes one of the first great literary meditations on the meaning of freedom in the English language and serves as a reminder that the Anglo-Saxons did not have a monopoly on this theme that was to become so important in broader British identity:

Ah! Freedom is a noble thing
Freedom makes man to have his liking;
Freedom all solace to man gives
He lives at ease that freely lives.[11]

If William Wallace and Robert the Bruce came out of the late thirteenth and early fourteenth century as nationalists and freedom fighters epitomizing a particularly Scottish identification of liberty as equating with liberation from the English, a more shadowy and legendary figure who emerged around the same time was to become an important icon of a broader and less nationalistic English conception of liberty. Robin Hood's historical origins and role are uncertain – modern scholarship tends to place him in the early thirteenth century – but by the mid fifteenth century he had come to be seen as a Saxon chivalric hero fighting Norman oppression and standing for the rights of the small man, with his project of robbing the rich to give to the poor being seen as an exercise in Christian social justice. In many of his later incarnations, not least as a dashing matinée idol in mid-twentieth-century cinema and television, Robin Hood was portrayed as being around at the time of Magna Carta, and as an opponent of the tyranny and arbitrary power of King John, championing the right of the people to rule themselves in freedom and dignity. His band of merry men, led by the sturdy yeoman Little John and the portly and benevolent Friar Tuck, helped to build up and reinforce several strong English, and later British stereotypes, including male bonding, the chivalric band of brothers and the jolly clergyman.

The Reformation further established the link between Englishness and the defence and promotion of liberty while also putting both concepts at the heart of a wider British consciousness. Its defining principles included the importance of the individual's relationship with God and a resistance to the authority of priests, prelates and church hierarchies, although in the event many Reformed churches went on to become highly authoritarian themselves. In its Lutheran origins especially, the Reformation was an essentially Germanic, Anglo-Saxon, Gothic movement. Its appeal in Britain was as much to the old Celtic as the Anglo-Saxon regions. In many ways, as we have already seen, it promoted a sense of closer identity among the Welsh, Scottish and English (and later the Protestant Irish). It also spread English influences more generally in the British Isles and played a significant role in Anglicizing Scotland and Ireland. Jonathan Clark goes so far as to describe the Act of Union of 1536 between Wales and England as 'a phase of the Protestant Reformation in England'[12]. The progress of the Scottish Reformation was greatly helped by the English, not least when the English fleet sailed up the Forth and drove out the French who were supporting the Catholic cause. To a considerable extent, indeed, the Reformation replaced the Auld Alliance of Scotland and France with a much closer alliance between England and Scotland, cemented by the 1603 Act of Union between the crowns and the 1707 Act of Union between the Parliaments.

It is no coincidence that several of the first serious propagandists for a united Britain were drawn from the ranks of leading Protestant Reformers in the later sixteenth and early seventeenth century. We have already noted the work of David Hume in Scotland (page 37). A similar enthusiasm for the creation of a new united Great Britain characterizes the writing of the leading English Reformer, John Bale, whose *Maior Britannia* (1548) called for a Greater Briton joining England, Scotland and Wales in a Protestant nation. The Reformation brought in its wake a much greater sense of England's 'Britishness', based in part on the sense that it represented a revival of the ancient, pure, independent anti-Roman Celtic or British church, comparable to the similar effect already noted in Scotland and especially in

Wales (see pages 98-99). This was often very Anglo-centred, as in the description of Britain by William Harrison that forms the first part of Holinshed's Chronicles, published in 1577. Edmund Spenser's *Faerie Queene* (1590-1596) is often taken as a key text in the development of England's British consciousness. It drew heavily on Arthurian legends to bolster the Tudor's 'British' project, as when Spenser had Merlin prophesy that the accession of Henry VII would mean the crown again being reclaimed by 'British blood' and that 'Thenceforth eternal union shall be made / Between the nations different afore.' Spenser turned the Palestinian St George into an English knight, a Saxon 'sprung out from English race' who will be remembered as 'St George of Merry England'. He also made him a Protestant saint, the champion of true religion and one of the elect, whose lady, Gloriana, Queen of Fairyland, stands for both the Church of England and Queen Elizabeth I, while her rival, Lucifera, is associated variously with the Papacy, Babylon, the Anti-Christ and Mary Queen of Scots.

For several recent historians, the ideal of a new united Protestant Britain championed by Spenser and other Elizabethan poets and propagandists represented an essentially Anglo-centric perspective. Alan MacColl in particular has argued that their conception of a new united Protestant Great Britain in reality involved an English takeover and that James VI and I's attempts to submerge the ancient identities of England and Scotland in a new united kingdom of Great Britain failed basically because of the feeling among most of his English subjects that 'British' meant English and did not incorporate any sense of Scottish identity.[13] I suspect that the reality is more complex. There was undoubtedly a certain Anglo-centric tendency and emphasis to the new British identity and consciousness created in the wake of the Reformation but it is wrong to see it simply in terms of an imposed English takeover. As the work of David Hume and the Welsh 'Cambro-Britons' discussed in the last chapter makes clear, there was plenty of enthusiasm for the idea of British identity and closer British union in Scotland and Wales. There were also complex counter-currents operating in the post-Reformation period, which actually promoted Scottish and Welsh particularist identity within the context of a general move towards a greater sense of Britishness.

This is evident in the impact made by the two great literary products and spiritual icons of the English Reformation, the Authorised, or King James, Version of the Bible and the Book of Common Prayer. Although both are especially associated with English identity and with the Church of England, their influence has been felt much more widely in the United Kingdom, and indeed, beyond it and, especially in the case of the Bible, their ownership and continuing use has by no means been confined to the Church of England or just to Anglican churches and communities. The King James Version was one of several English translations of the Bible made at royal instigation in the later sixteenth and early seventeenth centuries. The first, authorized by Henry VIII as part of the assertion of England's political independence from the Papacy, in Christopher Hill's words, 'played a large part in moulding English nationalism and asserting the supremacy of the English language in a society which from the eleventh to the fourteenth century had been dominated by French speaking Normans'.[14] Henry VIII was also keen to rejuvenate the Welsh language and to see the Bible translated into Welsh, a project that his daughter, Elizabeth I, brought to fruition when she authorized the Welsh translation of the Prayer book and New Testament by Richard Davies, bishop of St David's in 1567, and the whole Bible by Bishop Morgan of St Asaph in 1588. These translations played a significant part in the growth of a distinct and proud Welsh cultural and linguistic identity at the very time that Wales was undergoing legal and constitutional union with England and developing its sense of Britishness.

In Scotland and Ireland the move towards Gaelic translations was much slower – the complete Bible in Irish was not available in print until 1681 and the complete Scottish Bible was not completed until 1801 – and the English versions held sway and helped to define both the English and Protestant nature of the emerging British identity in both countries. The Authorised Version was, of course, in many ways an Anglo-Scottish project, initiated by a Scottish king following his accession to the English throne, involving academics and translators from both sides of the border and conceived as a major expression of James VI and I's desire to create a united kingdom of Great Britain based on the principles of reformed religion and religious tolerance. It remains today just as treasured in Scotland as in England and is still found on the lecterns, and still read at public worship, in a significant number of Church of Scotland churches.

The English prayer book, which first emerged in 1547, was revised in 1552 and attained its final form in 1662, was scarcely less important than the Authorised Version of the Bible in its influence on English language and identity. Although it belonged to the Church of England, where it formed the sole basis of virtually all worship until the introduction of the Alternative Service Book in 1980, it also greatly influenced the liturgies of Anglican churches in the rest of the United Kingdom and beyond and also of the Church of Scotland and other Protestant churches. Its resonant, mellifluous and poetic language, largely the work of Thomas Cranmer, in many ways defined the spiritual temper of Anglicanism and English spirituality more generally. It has proved particularly appealing to those on the edges of faith. In the words of the introduction to a recently published reissue of the first English Prayer Book of 1547: 'Cranmer expresses eternal truth in language as sublime as that of Shakespeare, which can be appreciated, without being taken literally, by the devout sceptic. Thus it may draw into the church many who would not count themselves as believers.'[15]

The Reformation did not take a uniform course throughout the British Isles. Whereas the Church of England had bishops and regarded the King as its head and supreme governor, the Church of Scotland was Presbyterian and adopted a decidedly equivocal attitude towards the Crown. In Wales, Protestant dissenters soon came to outnumber adherents to the established Anglican church and in Ireland the Reformation never really won over the hearts and minds of the people, most of whom remained Catholics. Despite these differences, however, it did bring certain common institutions and values to the new United Kingdom, chief among them the existence of established churches and a broad commitment to religious tolerance and liberty of conscience. Liberty meant different things to different people: to Anglicans it meant freedom from the authoritarian shackles and obscurantism of Rome, to Scots Presbyterians freedom from bishops and Anglicizing kings, while dissenters expressed it in terms of opposition to church establishment. If both church establishment and religious tolerance were to become hallmarks of British identity and character, they were by no means universally popular or accepted. Tolerance has always been a more conspicuous virtue among the English than the Scots, who have tended to take their religion much more seriously and even fanatically. Indeed, the tolerance that is so often taken to be a defining British characteristic is essentially English in origin, having been largely hammered out by Protestant dissenters in the seventeenth and eighteenth centuries in their struggle against the privileges and injustices of church establishment.

John Milton stands as the father figure of the radical Protestant Dissenting tradition, which largely forged the English and British tradition of liberty, tolerance and open-mindedness. This devout if unorthodox Puritan championed divorce three hundred years before it became legal in the United Kingdom and, in *Areopagitica* (1644), he produced one of the most powerful and eloquent apologias ever for religious toleration and the principles of free speech and a free press, valuing 'the liberty to know, to utter and to argue freely according to conscience above all liberties'. He based his argument on the centrality of the Christian concept of free will, the fact that humans are created by God with the freedom to choose between good and ill and that only the free exchange of opinions and ideas will allow the continuing active choice between good and evil and allow truth to advance. His refusal to extend toleration to Roman Catholics sprang from his sense that they put papal authority above individual conscience and denied the free exercise of choice and ideas.

In an interesting recent study, Joan Bennett has located Milton in what she calls a radical Christian humanist tradition and portrayed him as in many ways a natural successor to Richard Hooker, the sixteenth-century Anglican divine credited with providing the intellectual framework for the Church of England's pursuit of the *via media* and the principle of church establishment. For her, Anglicanism's great achievement was to counter the absolutism and infallibility of the Roman Church, not with an equally absolutist Kirk and infallible Scriptures as the Scots Presbyterians did, but with a balance between Scripture, tradition and reason and by emphasizing rational access to the natural order and the Scriptures. While Milton was no Anglican and rejected both monarchy and the principle of establishment, he also disliked Presbyterianism because of its dogmatic authoritarianism and emphasized a free Christian Commonwealth. For Bennett, Milton's great poetic works, *Paradise Lost* and *Paradise Regained*, can be read as allegories on the birth of Christian liberty in the mind of its creator who was above all 'Christ our liberator'. It is in that they are born free that humans are most obviously made in the image of God – the exercise of their freedom is the ultimate theological purpose of their human existence and human love is the exercise of human freedom.[16]

The other great seventeenth-century English champion of liberty and toleration, John Locke, represents another key strand of both English and British political thought in distrusting visionary politics and having a strong attachment to the virtues of peace and security and a quiet life. Based on the idea of a social contract and proposing limited government, his second treatise, *Of Civil Government*, draws on the Protestant idea of the law of God being the law of reason and providing moral guidance. Locke was a leading advocate of religious toleration. His *Essay Concerning Toleration* (1667) and his later letters on the same subject (1689, 1691 and 1692) argued that complete toleration should be given to every religious body whose doctrines are neither incompatible with civil society nor require their adherents to give allegiance to a foreign prince. His own religious sympathies were well expressed in the title of one of his major works, *The Reasonableness of Christianity* (1695), and conformed with the broad, rational latitudinarianism, not given to enthusiasms or extremes, which has been a hallmark of the English and especially the Anglican religious temperament.

The emphasis on tolerance and liberty pioneered in the work of Milton and Locke has continued to be a key feature of British political and religious thought and life. It is no coincidence that England should have produced perhaps the greatest proponent of the value of individual liberty, understood in terms of freedom from the dead weight of public opinion and social conformity as much as from arbitrary government and authority, in the person of the nineteenth-century philosopher, John Stuart Mill, author of the classic tract *On Liberty* (1859). At its best, the British emphasis on liberty and tolerance has encouraged diversity and an open society and allowed minorities of all kinds to flourish and to pursue their own social, political, cultural and religious goals instead of trying to cajole them into conformity with certain overriding principles as, for example, the French have tended to do. At its worst, the British approach has meant in reality a lackadaisical indifference which has fostered a fragmented and divided society where everyone is free to do their own thing and is left relatively undisturbed but where there is little sense of commonality or togetherness. Critics are increasingly pointing to this consequence of the British passion for tolerance and liberty in terms of the ghettoized nature of British cities and the extent to which different ethnic and religious groups are leading separate and parallel lives which never converge. Championing the very different French emphasis on an overriding secularism and on creating a secular public place where individuals renounce part of their personal particularity, Stuart Jeffries wishes the British could emulate their Continental neighbours but doubts that they will:

> *The key reason the British aren't more like the French is that we have no parallel revolutionary heritage. Instead of valuing égalité, we value the virtues of tolerance and liberty that were expressed best in the works of John*

Locke and John Stuart Mill. At best, this results in a cosmopolitan city such as London where we – different ethnic and religious, and non-religious groups – rub along without knowing or caring much about each others' cultures so long as they don't intrude too much on our own. But surely that is not good enough; nor does it produce the understanding of or respect for other cultures that is surely necessary for Britain if it is to defuse its growing ethnic and religious tensions. Worse yet, that Locke-Mill tradition has arguably produced the ghettoised populations of northern towns where the BNP has spread its defeatist message.[17]

It is undoubtedly true that there is a fine dividing line between tolerance and indifference and that in the new world created in part by globalization and migration where the presence of the other and the stranger is much more keenly and closely felt, tolerance is probably not enough and needs to be supplemented by the more demanding virtue of respect and by a greater sense of common bonds and purpose. But in a world which is also becoming markedly more intolerant, there is still much to be said for the value of tolerance and for championing it along with the other now somewhat threatened principles so ably and boldly articulated by Milton, Locke and Mill. We could certainly do with celebrating these founding fathers of British liberalism more enthusiastically. The 300th anniversary of John Locke's death in 1704 went almost completely unnoticed in Britain. One of the few who did remark on it, the *Guardian* journalist Martin Kettle, observed how characteristically British this neglect was and contrasted it with the action of the German foreign minister in making a detour to visit the grave of Immanuel Kant. Kettle urged his countrymen to celebrate and remember Locke, not just for what he had given them in the past, but also for the continuing relevance of his ideas today:

He is the essential philosopher of consensual constitutional government, the key expounder of the social contract, the sovereignty of the people, majority rule, minority rights and the separation of powers. He is our leading defender of individual civil liberty, the greatest advocate in our history of religious and civic tolerance, and the first proponent of progressive educational methods, as well as the principal godfather of all those attitudes of common sense, reasonableness, kindness and politeness that later eras have so often thought of as essentially British.

The things that Locke thought were important – government by consent, the parliamentary system, civil liberty, freedom of thought and religion, the rights of minorities, an education that is more than functional, the rule of law – have never seemed more modern than they do today. To the politics of the future, as of so much else, Locke still holds the key.[18]

The late seventeenth and early eighteenth century was a crucial period in the forging of a new British identity around the themes of Protestantism, parliamentary democracy, individual liberty and toleration. The so-called 'Glorious Revolution' of 1689 played a key role in bringing Scotland and England closer together in rejecting the absolutism and Catholicism of James II and jointly petitioning William of Orange to take the throne. It was, of course, an even more important event in forging Northern Irish identity with its adulation of King Billy and the apprentice boys and confirmation of a visceral and tribal attachment to the monarchy, the Union and the British way of life, defined in terms of bourgeois and Biblical morality and virulent anti-Catholicism. In wider terms, the Bill of Rights and other legislation that followed the 1689 settlement brought limited government, sovereignty vested in the Crown in Parliament and religious toleration to the United Kingdom. It represented the triumph of gradualism, that nostrum so beloved of Whig historians, the balance of oligarchy and democracy, monarchical and parliamentary sovereignty and slow evolutionary progress towards democracy which spared Britain the violence and excesses of the French and American revolutions of the later eighteenth century. 1689 was in many ways a victory for the Gothic Anglo-Saxon strain in the British constitution and psyche. William III was himself a very Gothic figure, rooted in Dutch Protestantism and hailed as the ruler who would restore ancient Saxon liberties. The importance of the shared sense of Gothic inheritance, running back through Magna Carta to the sturdy independent Anglo-Saxon yeomen, in forging a new sense of Britishness has been emphasized by the historian Colin Kidd:

Despite the hegemony of pre-existent national and regnal affiliations, and the lack of a convincing British identity, certain overarching loyalties furthered the process of ideological integration. Protestantism, a basic commitment to civil and political liberty, and a sense of having common

roots in a Gothic racial stock which manifested itself historically in the
evolution of similar mixed constitutions, together constituted a bedrock of
common Britishness.[19]

The extent to which the defence of Protestantism and liberty were linked together with anti-French and Spanish feelings to forge the new Britishness and specifically to promote Anglo-Scottish union is evident from the comment of the Scottish pamphleteer Andrew Brown in 1703 that he saw a union between England and Scotland as 'no improper expedient for the security of the Protestant religion, general liberty, and for the keeping even of the balance of Europe'.[20] The 1707 Act of Union between England and Scotland involved Scots in many ways buying into a very English vision of Britishness, with which many of them were very happy. It helped that the prevailing English sense of identity stressed heterogeneity, itself an aspect of the emphasis on tolerance and diversity. England was seen as a rich ethnic melting pot. Daniel Defoe noted in his *True-Born Englishman* (1701) how successive infusions of 'Roman-Saxon-Danish-Norman French' blood had produced that 'Het'rogeneous Thing, an Englishman'. Interestingly, Scots had much less sense of their variegated Pictish, Irish, British and Anglian roots and tended to see themselves as more homogeneous. When Defoe came to try and create a composite British identity in *The True-Born Britain* (1707), he fell back on the old myth 'Our Liniage we derive from antient Brute.' In fact, Lowland Scots at least could accept that they were Goths as much as Gaels. Michael Geddes, a Scot who became a clergyman in the Church of England, noted in 1706 that 'the Lowland Scots do seem to have been a Saxon, or German, and not an Irish nation,' a fact confirmed for him by their libertarian mixed institutions: 'In England and Scotland that German form of government remains to this day.'[21] As that observation suggests, more important than origin myths and ethnic identities were the shared religious, political and constitutional values and institutions which the Scots and English shared.

So it was that an essentially English identity – forged on the Saxon/Gothic myth of a pre-feudal libertarian past before the imposition of the Norman Yoke, strengthened by the Reformation and bolstered as much by virulent anti-Catholicism and antipathy towards the Continental powers of France and Spain as by the championship of liberty and toleration by Protestant dissenters – became in the eighteenth century the basis of a British national identity. A striking illustration of this is the way that certain anniversaries of what were largely English events came to be celebrated across Britain, notably Armada Day commemorating the defeat of the Spanish Armada and Guy Fawkes' night commemorating the discovery of the 1605 Gunpowder Plot. In his book *Bonfires and Bells* (Weidenfeld and Nicolson, 1989), David Cressy has chronicled how a unique calendar based on a patriotic sense of national identity, involving also the anniversary of the accession, coronation and birthday of the reigning monarch, was developed in Elizabethan and Stuart England as a counter to the Catholic feast days of Continental Europe and then later extended to the United Kingdom as a whole. It has lingered to this day with the result that Bonfire night is still celebrated with as much enthusiasm on 5 November in Scotland and Wales as in England.

The eighteenth century saw British identity and the constitutional arrangements of the United Kingdom firmly cemented on the solid Germanic foundations of 'the illustrious house of Hanover', whose stolid representatives on the British throne proved suitably high-minded and moral, if slightly stuffy, exemplars for the nation. Their impeccable Gothic pedigree was not lost on their subjects, with Bishop Edmund Gibson hailing George I as the living reaffirmation of shared Saxon origins. Respect for the Gothic monarchy went alongside enthusiasm for the Gothic inheritance of liberty, which was shared by the English, Scots, Welsh and Protestant Irish. As Colin Kidd points out in his *British Identity Before Nationalism*, while Anglo-Saxon England was seen as the source of the freedoms enjoyed by all the inhabitants of the United Kingdom, there was also acknowledgement of the role played by the Celtic British and even the Normans:

> *Englishmen enjoyed both an ethnic identity as descendants of the libertarian Anglo-Saxons and an institutional identity derived from the historic laws and mixed constitution of the realm, a long regnal history which encompassed the ancient Celtic Britons, the Gothic Saxons who displaced them from the fifth century onwards and the Normans who arrived in the eleventh century. Anglo-Saxonism predominated as the core identity of the English people, but, throughout the seventeenth and eighteenth centuries, the 'aboriginal' ancient Britons enjoyed significantly more than a walk-on part in the national pageant. The Normans too, although often cast as villains, played an integral (and sometimes positive) part in the unfolding history of English liberty.*[22]

As the idea of liberty as a distinctive British characteristic developed, the roles of Celts and Saxons in its early formation were seen as complementary rather than conflicting. This is well illustrated in the writings of Henry St John, Viscount Bolingbroke, one of the first of a long line of eighteenth-century writers to portray Britain as the home of liberty. Writing in 1730, he maintained that in all ages the island of Britain 'hath been the temple, as it were, of liberty. Whilst her sacred fires have been extinguished in so many countries, here they have been religiously kept alive.' Although himself standing very clearly in the English Gothic tradition, he was also happy to enlist the Celtic Britons on the side of liberty, even when they were fighting the Saxons: 'Their long resistance against the Saxons shows their love of civil liberty. Their long resistance against the usurpation of the Church of Rome … shows their love of ecclesiastical liberty.'[23] For Bolingbroke, the indigenous spirit of liberty common to both Saxon and Celt, which the Romans were not able to extinguish, proved too strong for the Danes and Normans who themselves became converts to it.

The most enduring literary expression of the idea of Britain as the divinely appointed dwelling place of liberty is the poem 'Rule Britannia', written in 1740 by the Lowland Scot, James Thomson. It picks up the prevalent Protestant idea of the elect and chosen nation with Britain arising 'at Heaven's command', its national charter of freedom promoted by guardian angels and its future destiny, flourishing 'great and free', guaranteed by Providence while other nations, 'not so blest as thee, must in their turn to tyrants fall'. The Covenant theology and accompanying sense of manifest destiny and a chosen people so evident in Thomson's poem was by the mid eighteenth century much stronger among Scots than the English who had largely abandoned it. It went with a strong continuing Scottish attachment to freedom that harked back to ancient times and found expression in the stirring anonymous patriotic song 'In the garb of Old Gaul', written around 1760:

> In the garb of old Gaul, with the fire of old Rome,
> From the heath-covered mountains of Scotia we come,
> Where the Romans endeavoured our country to gain
> But our ancestors fought, and they fought not in vain.
> Such our love of liberty, our country and our laws,
> That like ancestors of old, we stand by freedom's cause;

We'll bravely fight, like heroes bright, for honour and applause,
And defy the French, with all their art, to alter our laws.

What is fascinating about this song, written soon after the second Jacobite uprising, is that it makes no mention of the anti-English legacy of Bruce and Wallace. Scotland's enemies are seen rather as the Romans and especially the French. Just as much as 'Rule Britannia', and even more explicitly, 'In the garb of old Gaul' celebrates the Gothic British tradition of freedom against the absolutist tendencies of Continental Europeans. It was written when the British army, with a substantial Scottish contingent, was fighting the French in Canada. The fifth verse of the song makes specific allusion to this war and to the 'pride of old France' quaking before the claymores of the Scottish soldiers. The last verse clearly articulates the twin themes of defending freedom and anti-French feeling which were so important in moulding British identity in the mid eighteenth century:

Then we'll defend our liberty, our country, and our laws,
And teach our late posterity to fight in freedom's cause;
That they like our bold ancestors, for honour and applause,
May defy the French, with all their art, to alter our laws.

Colin Kidd is convinced that the rhetoric of Gothicism strengthened the process of British integration in the eighteenth century. Post-Enlightenment Scotland, Protestant Ireland and Colonial America all picked up on the common political language and sense of shared Gothic heritage and identity embodied in the 1689 settlement and the Hanoverian succession. Scots, he suggests, had no difficulty with the Anglicization that came in the wake of the 1707 Act of Union because 'it held out the prospect of a return to the ancient Gothic freedom once enjoyed by earlier generations of Scots, but which had evaporated with the Romanist corruptions involved in the establishment of the French-inspired College of Justice.' Furthermore, 'To eighteenth century North Britons Anglicisation entailed incorporation within a liberal world of civilized, post-feudal modernity.'[24] Jonathan Clark, another modern historian who has written illuminatingly on this theme and period, has no doubt that "Britishness" in its prevalent sense rested in large part on the ancient and massive foundations of Englishness, and the equally ancient if differently formulated identities of England's neighbours.'[25] He has demonstrated the extent to which the language of liberty was based on appeals to Magna Carta, the 1689 Bill of Rights, the Hanoverian succession and above all to Protestant religion. For Clark, the roots of the British love affair with liberty were religious and spiritual. Protestantism naturally brought diversity and pluralism in its wake, as well as an emphasis on individual interpretation and a dislike of authorities. These factors were to be very important in the development of liberty and toleration in Britain.

Jonathan Clark has also shown how in Britain the Enlightenment did not involve a process of secularization, as it did on the Continent, but was rather underpinned by theological and ecclesiological argument. The British attachment to liberty was developed in opposition to the perceived priest-craft and tyranny of Roman Catholicism. It took particular exception to the exclusive claim of the Church of Rome that no one could be saved outside of the church. English common law was held up as the great bulwark against the centralizing authoritarianism of Roman law and Roman Catholicism. Protestants outside England were happy to claim and celebrate this inheritance. David Williams, a Welsh Dissenting minister, argued in 1777 that the British constitution was the work of Saxons from Germany, 'filled up and perfected by Alfred', defaced by feudalism and the Norman Conquest, and restored by the 1689 Glorious Revolution.[26]

The sense of Britishness forged out of this common anti-Catholic consciousness was not homogeneous and monochrome. Protestantism by its very nature breeds diversity and dissent. The Toleration Act which together with the Bill of Rights formed the basis of the 1689 constitutional settlement, allowed freedom of worship for Protestants of all kinds. The 1707 Act of Union acknowledged the diversity of religious practice in the newly created United Kingdom by securing the maintenance and protection of two completely different national established churches, Presbyterian in Scotland and Anglican in England. It thus established, through what Kidd somewhat disparagingly calls 'the lame Erastian compromise of 1707', a multi-confessional British state.[27] In fact, as will be argued later, the model which it formally confirmed of religious toleration coupled with broad national established churches has provided a unique British way of combining pluralism and common identity that may still have much to offer today. It was to take some time before full religious toleration was granted, especially to Roman Catholics, but it was thanks in no small measure to the constitutional and ecclesiastical framework constructed at the beginning of the eighteenth century that Britain became a beacon of tolerance and liberalism and a refuge for those seeking asylum and fleeing persecution for the next two hundred years.

While both Anglicans and Dissenters agreed in equating Britishness with liberty, there were differences in the way in which they envisaged the connection. Pasi Ihalainen, a Finnish historian, has made an extremely interesting comparative study of sermons preached between 1685 and 1772 in the Church of England, the Dutch Reformed Church and the Swedish Lutheran church. What he finds striking about the Anglican sermons in this period is the way that they conceived national identity not in terms of the Old Testament model of the chosen nation of Israel but rather as a more secular construct based around the idea of liberty. Indeed, liberty even more than Protestantism was taken to be the defining and God-given characteristic of both England and Britain. For Anglicans this went with strong anti-French and anti-Catholic feeling but also more positively with a sense that tolerance was a uniquely British characteristic and that Britain had a special role both as a home of liberty, welcoming refugees and those seeking asylum, and also as a fighter for liberty abroad. Protestant Dissenters in England, fighting Anglican hegemony and the privileged Anglican establishment, developed a rather different understanding of liberty which was more inclined to be anti-monarchical, anti-hierarchical and anti-episcopal. Building on the pioneering work of Milton and others, eighteenth- and early nineteenth-century Dissenters did much to consolidate the identification of Britain with liberty and freedom. In doing so, they also struck a proudly patriotic note, none more so than Isaac Watts, the Independent minister and founder of English hymnody, who rewrote the Psalms in 1719, substituting 'Great Britain' for 'Israel' and had no qualms about invoking the concepts of divine favour and the chosen nation:

Shine, mighty God, on Britain shine,
Amidst our isle, exalted high,
Do thou our glory stand,
And, like a wall of guardian fire,
Surround the fav'rite land.

William Blake combined dissenting Protestantism and radical political views with a profound mysticism and conservative patriotism. It is no coincidence that one of his most significant poetic works should have been both dedicated and devoted to John Milton, whom he described as 'Milton of the land of Albion' and who was a huge influence on his own work. Blake was fascinated by the antiquities, the myths and what he took to be the deep spirituality of Britain's Celtic past – the world of Druid priests and Welsh wizards. He was heavily influenced by the legend of the lost continent of Atlantis, of which the British Isles were the only surviving remnant. He was also deeply imbued with the Gothic strain in British identity, desiring to return to the world of Saxon freedom and Biblical principle. Like so many English radicals, he looked nostalgically back to a lost golden age as much as he looked forward. His attachment to both the Celtic and the Gothic, to Christian and pagan mythology and to nostalgia and radicalism came together in a fascination with Albion, the old name of Britain.

This is most strongly worked out in his two last works, *Milton* and the massive poem *Jerusalem: The Emanation of the Giant Albion*, written between 1804 and 1820, in which Albion is anthropomorphized or at least turned into a giant body and becomes almost a paradigm for the whole Creation-Fall-Salvation drama of Christianity. As with much of Blake's work, the meaning is obscure and ambiguous. It is never entirely clear whether Albion stands for England or Britain. At times he seems to equate the two, as when he writes: 'And England, who is Britannia, awoke from Death on Albion's bosom.' Yet, although most of his references are to English landscapes, he does at times suggest a wider compass which certainly takes in Scotland, as in his vision of souls descending:

There are two gates through which all souls descend, one southward
From Dover Cliff to Lizard Point, the other toward the North,
Caithness and rocky Durness, Pentland and John Groat's House.

There is also a strong sense of the ethnic melting pot that is Britain, even if the English seem to emerge as its ultimate embodiment:

What do I see! The Briton, Saxon, Roman, Norman amalgamating
In my Furnaces into One Nation, the English, and taking refuge.
In the Loins of Albion.[28]

Blake's vision of Albion mixes fierce patriotism with revolutionary radicalism and apocalyptic mysticism. He sees the nation as having a great destiny and constantly calls on it to awake, shake off its sloth and sin and inaugurate a new age in which the values of the Kingdom of God will prevail. For him, Albion, or sometimes just London, is seen as Jerusalem, the heavenly city, and even more explicitly as the new Jerusalem mentioned in the Book of Revelation. This identification is most clearly made in the short poem that begins *Milton* and which has become an anthem of Britishness, sung at the Last Night of the Proms and by women's institutes across the land. It is possible to take the two verses that begin 'And did those feet in ancient times' in several different ways: as a lament for the loss of England's 'green and pleasant land' to 'the dark satanic mills' of industrialization and commercialism; as a retelling of the legend that Jesus came to England as a companion of Joseph of Arimathea; as a mystical romantic's protest against the forces of post-Enlightenment rationalism; or as a utopian socialist call to build the New Jerusalem based on the values of social justice and equality in Britain. It is only in the last hundred years that it has become such an iconic expression of national identity. Neglected for a century after it was written, it was resurrected by the poet laureate Robert Bridges during the First World War for his anthology *The Spirit of Man* and set to music by Hubert Parry in 1916 for a meeting of the 'Fight for Right' movement which had been set up 'so to brace the spirit of the nation that the people of Great Britain, knowing that they are fighting for the best interests of humanity, may refuse any temptation to conclude a premature peace'.[29]

In a very British way, 'Jerusalem' managed throughout the rest of the twentieth century to be simultaneously a socialist anthem regularly sung at trade union meetings and Labour Party conferences and a favourite hymn in public school chapels and at society weddings. It has also succeeded in achieving British-wide popularity despite mentioning only England in its text. When the committee producing the new 2005 edition of the Church of Scotland hymn book chose to excise it, there were numerous protests from Scots who identify strongly with it and wish to go on singing about and celebrating England's green and pleasant land. It is, indeed, a sad reflection of the narrower and more nationalistic spirit now prevailing in Scotland that such an icon of Britishness as Blake's 'Jerusalem' should be removed from the pages of the national church's hymnary on the grounds that it is too English.

A more explicit equation of Britishness with freedom was made by another

English poet writing at the dawning of the nineteenth century, when William Wordsworth wrote in 1807 of

> *The Flood*
> *Of British freedom, which, to the open sea*
> *Of the world's praise, from dark antiquity*
> *Hath flowed, 'with pomp of waters, unwithstood'*[30]

Wordsworth's lines, which appeared in a book significantly entitled *Poems Dedicated to National Independence and Liberty*, provided literary expression to an ideal of Britishness which was represented in many different ways in the late eighteenth and early nineteenth centuries. The figure of John Bull, created by cartoonists and satirists as the corpulent, peaceable personification of English liberty well fed on beef and beer, often portrayed as farmer or shopkeeper, stood against the equally stereotyped caricature of the excitable, bellicose, atheist, radical, libertine Frenchman. Bull was not a one-dimensional figure – sometimes radical and at other times fiercely loyalist, he gave out the message that you could not ever quite take the Englishman for granted. Even horticulture was enlisted in the national identification with the principle of freedom, with the English tradition of landscape gardening being seen as indicative of a predisposition towards freedom in contrast to the regimented formality of French parks and gardens. Britain's attachment to freedom was made much of by those fighting to abolish the slave trade, and later slavery as a whole, from the British Empire.

The abolitionist movement was one of the more recent British achievements commended by Gordon Brown in his key British Council speech in 2004. After admitting that there are many examples in history of how the British failed to live up to their ideals, he pointed out:

> *The idea of liberty did mean, in practice, that for half a century it was*
> *Britain that led the worldwide anti-slavery movement with engraved on*
> *the badge of the anti-slavery society a figure of a black man and the quote,*
> *'Am I not a man and a brother?'*

In fact, it is debatable whether it was the idea of liberty so much as evangelical Christian compassion and missionary zeal that really impelled the British anti-slavery movement. The leaders of the abolitionist crusade, from William Wilberforce onwards, were predominantly conservative evangelical Christians who were motivated less by abstract notions of liberty than by a burning sense of the negro slave's importance to God and the urgent need for his soul to be redeemed and saved.

The anti-slavery movement points to an important feature of the British love affair with freedom – that it has been largely conceived and expressed in religious terms rather than worshipped as an abstract secular ideal, as in France. This has been broadly true of the approach of the three main political traditions in Britain over last three hundred years, Whiggery/Liberalism, Conservatism and Socialism. British Conservatism has been deeply attached to the principle of individual liberty; Edmund Burke famously spoke of the freedom of Englishmen as a patrimony and inheritance derived from their forefathers and enshrined in the 'prejudice' or 'prescription' of the ancient constitution of the-realm.'[31] Christian notions of original sin and patriarchal/paternal authority have moulded and tempered the Conservative approach to freedom. For British socialists a commitment to democracy and free institutions has run alongside a passion for social justice and equality, producing a Labour Party which has eschewed revolutionary rhetoric in favour of gradualism and famously owes more to Methodism than to Marxism. British politicians and political theorists have for the most part been very uneasy about the attachment to grand principles and abstract theories often found among their counterparts on the Continent. They have also generally eschewed atheism and secularism in favour of a pragmatic but principled gradualism with a religious and ethical foundation. This dislike of grand theories and ideologies is especially evident in the English. John Stuart Mill, who in many ways did exhibit a Continental taste for liberty as a big over-arching theory, admitted when writing to a French confidant that 'the English habitually distrust the most obvious truths if the person who advances them is suspected of having any general views.' Alexis De Tocqueville, from his French perspective, agreed, noting that 'the English seem to me to have great difficulty in getting hold of general and undefined ideas.'[32] When much of the Continent was engulfed in violent revolution and under the sway of atheist republicanism in 1848, The Economist reacted with the simple and heartfelt prayer: 'Thank God we are Saxons.'

The clearest expression of this passion for liberty conceived not in terms of an abstract general principle and ideal but rather as an adjunct of religious belief is to be found in the British Liberal tradition. It is, perhaps, the most British of the three major political traditions. Conservatism has always been predominantly and distinctively English, Socialism has had its heartlands in Red Clydeside in Scotland and the coal-mining valleys of South Wales. Liberalism has been spread more evenly across the United Kingdom, with perhaps a bias towards its Celtic fringes. Indeed, the British Liberal party has been described as 'the last protest of the Celt against the Anglo-Saxon'.[33] It is striking that, of the thirteen leaders of the Liberal Party over the last hundred years, six have been Scots (Henry Campbell-Bannerman, Archibald Sinclair, Jo Grimond, David Steel, Charles Kennedy and Menzies Campbell), five English (H. H. Asquith, Herbert Samuel, Jeremy Thorpe, Paddy Ashdown and Nick Clegg) and two Welsh (David Lloyd George and Clement Davies). If it has fed politically on Celtic identity, however, British Liberalism has supped intellectually at the same table that nourished Milton, Locke and Blake, the great English radical Dissenting tradition. As Gilbert Murray wrote, 'Liberals are politically the descendants of the Puritans' combining, just as Milton did, 'the search for righteousness and the belief in freedom'.[34] Lord Acton, the Victorian Roman Catholic statesman and intellectual who devoted much of his life to a monumental history of liberty, believed that the British Puritan¬Whig tradition of tolerance was its greatest manifestation. There were many Victorian Liberals who, like Henry Lunn, the Methodist travel agent, 'derived their Liberalism not from Manchester but from Nazareth'. The Nonconformist conscience that provided the backbone of British Liberalism in its most glorious period was both a British-wide and yet also a peculiarly English phenomenon as the journal, the *Nonconformist*, acknowledged in 1880:

> *Britain has had some inspiring visions of the Kingdom of justice one day to be established among men. The Liberal Party has striven to follow the fiery pillar of conscience into this promised land. It has striven to be the party of moral principle as against that of selfish and corrupt interests, the party of peace as against that of violence, the party of popular improvement and reform as against that of resistance to progress, the party of justice as against that of despotic force or social disorder. The backbone of this party has been the religious Protestantism and Puritanism of England.*[35]

The figure who supremely incarnated Victorian Liberalism, W. E. Gladstone, is perhaps the most truly British statesman in history, exhibiting in his own family background, life and concerns that wonderfully perichoretic sense of interpenetration and overlapping identities that I have extolled and which he would certainly have recognized as an enthusiastically Trinitarian Christian. He also stands as the most fervently pro-European Prime Minister that the United Kingdom has ever had and as a reminder that Britishness does not necessarily equate with a Little Englander mentality, xenophobia and dislike of the Continent. Both Gladstone's parents were Scottish – his mother from the Highlands and his father from the Lowlands. He was brought up in Liverpool and retained a trace of its distinctive accent throughout his life. He was educated at Eton and Oxford, married the daughter of a Welsh landowner and established his non-London home in North Wales. In Parliament, he successively represented constituencies in England and Scotland. His abiding political mission was to pacify the Irish and he devoted what many of his contemporaries thought was a disproportionate amount of time to the affairs of Ireland, disestablishing its church and eventually splitting his party through his commitment to its Home Rule. Gladstone's attitude and policies towards Ireland showed that he was no Unionist, yet in other respects in both his personality and politics he was Britishness personified, exemplifying some of its most characteristic paradoxes and tensions. He was a committed High Anglican who loved the established church and yet found many of his staunchest allies and supporters in the ranks of provincial Nonconformity, a man whose natural sympathies lay with the aristocracy and who possessed an innate conservatism yet championed radical social, political and economic reforms and became steadily more left-wing as he grew older. Above all, he was motivated by a love of liberty and passion for self-improvement grounded in strong Christian faith and deep immersion in classical learning and literature.

Post-Gladstonian Liberals continued to emphasize the religious origins and basis of their political commitment to liberty even as belief in Christianity waned. T. H. Green, hailed as the founding father of a British school of idealism very different from the more abstract and secular Hegelian Continental model, continued to see liberalism as the fulfilment of Puritanism and sought through an emphasis on conscience, responsibility and positive ideas of freedom to keep alive the ethical principles of Christianity on rational grounds when its supernatural under-girding seemed to be disappearing. British liberalism differs significantly from both US and Continental liberalism. Unlike the USA's essentially metropolitan and secular movement, urbane, sophisticated and rationalistic, liberalism in Britain has been rugged, restless and anti-establishment, reflecting its origins in religious Puritanism and provincial radicalism. Its nurseries have been solid and somewhat forbidding Nonconformist chapels and temperance halls rather than the smart salons and pavement cafes frequented by the East and West coast elites.

Liberalism can also, perhaps, make some claim to be the distinctive expression of the British political outlook because of its espousal of the middle way. I am thinking here not just in party political terms, although in its role as the third party for much of the twentieth century the British Liberal Party did often present itself and was perceived by electors as offering a middle way between Conservatism and Socialism. It is also true, as the historian Michael Brock has suggested, that one of the distinguishing characteristics of British Liberalism is 'the belief that moderation and reason are the prime requirements in the ordering of human affairs'.[36] Attachment to the middle way goes well beyond the ranks of paid-up Liberals, however, and has been a guiding principle for many Conservative and Labour politicians as well. Explaining his defection from the Conservative to the Labour benches in 2005, the MP and academic Robert Jackson said that it was because he felt that the former party had deserted the middle way and the latter increasingly espoused it. For him, that middle way was epitomized by the 'One Nation tradition in the middle, and the heart of British politics. It expresses the central aspirations of the British people. It also covers ground that has not, historically, been possessed exclusively by either of the two great British political parties.'[37]

Jackson went on to comment, very tellingly, 'The middle way is England's greatest contribution to Britishness' and to suggest that the phrase was first deployed in the preface to the Church of England's 1662 Book of Common Prayer. In fact this is not strictly true but certainly the idea of a middle way was a principle guiding those who composed this book, as expressed in the preface where they wrote that: 'It hath been the wisdom of the Church of England, ever since the first compiling of her Publick Liturgy, to keep the mean between the two extremes, of too much stiffness in refusing, and of too much easiness in admitting any variation from it.' This could stand as an encapsulation of the English temperament, especially in matters religious, where a natural conservatism and resistance to radical uprooting and change is tempered by an acknowledgement that all things in this life are provisional and transitory (a sentiment also beautifully expressed in the Book of

Common Prayer Communion service) and to that extent relative and malleable. In a wider and deeper sense, of course, the Church of England has been seen as holding a middle way between Rome and the Reformers and, perhaps more of late, between liberals and conservatives, balancing the authority of Scripture, reason and tradition, trying to hold widely different views in tension and those who adhere to them in brotherly love and charity. To that extent, its clergy and bishops have been perhaps most characteristically English, if not British, when they have pursued the *via media* and the great broad church tradition, so tempting to caricature in its soft, comfortable sogginess as John Betjeman did in his wonderful poem about the archetypal Wykehamist:

Broad of Church and broad of mind,
Broad before and broad behind,
A keen ecclesiologist,
A rather dirty Wykehamist.

It is easy to make fun of the Anglican broad-church tradition and it is true that it is born in many ways of the privilege of establishment and a public school education. Yes, it may seem all too cosy and comfortable. It infuriates those who want sharply defined boundaries and mission statements and goes wholly against the prevailing tendency for focus groups, niche marketing and clearly defined products.

Perhaps its last great exemplar was Robert Runcie, Archbishop of Canterbury from 1980 to 1991 and himself a good example of the overlapping identities implicit in Britishness in being of Anglo-Scottish background. A supreme exemplar of the very English qualities of openness, liberalism, tolerance and the middle way, he stated his view of the Church's role in his enthronement sermon at Canterbury Cathedral: 'The cry is "The Church must give a firm lead." Yes. It must – a firm lead against rigid thinking, a judging temper of mind, the disposition to oversimplify difficult and complex problems.' During his years as Archbishop, he came under considerable criticism for being weak, indecisive and uncertain in his leadership, not least in the infamous *Crockford's* preface of 1987, which observed that 'he is usually to be found nailing his colours to the fence'. As his son James wrote in a moving tribute shortly after his father's retirement, it is easy to see doubt where there is really ambivalence, indecision where there is forbearance, dithering and weakness where there is thought, pause and reflection. James Runcie admitted that he got so fed up with his father being pilloried in the press that he once implored him, 'Can't you do anything? Can't you be clearer, stronger?' The reply from his father, was almost angry: 'I am strong on forgiveness and tolerance. I am clear. Clear in my faith in Jesus Christ. And I believe in authority – the authority of love.'[38]

It is noticeable that while many of its own members castigate it for its wishy-washy fuzziness and openness and for being the Church Hesitant rather than the Church Militant, the Church of England finds many of its most eloquent admirers and defenders from outside its own ranks. The Roman Catholic peer William Rees-Mogg is one of them, believing that 'the Church of England stands for the quiet virtues of moderation, peace, tolerance, good nature, tranquillity, decency and order – the traditional virtues of the English.' He takes issue with those within the established church who would wish it to be less national and less conservative, less attached to good manners and respect and to adopt a more aggressive and militant posture and 'go dragon¬hunting' in the spirit of St George. Its cultivation of an atmosphere of peace, he suggests, 'should not be regarded as a weakness, as a mawkish avoidance of necessary conflict, but rather as a contributor to good social relationships and as a preparation for prayer'.[39]

Much of the Church of England's broad-church tradition and its historic openness and pursuit of the middle way is a function of its establishment. The other established national church in the United Kingdom, the Church of Scotland, also exhibits many of the same characteristics of breadth, fuzziness and a blurring of hard edges and rigid boundaries. It too contrives 'to hold together those of widely different theological views. It is ironic in many ways that the British – and especially the English liberal tradition, with its emphasis on diversity and tolerance, was hammered out largely by Dissenters in opposition to the established church.

Disestablishment came to Ireland in 1871 and to Wales in 1920, in both cases at the instigation of Liberal governments and because Anglicans were in a small minority in both countries. There is now considerable pressure for church disestablishment in England, not least from within the Church of England itself, less so in Scotland where the form of establishment is much weaker and does not involve state interference in the affairs of the church. It is striking that some of the most enthusiastic supporters of the principle of established churches are drawn from the leadership of Britain's non-Christian faiths who see the benefits of having public acknowledgement and recognition of religion at the heart of the state and call for an open and hospitable establishment as a key element in fostering more respect for religious minorities in Britain (see pages 204-6). I will return to this argument later, but for the moment I just wish to say something about how established churches have contributed to British identity and to its liberal, open and tolerant emphasis.

There is no doubt that the existence of established churches has contributed strongly to national identity in the United Kingdom. Historically, it could be argued that they have reinforced loyalties to England and Scotland more than to Britain as a whole. Both the Church of England and the Church of Scotland have been important vehicles for representing and carrying images and ideas associated with national consciousness – the Church in Wales and the Church of Ireland have also had this role, not least in the way that they have celebrated their respective national patron saints. They have also reached out to embrace those within the great unchurched majority. This, of course, is one of the great Christian justifications for having established churches: that they provide the ordinances of religion for those who are not regular churchgoers, reaching many, if only occasionally as at weddings and funerals, who would never otherwise darken the doors of any church. Their privileged status and official recognition also allows them to bring spiritual and religious teaching, values and pastoral care into public places and institutions like schools, hospitals, prisons and universities. Even at a time when both membership of and attendance at established churches have massively declined, it remains' the case that they still command the loyalty and allegiance of a significant part of the population (see page 68).

This continuing identification with the national established churches of England and Scotland, however tenuous, is an important element in the persisting latent, unconscious, implicit folk religion that makes seventy-two per cent of the British population still describe themselves as Christians. As such, it is also a major factor in British spiritual identity. Established churches also play a more active role in promoting British consciousness. The Church of England stage-manages, generally very effectively, great state occasions, especially those connected with the monarchy such as royal weddings and funerals. It is particularly good at worshipping what has been somewhat disparagingly referred to as 'the transcendent God of the state occasion', With a little bit of help from the Church of Scotland, it presides over coronations, those occasional rituals loaded with pageantry and symbolism which perhaps come closer than any other public ceremonies to embodying the spiritual heart of Britishness. Together with the Church of Scotland and, to a lesser extent, the Church in Wales and Church of Ireland, it mounts services to mark significant national events and anniversaries. The Remembrance services held in parish churches and at war memorials across the United Kingdom on the Sunday morning closest to 11 November mark a significant moment of national consecration and dedication which, like the two-minute silence observed on the day itself, is gaining rather than losing support, especially among the young. While it is pre-eminently the Church of England that flies the flag of civic religion for the whole of the United Kingdom, the Church of Scotland also performs this role to a lesser extent. I am not just thinking here of the number of Union Jacks that one sees hanging in Church of Scotland churches, although I do take a certain delight in showing them to patriotic Anglicans venturing north of the border, but rather of the extent to which Moderators of the General Assembly are involved in national UK-wide celebrations and state occasions.

More importantly, perhaps, senior figures in both the Church of England and the Church of Scotland take seriously their responsibilities as leaders of national churches to reach out to and represent those outside the narrow confines of church membership, and not least those of other faith communities. In this, they exhibit the 'hospitable establishment' commended by George Carey as Archbishop of Canterbury and use their privileged status and access to ensure that ethical and moral concerns are represented in the highest councils of the land and that religion as a whole is given public space and recognition and not marginalized and privatized. This is one of the main arguments in favour of establishment – that, in the words of Adrian Hastings, 'it makes the wielders of secular sovereignty a little more aware of the reality of a different sovereignty.'[40] It is put in more theological language in terms of an acknowledgement of the ubiquity of divine presence and a strong endorsement of the prevenience of God's grace by the Church of Scotland theologian Ruth Page:

> *To be established is to proclaim that God is always involved in all that happens within our countries. A further implication of this belief in the spatial and temporal omnipresence of grace is that God cannot be thought of as sending his grace from time to time here and there over an infinite*

void, but rather is to be seen as a continuing gracious presence with us which
both sustains and disturbs … An established church has the responsibility
to see that the grace of God prevenient in his presence is in fact known and
expressed in every corner of the country. Mission is not the planting of lights
here and there in a dark world but the making known of the light which
shines already.[41]

Established churches particularly fit the British, and more especially the English, psyche and temperament because they encourage liberalism, openness and broad-mindedness. The *Financial Times* journalist John Lloyd came to St Andrews recently to ask me why Britain has not succumbed to the religious fundamentalism found increasingly in the USA and growing in so many parts of the world. My immediate answer was 'because we have established churches'. The establishment mentality is the opposite of the sectarian mentality. Because established churches are intimately engaged with and active in public institutions like parliaments, local government, universities and hospitals, they must remain broad, moderate, open and inclusive. They promote pluralism and diversity, embracing a much wider variety of viewpoints than other more narrowly focused churches which lack their national role and responsibilities. Adrian Hastings has identified pluralism as the defining characteristic of British Christianity. This has been achieved without the privatization that has occurred in the pluralistic religious culture of the USA. It has something to do, I think, with the existence of established churches, the public religious culture that they have helped to create and the healthy culture of dissent and nonconformity that has also developed in opposition to them. Disestablishment would further privatize Christianity and religion in Britain and it would also tend to push it in a more conservative and fundamentalist direction. Frederick Temple, the great liberal Archbishop of Canterbury at the end of the nineteenth century, understood this when he opposed calls for disestablishing the Church of England. He did so by appealing to the British tradition of liberty and the exercise of free independent thought and conscience that have motivated so many of the calls from Dissenters and Nonconformists for disestablishment, arguing that

Liberty in the Church of England had saved valuable schools of thought from
extinction and given it a more truly catholic character than any other body of

Christians. Liberty alone had made the Church national, and he feared that disestablishment, if it came, would hand the Church over to narrow-minded dogmatists.[42]

To their critics, established churches exemplify the wishy-washy relativism and lack of firm and clear beliefs that are sometimes taken to characterize Britishness as a whole. Is the much-famed British tolerance in reality a lackadaisical indifference?

In his magisterial essay *On Compromise* in 1874, the liberal intellectual John Morley identified as a besetting sin of the British 'a flaccid latitudinarianism, which thinks itself a benign tolerance for the opinions of others, but which is in truth only a pretentious form of being without settled opinions of our own, and without any desire to settle them'.[42] More recently, the *Guardian* columnist, Stuart Jeffries, has suggested that tolerance in modem Britain means, in effect, 'I don't give a monkey's what you do in your own home, but if your barbecue smoke wafts into my duvet cover when it's drying on the line, I won't speak to you again but you will feel the frown through the net curtains for the next 20 years.' For him:

> *Britons don't love their neighbours, but, so long as you keep the noise down, you can sacrifice goats to your God under the full moon as far as we're concerned. Indifference has become Britain's most widely practised civic virtue and is, quite possibly, a reason we adjusted to becoming a multi-ethnic society less painfully than one might have expected. It also means, though, that Britons have rarely felt it incumbent on them to learn about their new neighbours' cultures, still less about their religions.*[44]

This mixture of tolerance and indifference is a complex aspect of the national psyche producing consequences that conflict as well as overlap with one another. It goes with a sense of reserve that can often be taken to the point of seeming coldness and unfriendliness but perhaps its strongest and most positive effect is to let people do their own thing and not be censorious about other people's beliefs or behaviour. The great cry of John Stuart Mill against the despotism of public opinion has been heeded and in that sense the British, and especially the English, have been postmodernists long before the phrase was coined and discovered by the rest of the world. Do they also have the lack of overarching values and suspicion of meta-narratives that goes with postmodernism? Certainly there has long been a suspicion of ideologies, whether the French trinity of *liberté, égalité* and *fraternité*, the Hegelian abstracts and Kantian absolutes favoured by Germans, or the frightening mixture of cheesy patriotism, free-market economics and religious fundamentalism increasingly espoused in the United States of America.

There is, however, no room for complacency about the continuing flourishing of tolerance and broad, pragmatic open-mindedness in contemporary Britain. They are under strain and perhaps even in retreat along with other values nurtured and fostered especially by the Gothic Anglo-Saxon strain in the national make-up and psyche that has been the subject of this chapter. Certainly many of the institutions which are particularly associated with this strain are in decline in terms of public standing and popular support. This is true of Parliament and the established churches of England and Scotland. The eirenic, open, undogmatic liberal broad-church tradition in the Church of England is in retreat. The Nonconformist and Dissenting tradition that gave birth to British liberalism and tolerance has almost completely disappeared, the denominations that once proudly and fiercely embodied it, notably Methodists, Presbyterians, Congregationalists and Unitarians, reduced to a tiny surviving rump or swallowed up through amalgamations. Universities are in danger of forsaking the values of liberal education in favour of narrow instrumentalism, managerialism and a jargon-laden research culture which prefers abstruse and nit-picking academicism to broad enlightenment and learning. In many areas of life, there seems to be less openness and less room for eccentricity and originality but rather more and more conformity, bureaucracy and playing for safety.

The Labour Governments elected in 1997, 2001 and 2005 have been characterized by an interventionist managerial reformism and an obsession with audits, targets and accountability. In banning fox hunting and proposing compulsory identity cards, they have also shown scant regard for the traditional British love of liberty and personal freedom. The rising threat of terrorist attacks, and perhaps even more the rising level of fear and suspicion that they have engendered, have led to legislation in the last few years which has gone against the principles enshrined in Magna Carta and *habeas corpus* and introduced control orders, arbitrary house arrest and imprisonment without trial. The decision to go to war against Iraq seemed to flout the principles of the rule of law. Legislation to ban protests within the precincts of Parliament and to make it a criminal offence to incite religious hatred has aroused widespread opposition for flying in the face of the long-held British commitment to freedom of speech and opinion. Several of the key principles in the English attachment to liberty that Gordon Brown so eloquently identified as the defining characteristics of Britishness in the speech quoted at the beginning of this chapter appear not to mean or matter much to the Government in which he has played so prominent a part. As the *Guardian* journalist Martin Kettle has perceptively remarked, 'It is some consolation that politicians like Blunkett and Brown are prepared to talk and think about Britishness, but they are still a long way from understanding liberal England.'[45]

Yet, despite these negative signs, there are also many positive indicators of the persistence of those values that have been identified in this chapter as the special Gothic Anglo-Saxon contribution to Britishness. The Government's attempt to allow terrorist suspects to be kept in custody for up to ninety days without charges being brought was defeated in the House of Commons in 2005 by an alliance of Conservatives, Liberal Democrats and Labour rebels. Commenting on this victory for the principle of individual freedom, Michael Kinsley, a syndicated newspaper columnist in the USA, reflected that it showed the superiority of the 'metaphysical conceit' posing as the British constitution, an ill defined set of ideas and values floating in the ether', over the US constitution with its Bill of Rights and detailed legislative checks and balances:

> In which country are individual rights more secure? Legally, the clear
> answer is the United States. But there's something else, something hard to
> describe because it's essentially a 'love of freedom'. But it's earthier than that,
> more deeply rooted in the old country than the new one which actually broke
> itself off from the old one over precisely this issue of human freedom.
>
> A bone-deep desire to be left alone, a tolerance for eccentricity; a
> quick resentment of bullies – these are qualities that Britain has more than
> America. And they might be more important.[46]

The United Kingdom remains one of the freest and most tolerant societies and states in the world, a favoured destination for asylum seekers and refugees who find it a beacon of liberty, fair-mindedness and civilized values. The BBC World Service is still respected throughout the world for its impartiality, free comment and calm authority. Protestantism may be in massive and possibly even terminal decline but the pluralism, diversity and respect for individual conscience and human rights that it did so much to engender is still a marked characteristic of British public and private life. As in so many other areas, it is the new Britons from the ethnic minorities who often appreciate this aspect of Bntishness more than many in the white majority and who are determined to see it defended and maintained. Shami Chakrabarti, the British Asian who heads the civil rights pressure group Liberty, is in no doubt about what constitutes the essence of Britishness and how important it is to defend it: 'There's far too much navel-gazing about British identity. What is Britishness? It's not about whether you know the recipe for fairy cakes or which cricket teams you support. It's about free speech and fair trials.'[47]

5 Moral Fibre and Muscular Christianity

The Scottish Contribution

I originally conceived of entitling each chapter of this book with a line from a patriotic song but later gave up the idea except for the heading of Chapter 2, which begins with the question 'Red, white and blue, what does it mean to you?' from the song 'There'll Always Be an England'. This chapter was to have been entitled 'The Boys of the Bulldog Breed', a phrase from the stirring song 'Sons of the Sea', which was written in 1897 and sung during the Boer War. With its reminder that 'the Sons of the Sea' are 'all British born' and 'made old England's name', it was, in fact, the work of an Irishman, Felix McGlennan, and as such is an appropriate reminder of the hybrid and perichoretic nature of British identity. So too is the song 'Rule Britannia', whose recurring last line 'Britons never, never, never shall be slaves' I was going to use for the title of Chapter 4. It was the work of a Scot, James Thomson, and stands as a suitable testament to the considerable Scottish contribution to Britishness.

As we have already seen, some of the most eloquent and fervent calls for the union of the different nations of the British Isles and the creation of a United Kingdom have come from Scots from David Hume onwards. James VI of Scotland was in many ways the architect of the United Kingdom, the first modern monarch to style himself king of Great Britain and an enthusiastic exponent of a new united British identity. Following the parliamentary union of 1707, it was Scots rather than

English who largely espoused the notion of Britishness, often describing themselves as North Britons. Indeed, it is hardly too much to see the post-1707 notion of Britishness as a largely Scottish invention. Scots have even done much to contribute to notions of English identity. For the second half of the eighteenth century and much of the nineteenth, the standard work on English history was the six-volume *History of England* by David Hume (no relation of his sixteenth-century namesake), the Edinburgh philosopher and leading figure in the Scottish Enlightenment. Published between 1754 and 1762, it ran from the arrival of Julius Caesar to the Glorious Revolution of 1689.

As well as being arguably the most enthusiastic proponents of the concept of Britishness within the United Kingdom, Scots have also contributed something very important and distinctive to it. If the Irish and Welsh have brought spirituality and Celtic fire and the English a love of liberty and tolerance, the Scottish contribution has been in the area of moral fibre and earnestness, an unbending sense of duty and responsibility and a strong commitment to the common good and to social and civic action. In these contributions they have been joined by many in the Protestant Unionist community in Northern Ireland, which is largely descended from the Scottish Presbyterians who settled in Ulster, especially during the plantations of the seventeenth century. I am conscious that there is very little about the Northern Irish in this book, which may seem a particularly strange lacuna given that they are the most self-consciously British and unionist element in the population of the United Kingdom. This is because I am increasingly persuaded (by the Northern Irish themselves) that Northern Irish identity is, in fact, *sui generis*, neither really British nor Irish. Stephen Howe, Professor of History and Cultures of Colonialism at the University of Bristol, has recently identified a variety of Britishness exemplified in Belfast and other Northern Irish urban centres in the nineteenth and much of the twentieth century. He characterizes it as profoundly masculinist and intensely localized and argues that the collapse of both Protestantism and Britishness as sustaining forces has left Ulster loyalism, which he rightly distinguishes as a distinctively Irish culture, demoralized, uncertain and ambiguous about its identity and future. 'Ulster loyalism,' he notes, 'seems doomed to imprisonment by a terminally declining form of Britishness,' by which he has in mind traditional urban, working-class culture.[1] It is certainly true that many in Northern Ireland are struggling to come to terms with a hybrid identity of British-Irishness or Irish-

Britishness. Possibly the revival of Celtic Christianity and of some of the myths and themes discussed in Chapter 3 can help in this process. What is undeniably true on the more positive side, however, is the extent to which Ulster Protestantism has contributed significantly to many of the characteristics of Britishness which I will be outlining in this chapter and attributing particularly to the Scottish influence.

In describing this joint contribution, as I originally intended to do, as coming from 'the boys of the bulldog breed', I am aware that I would have been using a phrase that has now come to take on rather negative connotations. The image of the snarling bulldog with studded collar that is, as we have seen, one of the bestsellers among the T-shirts sold in the Glorious Britain shops in UK airports, suggests an aggressive kind of xenophobia more usually associated with the National Front and the British National Party. That is not what I had in mind here, although it is perhaps fair to point out that the Scots and Northern Irish are the least tolerant and potentially the most racist of the long-term inhabitants of the British Isles. I was thinking rather of those bulldog qualities epitomized by Sir Winston Churchill: resilience, tenacity, dependability and the stiff upper lip. Daniel Jenkins identified an important aspect of the 'bulldog' qualities of the Scots when he observed that they

> *remain more likely than most of the English to see that there are certain issues which cannot be resolved simply by a little give and take here and there and a sensible readjustment of perspective, while the continuities are preserved. They put a little iron, a little intellectual rigour, into British moderation which in its English, and especially its Anglican form, it needs.*[2]

Even more than with the other contributions to Britishness so far delineated in this book, the particular cluster of characteristics that forms the subject of this chapter is embedded in Protestantism. They include the classic Protestant virtues, as explored by Max Weber and Richard Tawney, and especially the classic Presbyterian virtues of self-discipline, intellectual rigour and seriousness and an unbending and unwavering sense of duty. Despite what both Weber and Tawney argued, they have not always been harnessed to individualism and ruthless competitiveness. Scottish Presbyterianism has always had a strong social, communal and civic dimension and a concern for the good of society as a whole. These and other aspects of the Scottish contribution are epitomized by Gordon Brown, himself a son of the manse and the great contemporary apostle of Britishness, a touch dour in his personality, a formidable workaholic seriously committed to moral issues and social causes. It is significant that when he identifies what he sees as the key characteristics of Britishness, 'a sense of civic duty and commitment to the public space' feature alongside tolerance, openness to the world, fair play and commitment to liberty and democracy. For him, indeed, duty stands alongside liberty as the defining British value:

> *At every point this British belief in liberty has been matched by a British idea of duty as the virtue that reinforces neighbourliness and enshrines the idea of a public realm and public service. A belief in the other is an essential element of nationhood in every country but whether it arose from religious belief, from a 'noblesse oblige', or from a sense of solidarity, duty in Britain – for most of the time an unwritten code of behaviour rather than a set of legal requirements – has been, to most people, the foundation of rights rather than their consequence.*[3]

In his 2004 British Council speech, Brown went on to point out that 'the call to duty and to public service' was 'often impelled by religious convictions' and had led to the 'mushrooming of local and national endeavour, of associations and clubs, a rich tradition of voluntary organizations, local democracy and civic life'. He could have been describing the particular legacy and contribution of Scots Presbyterianism as much as the more general nature of Britishness for which he is such an enthusiastic apologist.

Scottish enthusiasm for the concept of British identity goes back a long way. It is evident in the work of one of the first modern historians of Britain, John Major, who styled himself 'a Scottish Briton' and whose *History of Great Britain* (1521) called passionately for the unification of Britannia. The Ulster plantations of the early seventeenth century linked Scotland and England through the colonization of Northern Ireland and were a key element in the historical foundation of Britishness: Francis Bacon described them as 'a second brother to the Union'. When James VI united the crowns of Scotland and England in 1603, he hoped to bring Ireland into his new united kingdom. In the event, although that did not officially happen until the Act of Union of 1800, the descendants of the Scottish settlers in Ulster became the most fervently pro-British and pro-Unionist subjects of the United Kingdom monarchy.

The Scottish Enlightenment in the eighteenth century encouraged enthusiasm for Britishness north of the border, as Alexander Wedderburn and his fellow contributors to the *Edinburgh Review* coined the term 'North Britain' to describe their land. Edinburgh came to think of itself as the capital of North Britain, as exemplified by the name given to the massive railway hotel built over Waverley Station, 'The North British', sadly changed in 1991 to 'The Balmoral'. The espousal of Britishness by enlightened Scots like Wedderburn in no sense diminished their sense of Scottishness. Rather this early display of hybrid or hyphenated identity gave their Scottishness a new dimension and hope. In the words of the contemporary Scottish poet and literary historian, Robert Crawford:

> *Such figures were pro-British because they were pro-Scottish: it was in the promise of 'Britain' that they saw the richest future for a Scotland that would soon improve' … To many it appeared that the way to advance as a Scot was to appear as English as possible, while at the same time upholding an idea of Britishness in which Scotland would be able to play her full part.4*

In his book *Devolving English Literature*, Robert Crawford has argued persuasively that the whole academic discipline of English literature is essentially an eighteenth-century Scottish invention, coming out of the teaching of rhetoric and *belles lettres* in the Scottish universities and developed in the context of the new enthusiasm for Britishness in the aftermath of the 1707 Union. It went alongside the Anglicizing of Scottish speech and language, a project of which evangelical Protestantism was in the van in the Highlands and Islands. As Crawford points out, while post-1707 English writers made no concession to the concept of Britishness, as opposed to Englishness, Scots took it enthusiastically on board: 'Insightfully, awkwardly, entrepreneurially, Scottish writing entered its British phase. It is this Britishness which, more than anything else, distinguishes Scottish from English literature in the eighteenth century.'5

This 'British' phase of Scottish writing has given Britishness some of its most enthusiastic and eloquent laureates and exponents – chief among them, of course, James Thomson of 'Rule Britannia' fame. A son of the manse, Thomson was born in 1700 in Ednam in the Borders, went to school at Jedburgh and studied Arts and Divinity at Edinburgh University. Thereafter he turned from his early ambition to follow his father into the ministry and went to London to pursue a literary career. By the time of his death in 1748, he was living in some comfort and style in Richmond and was a successful poet. Thomson's highly coloured effusions to Britain were no doubt written partly to suit the growing market for patriotic poetry in Hanoverian England but he himself also clearly believed in them. He was especially keen to promote Britain as a cultural and ethnic amalgam embodying the principle of diversity in unity. Like many of the Scots who took up the idea of Britishness, he did so partly to make clear that Britain included more than England. Sending an early draft of his poem, 'Summer: A Panegyric on Britain', which begins 'Happy Britannia', to his fellow Scottish poet, David Mallet, he wrote, 'The English People are not a little vain of Themselves, and their Country. Britannia too includes our native country, Scotland.'

Thomson's most enduring contribution to British identity was written in 1740 for a masque celebrating the England of Alfred the Great, which he co-authored with Mallett. It is, of course, Britain as a whole rather than just England that 'Rule Britannia' serenades and identifies with freedom. Thomson had earlier made a similar association in a poem called *Liberty* (1734-1736), in which the goddess Liberty having vainly journeyed through Continental Europe finds her true home with Britannia:

> *She rears to freedom an undaunted race:*
> *Compatriot zealous, hospitable, kind,*
> *Hers the warm Cambrian: hers the lofty Scot,*
> *To hardship tamed, active in arts and arms,*
> *Fired with a restless, an impatient flame,*
> *That leads him raptured where ambition call;*
> *And English merit hers – where meet combined*
> *Whate'er high fancy, sound judicious thought,*
> *An ample generous heart, undrooping soul,*
> *And firm tenacious valour can bestow.*[6]

In this poem, Thomson shows his Scottishness and the legacy of his childhood in a Presbyterian manse when he insists that British freedom can only be sustained by the three virtues of sturdy independence, integrity and a passion for the common welfare:

> *By these three virtues be the frame sustained*
> *Of British freedom – independent life;*
> *Integrity in office; and o'er all*
> *Supreme, a passion for the commonweal.*[7]

We have already noted that the idea of liberty was taken up enthusiastically by Scots in the mid eighteenth century, as evidenced by the rousing song, 'In the Garb of Old Gaul'. It is noticeable that after the opening panegyric to liberty (quoted on page 128), the song goes on to extol the more distinctively Scottish virtues of moral fibre and masculinity:

> *No effeminate customs our sinews unbrace,*
> *No luxurious tables enervate our race;*
> *Our loud-sounding pipe breathes the true martial strain,*
> *And our hearts still the old Scottish valour retain.*

The eighteenth-century Scottish invention and assertion of Britishness as a paradigm of diversity in unity was expressed in fiction as well as poetry. Robert Crawford, with much justification, calls the Dumbarton born and educated Tobias Smollett the first British novelist. The opening words of his first novel *Roderick Random* (1748) – 'I was born in the northern part of this united kingdom' – signal both Scottishness and Britishness, and the book goes on to examine the various ways in which these two identities interact. Roderick is accepted as a Scot within the British union and his marriage at the end of the novel to an English bride signifies the unity of the kingdom. Smollett's *Humphry Clinker* (1771) is, for Crawford, the first fully British novel. It deals with cultural crossovers, telling the story of a party from rural Wales who undertake a tour of England and Scotland, celebrating the varieties of Britishness, the breaking down of prejudices between (especially) the English, Scots and Welsh and the forging of union between them.

Robert Crawford gives several other examples of the 'Britishness' of Scottish literature. There is the role of James Boswell in presenting Dr Samuel Johnson to the world as the supreme embodiment of the John Bull type of Englishman. Indeed, the figure of John Bull himself owes much to the work of the Scottish humorist, John Arbuthnot. Robert Burns is, for Crawford, above all a British poet who signs himself 'a Briton' and whose democratic philosophy, summed up in his song 'A Man's a Man for a'that' sung at the opening of the Scottish Parliament, provided an anthem for British socialism as much as Scottish nationalism. This 'British' strand in Scottish literature reached its apogee in the work of Walter Scott, regarded by Crawford as the greatest novelist of Britishness. His *Waverley* (1814) tells the story of an English chivalric hero who comes to Scotland and, like Smollett's novels, celebrates both the cultural mix and diversity and the unity of Britain. As in *Roderick Random*, a marriage between the English Waverley and the Scottish girl, Rose Bradwardine, symbolizes the unity of the two kingdoms. Scott's *Ivanhoe* (1819) features Saxons, Normans, Christians and Jews and can be read as a tribute to British multiculturalism.

Walter Scott stands, indeed, as one of the first examples of Scottish-British dual consciousness and hyphenated identity. He was at once a proud Scottish patriot with a plaster cast of the head of William Wallace over the fireplace of his home at Abbotsford and a keen admirer of British martial valour, extolling the bravery of Wellington's soldiers on the field of Waterloo. He also felt a strong European identity. Like Burns, he mixed English and Scottish phrases in his writing. He helped to make the Hanoverian dynasty more British and acceptable in Scotland by swathing George IV in tartan when the King visited Edinburgh in 1822 and paved the way for the British monarchy's love affair with the Scottish Highlands. He was also a leading proponent of the notion of chivalry that was to play a significant part in the Victorian reconstruction of Britishness. An instinctive conservative, royalist and romantic, Scott wrote the articles on chivalry and romance for the *Encyclopaedia Britannica* and did much though his poetry to propagate and keep alive the legends of King Arthur and the Knights of the Round Table. His poem *The Lady of the Lake* (1810) managed to bring not just Arthur but Robin Hood and Merrie England into an essentially Scottish story and setting and also did much to stimulate English tourism in Scotland. In *The Field of Waterloo*, he linked both Britannia and St George to the cause of chivalry and portrayed modern British soldiers as successors to medieval knights in fighting for the cause of right:

> *Now, Island Empress, wave thy crest on high,*
> *And bid the banner of thy patron flow,*
> *Gallant St George, the flower of Chivalry,*
> *For thou hast faced, like him, a dragon foe,*

And rescued innocence from overthrow,
And trampled down, like him, tyrannic might,
And to the gazing world mayst proudly show
The chosen emblem of thy sainted Knight,
Who quelled devouring pride, and vindicated right.

Walter Scott was not the only nineteenth-century Scot to make a significant contribution to the rediscovery and reinvention of chivalry that played so central a role in Victorian constructions of Britishness. Thomas Carlyle, son of an Ecclefechan stonemason, championed two very important aspects of it in his gospel of work and cult of the hero. Carlyle's own great hero, Oliver Cromwell, although a very English figure, rightly described by his modern biographer, Christopher Hill, as 'God's Englishman', could also be presented as a very British leader, conquering England and Ireland and embarking on an imperial mission. Particularly in the way that Carlyle portrayed him, he is also a very Scottish figure – Protestant, puritanical, gripped by a sense of divine calling and election, driven by the stern imperative of duty and displaying both a passion for liberty and a fierce intolerance. Carlyle's Cromwell is a prototype of the muscular Christianity that was to exemplify Britishness in the age of Victorian imperialism and for some time beyond it.

Muscular Christianity was as much an English as a Scottish characteristic, which had its roots in Protestantism and probably owed more to the Gothic Anglo-Saxon than the Celtic strain in Britishness. The phrase seems to have been first used in 1857 with reference to Charles Kingsley, the English country clergyman and author, who had

> *set himself the task of spreading the knowledge and fostering the love of a*
> *muscular Christianity. His ideal is a man who fears God and can walk a*
> *thousand miles in a thousand hours – who, in the language Mr Kingsley has*
> *made popular, breathes God's free air on God's rich earth, and at the same*
> *time can hit a woodcock, doctor a horse, and twist a poker round his finger.*[8]

A modern study, which portrays muscular Christianity as the embodiment of the Victorian age, describes Kingsley as wanting to propagate the image of a 'masculine, charismatic, and authoritative Englishman who stands as a representative of a resolutely Anglo-Saxon and Protestant nation-empire'. There was a strong anti-Catholic strain in the writing of Kingsley and his fellow Victorian exponents of muscular Christianity. They associated Catholicism with moral degeneracy, priest-craft, subservience and the effeminacy of lace cottas, stoles and incense. The manly Christianity which they championed was firmly Protestant, fiercely patriotic and based on the chivalric spirit of self-sacrifice. It was also simple and straightforward, if demanding. Kingsley wrote in the Christian Socialist journal *Politics for the People*: 'All that is wanted is the Spirit of self-sacrifice, patriotism, and brother-love – which God alone can give'.[9]

Muscular Christianity followed on in many ways from the Anglo-Saxon heritage of sturdy independence and self-reliant vigour which was explicitly celebrated in Kingsley's novels *Alton Locke* and *Westward Ho!* However, it did not produce a creed of competitive individualism but rather was one of the main influences behind the Christian socialist movement, which began in mid-Victorian Britain. Alongside Kingsley, the leading figures in this movement included Thomas Hughes, Liberal MP and author of the classic novel about English public school life, *Tom Brown's School Days*, and W. D. Maurice, perhaps the greatest British theologian of the nineteenth century, who emphasized Christ's headship over the whole of humanity. Originally a Unitarian, Maurice became an Anglican largely because of his enthusiasm for the theological breadth and the commitment to national service that he saw exemplified in the institution of the established church. He articulated a very British set of theological values, being liberal on atonement but emphasizing the themes of sacrifice and service and preferring social action to abstract intellectual theorizing. He once remarked that he learned as much theology from the hospital wards in which he served as chaplain as from books and in the Divinity classrooms where he lectured.

Although Maurice was English, he had an important Scottish circle of friends and disciples. They included Thomas Erskine, A. J. Scott and John Macleod Campbell, who shared his belief in the inherent goodness of humanity and reacted against the forbidding Calvinistic doctrines of limited atonement and double predestination. One of Maurice's closest friends and disciples was the Scottish poet, preacher, novelist, fantasist and fairly-tale writer, George MacDonald, whose writings had a profound influence on both C. S. Lewis and J. R. R. Tolkien. It has recently been argued that MacDonald's fairy-tales *The Princess and the Goblin* and *The Princess and*

Curdie provide a more nuanced and feminized version of muscular Christianity, in which physical frailty is mixed with spiritual strength and the emphasis is on persistence, never yielding and rising when you are fallen.'[10] These particular qualities have certainly long had a special place in Scottish hearts, witness the influence of the story of Robert Bruce and the spider with its moral, 'If at first you don't succeed, try, try and try again.' It is also noticeable that muscular Christianity found several prominent devotees in the established Church of Scotland. John Caird, Professor of Divinity and later Principal of the University of Glasgow, preached a memorable sermon on 'Christian manliness' to the student body at the opening of the academic year 1871-1872. Norman MacLeod, minister of the Barony Church in Glasgow and Queen Victoria's favourite preacher, put the central precepts of muscular Christianity into his hymn 'Courage, brother, do not stumble', written originally for the many working men in his congregation and sung with considerable effect at the funeral of John Smith, leader of the Labour Party, in 1994. With its simple exhortation that 'though the road be rough and dreary and the end far out of sight, foot it bravely, strong or weary, trust in God and do the right,' it is a spiritualized version of Harry Lauder's music hall song 'Keep right on to the end of the road'. In MacLeod's case, the gospel of persistence and simple trust derived from his boyhood in a Highland manse. As he himself observed:

> *If ever 'muscular Christianity' was taught to the rising generation, the*
> *Highland manse of those days was its gymnasium. After school hours, and*
> *on 'paly days' and Saturdays, there was no want of employment calculated*
> *to develop physical energy. The glebe and farm made a constant demand for*
> *labour which it was joy to the boys to contribute.*[11]

It was perhaps no coincidence that the cult of manliness that grew out of muscular Christianity in the late nineteenth century and under-girded British imperialism in its high noon found its supreme literary expression in the pages of the *Scots Observer*. Its English editor, W. E. Henley, pursued a crusade against what he took to be the decadence of the aesthetic movement and gave Rudyard Kipling his first literary platform on his arrival home from India. Kipling became a leading propagandist for the male virtues of the stiff upper lip, sense of duty and purpose and readiness to shoulder 'the white man's burden' that came to be associated with British imperialism, as well as some of its less appealing values like racial superiority and imperiousness. Imperialism and Britishness are closely intertwined in many definitions, especially by those who are hostile to both concepts. Scots made a disproportionate contribution to the Empire and Scottish values perhaps also had a similarly disproportionate influence on constructions of Britishness in the heyday of imperialism.

One aspect of the British character often associated with the gung-ho masculinity of the imperial project is its anti-intellectualism. It is epitomized in words written by one of the great nineteenth-century enthusiasts for chivalric revival, Kenelm Henry Digby, in his book *The Broad Sword of Honour* (1822):

> *The scholar may instruct the world with his learning, the philosopher may astonish and benefit it by his researches, the man of letters may give a polish and a charm to society, but he who is possessed of simple faith and high honour, is, beyond all comparison, the more proper object of our affection and reverence.*[12]

Just to confound all that I have said about the Protestantism of this particular element in British identity, Digby was himself a committed Roman Catholic. He was, however, sufficiently imbued with the spirit of muscular Christianity to feel that 'the effects of exercise and activity, and even of the violent amusements of ancient chivalry and of our modern youth are, I conceive, unquestionable in warming the heart and in exciting the love of virtue.' Quoting these words in his fascinating study of the revival and reinvention of the code of medieval chivalry in Britain between the late eighteenth century and the 1914-1918 war, Mark Girouard observes, 'How many rugger playing Victorian prefects are implicit in those sentences.'[13]

It is with the development of the institution of the Victorian public school that the British obsession with character, team spirit and moral and muscular fibre has perhaps been most closely associated. Certainly, the ranks of Victorian headmasters produced some of the most fervent devotees of the gospel preached by Digby. Henry Hart, headmaster of Sedbergh, declared in 1880 that 'character more than scholarship was the aim of his teaching.' It is striking that the most firmly committed of all Victorian public school headmasters to these values was a Scot, Hely Hutchison Almond, who ruled Loretto School for forty years from 1862. The regime during his time there is well described by Richard Holt:

Every moment had to be filled with useful or energetic activity and there
was a timetable that showed exactly how time was to be spent. There were
compulsory games every day. Even the school uniform with its open shirts and
long shorts looked like a football strip. If ever a man took Kipling's maxim of
'filling the unforgiving minute' it was Almond. Rugby was the main game
and its virtues were extolled in the school song' Go like blazes'. Running was
another of Almond's enthusiasms and boys would be cheerfully chucked out
into the depths of a bad Scottish winter when 'the roads were hedge high with
snow' and 'every now and then they would fall into a drift'.[14]

Sport came to be one of the main vehicles through which the British ideals of
Christian manliness, fair play and team spirit were carried across the Empire. In his
book on *Sport and the British*, Holt cites a classic example of what he calls this process
of 'cultural reproduction' in the person of the black historian, novelist and socialist, C.
L. R. James, who came from a modest, respectable and religious family in Trinidad.
James won a scholarship to a racially mixed secondary school steeped in the British
public school tradition and, in Holt's words, immersed himself 'in the middle-class
culture of the British boy, reading the *Boy's Own Paper* and *The Captain*, worshipping
at the shrine of W. G. Grace and memorizing the averages of C. B. Fry with the awe
of a young Harrovian reading *Wisden*'. The impact of this education on James was' a
subtle blending of "high" culture with physical culture'[15]. Despite becoming a socialist,
he could never stomach Nye Bevan's mocking of the 'Tory' morality of 'playing with a
straight bat', nor did he later sympathize with those who supported the West Indies
cricketers largely for their potential to inflict humiliation on the former colonial power.
This 'wasn't playing the game'. James maintained an attachment to the principles of
fair play and keeping a straight bat despite their imperial provenance. So did several
other colonial radicals who saw no contradiction in supporting the British sporting
ethos whilst denouncing British exploitation and colonialism.

The British ideal of the sporting hero, and its capacity to embrace more than
just the clean-limbed young Englishman, is well explored in the film *Chariots of
Fire* (1981), based around preparations for the 1924 Olympic games. Its opening
sequence provides a powerful evocation of the team spirit at the heart of early
twentieth-century Britishness, with a group of men running together along the
West Sands beach at St Andrews on the east coast of Scotland, each identically clad

with a Union Jack emblem on their shirts. The location on the edge of the seashore enhances the atmosphere of an island nation. The two central figures in the film are both outsiders and yet quintessentially British in their different ways: Harold Abrahams, the Gilbert and Sullivan-loving Jewish athlete educated at Cambridge University, who runs round his college quad to the strains of 'He Is an Englishman' from *HMS Pinafore* and goes on to win the gold medal for the 100 metres; and Eric Liddell, the high-minded Scottish Congregationalist who refused to run the 100 metres for which he had trained when he discovered that the heats were to be held on a Sunday, went on to win the 400 metres and spent the rest of his life as a missionary in China, dying at the age of forty-three in a Japanese concentration camp. Both men could have stepped out of the pages of the *Boy's Own Paper* and exemplified different facets of the British sporting hero while yet remaining in key respects on the fringes of conventional British identity.

The way in which Scottish high-mindedness and muscular Christianity went along with the spirit of enterprise and capitalism that is also associated with the land of Adam Smith in making the British Empire is most famously epitomized in the figure of David Livingstone, missionary and explorer who went to Africa, in his own words, 'to make an open path for commerce and Christianity'. Opening up the remote comers of the Dark Continent, seeking to convert the natives and developing new markets for trade were not the only ways in which Scots showed their enthusiasm for British imperialism. Nearer home, the Church of Scotland minister, James Cooper (1846-1922), dreamed of the establishment of a single church to minister to the peoples of the British Isles and the Empire. Cooper, for three decades a parish minister and then professor of church history at Glasgow University, was, as we have already noted, a considerable enthusiast for Celtic Christianity (page 102). He was also passionately committed to a scheme of 'imperial reunion' in which all the churches of Great Britain and the Empire would join together on the basis of their common Celtic heritage. He first advocated a United Church for the British Empire in a sermon in 1902, in which he pointed to the contrast between the divided state of the church and 'the remarkable drawing together of the different populations of the British Empire, a new loyalty to King and country, a new spirit of imperial unity'. As a first step towards the creation of this united church, Cooper strove hard to achieve a union between the Church of England and the Church of Scotland. In a sermon in St Paul's Cathedral in 1918, he deplored the scandal of ecclesiastical disunity in the United Kingdom and pressed strongly 'the obligation lying upon us as British Christians and British Churches so to agree that we may yield to our Divine Lord and Master a United Church for the British Empire'. A fused British church, uniting at least the established churches of England and Scotland, would 'seal and consecrate the British Empire' and hold out an olive branch to the rest of Christendom.[16]

Three towering Scots of the twentieth century, all deeply imbued with the values of muscular Christianity, moral seriousness and communal purpose, made a significant and enduring contribution to the notion of Britishness that emphasized especially its spiritual underpinning. The contributions made by John Buchan, novelist, politician and colonial administrator, John Reith, founder and first Director General of the BBC, and George Macleod, founder of the Iona Community, are worth recalling in some detail because they show very clearly the huge importance of the Scottish dimension in modern British identity and its strongly religious and spiritual character. The first of the trio, John Buchan (1875-1940), is a wonderful exemplar of hyphenated identity, his life a mixture of English and Scottish themes and places with interludes in far-flung corners of the Empire. Educated at Glasgow and Oxford, his favourite landscapes were the Scottish Borders and the Cotswolds, with the South African veldt and the frozen wastelands of Northern Canada as close runners-up. He epitomized the strenuous puritan strain in the British character, drawing not just on his Scottish Presbyterian roots which remained dear to him throughout his life but also on the English Dissenting tradition – perhaps no book influenced him more among the many he read in his boyhood than John Bunyan's *Pilgrim's Progress*, which he was to quote movingly at the end of his novel *Mr Standfast* (itself a title based on a character in Bunyan's book).

John Buchan displayed the characteristic British penchant for a life of action rather than just of intellectual or cultural pursuits. Like the heroes of what he deprecatingly called his 'shockers', he enjoyed climbing, deer-stalking, fishing and as many other healthy and manly outdoor pursuits as his congenital stomach trouble would allow him. A politician as well as a writer, his politics display a fascinating mixture of conservatism, liberalism and an over-arching Unionism. He made his maiden speech in Parliament defending the principle of hereditary peers in the House of Lords and his second speech defending the 1707 Act of Union between England and Scotland. Yet he was a progressive on many issues, including the welfare state and Scottish devolution, strongly supporting the setting up of a Scottish office in Edinburgh. A devoted and romantic Scot, he also believed passionately in Scotland as part of something greater, the United Kingdom and the British Empire. He was devoted to the Church of Scotland throughout his life. When he lived in London, he worshipped at St Columba's Church of Scotland where he became an elder although, when he later moved to Elsfield, near Oxford, he worshipped at the local Church of England parish church. He was thrilled towards the end of his life to be appointed as Lord High Commissioner to the General Assembly of the Church of Scotland – a role in which he represented the sovereign and which, in the words of his biographer Andrew Lownie, 'had developed into representing Scottish national identity within the Union'.[17]

This was one of the many values that Buchan had imbibed from his father, a quiet, serious, gentle minister of the Free Church of Scotland who gave his son a love of Scotland through ballads and stories but taught him also that there was no reason to dislike the English, a lesson that he had to reinforce when his children were rude to an English cousin who stayed the night in the manse:

> *Why, you silly little people, don't you know that England and Scotland are one, have been for hundreds of years? Our interests are the same; we work together, play together, and, if need be, fight together. Every Scot worth the name thinks his country is the best and wants to do it credit, but we're not shedding any glory on Scotland when we're rude to a guest because she's English.*[18]

John Buchan put much of himself into the hero of his first novel with a contemporary setting, *The Half-Hearted* (1900). Towards the end of it, Lewis Haystoun, laird, traveller, writer and would-be Conservative politician, makes a heroic one-man stand against enemy troops invading India. As he single-handedly attempts to hold a pass against them, knowing that he is bound to be killed, his thoughts turn to his beloved Scotland many thousands of miles away and he momentarily feels the extreme loneliness of an exile's death. Yet he realizes also that 'the heritage of his land and people was his in this ultimate moment a hundredfold more than ever.'

> *To the old fighters in the Border wars, the religionists of the South, the Highland gentlemen of the Cause, he cried greeting over the abyss of time.*

He had lost no inch of his inheritance. Where, indeed, was the true Scotland?
Not in the little barren acres he had left, the few thousands of city-folk, or
the contentions of unlovely creeds and vain philosophies. The elect of his race
had ever been wanderers. No more than Hellas had his land a paltry local
unity. Wherever the English flag was planted anew, wherever the last stand
was made in the march of Western progress, wherever men did their duty
faithfully and without hope of little reward – there was the true land of the
true patriot.[19]

What is fascinating about this passage is the way that it locates 'the true Scotland' not in the lochs and glens of home but in the far reaches of empire 'wherever the English flag was planted anew' (not even the Union flag) and wherever men are doing their duty faithfully and without hope of reward. It is a very masculine and a very imperialist vision of Scottishness in Britishness. Buchan himself epitomized the Scottish involvement in the British Empire in his own public career, working as a young man with Lord Milner's kindergarten in South Africa and going to Canada at the end of his life to serve as Governor-General. While he was not naively starry eyed about it, he had a deep romantic attachment to the British Empire which was for him essentially a spiritual and Christian entity. For his speech as Lord High Commissioner on the last day of the 1933 General Assembly of the Church of Scotland, he took as his theme the Scottish Church and the British Empire and expounded the essence of his creed: 'The true bond of Empire is the spiritual bond. Its cohesion is in its ideal and not in its form of government ... The true empire is a spiritual thing based essentially upon Christian ideals.'[20]

Buchan's novels are populated by a largely male world of clubbable, clean-limbed, chivalrous, straightforward imperial heroes. In the words of Benny Green, 'like half the games masters in the Empire, he thought that cold baths and long walks in the heather were better calculated to boost a fellow's religiosity than rolls in the clover.'[21] Although he was happily married, his novels largely shun any romantic interest and are almost entirely about all-male bonding and escapades. One of his earliest sallies into fiction, a short novel entitled *Sir Quixote of the Moors*, ends with the hero riding away from the lady he loves, showing that he loves honour more. Tellingly, when the book was published on the other side of the Atlantic, his American publishers insisted on adding a paragraph in which, after an hour of riding away, the hero turns back to return to his love. Yet his fiction is not all stiff upper lips and suppressed emotions – there are occasional outbursts of passion and there are also recurrent darker undercurrents, notably the tensions between paganism and Christianity and between order and chaos. For all his romantic idealism, Buchan had a quintessentially Scottish and British preference for practicality and getting things done. He was also a great believer in the English virtues of moderation and compromise, lauding the moderate leader, like his great hero the first Marquis of Montrose, who 'knows that most of our rules of life are not eternal truths, but working conventions, which must often be drastically overhauled to make certain that they have not survived their usefulness'[22]. He also valued competence, as illustrated in another passage in *The Half-Hearted* where the Conservative MP, Wratislaw, challenged by Haystoun as to what he would regard as the highest happiness, answers 'the sense of competence':

> *And what do we mean by competence? Not success! God knows it is something very different from success! Any fool may be successful, if the gods wish to hurt him. Competence means that splendid joy in your own powers and the approval of your own heart, which great men feel always and lesser men now and again at favoured intervals. There are a certain number of things in the world to be done. And we have got to do them. We may fail – it doesn't in the least matter. We may get killed in the attempt – it matters still less. The things may not altogether be worth doing – it is of very little importance. It is ourselves we have to judge by. If we are playing our part well, and know it, then we can thank God and go on. That is what I call happiness.*[23]

This is a fascinating exposition of a very British outlook which links the cult of heroic failure and the second-best with the sentiments of Henry Newbolt's classic Victorian public school poem *'Vitaï Lampada'* ('Play up, play up and play the game') and the song 'We're Here because We're Here' that kept the Tommies going in the trenches of Flanders in the First World War. There is more here, however, than stoicism or public school gamesmanship. At its root, perhaps, lies the idea of getting on with the job and doing it well, however humdrum or however dangerous it may be. It is the creed expounded in George Herbert's 'Teach me my God and King' with its line 'Who sweeps the room as for thy cause, makes that and the action fine' and in John

Keble's similar observation in 'New every morning is the love' that 'The trivial round, the common task, will furnish all I need to ask'. In many ways, it is a very bourgeois attitude and it is noticeable that for all his admiration of both aristocrats and working men, John Buchan has a particularly soft spot for the unassuming British middle classes, represented wonderfully in his novels in the person of Dickson McCunn, the Glasgow grocer, who, it is observed in *Huntingtower*, 'is the stuff which above all others makes a great people. He will endure when aristocracies crack and proletariats crumble.'[24] It is the British middle classes who provide the moral backbone that prevents anarchy and who make Britain, in the eyes of Saskia, a refugee from the Russian revolution, 'the safest place in a mad world'.

This steady, stoical competence is not without its uplifting, sacrificial side. In *The Half-Hearted*, Wratislaw expresses another very British sentiment when he reflects, 'The great things of the world have all been done by men who didn't stop to reflect on them... A man must have that direct practical virtue which forgets itself and sees only its work.' This for him is true self-sacrifice, and it leads him to reflect that, if he had some desperate frontier work to get through with and a body of men to pick for it', he would go for the Calvinists and fanatics for choice – 'They would have the fear of God in them, and that somehow keeps a man from fearing anything else. They would do their work because they believed it to be their duty.'[25] We are back yet again to the Protestant Puritan streak in the Scottish and the British make-up, with Presbyterian divines preaching duty and self-sacrifice and with a strong moral concern for upholding the right, supporting the weak and promoting the common good. These themes run through Buchan's novels – as do other Puritan themes like the chase and the pursuit, the curious dispositions of Providence and the sense of overarching moral order. They are complemented and to some extent countered by other themes not always associated with Puritanism: the sacredness of place, a powerful mysticism and fascination with surviving traces of paganism and 'the old religion' of Britain.

It is this amalgam of themes that make John Buchan's famous 'shockers' such quintessentially British stories. Indeed, he seems to me to be perhaps among the most British of all novelists in terms of his plots, characters and style. This is not just in the narrow sense recognized by some of his more sneering reviewers like William Plower, who wrote of *A Prince of the Captivity* when it came out in 1933, 'It is a British book, for boys of all ages if not of all kinds, and will find a niche in school libraries. It discloses a "decent" scout-masterly attitude to life, and a wildly romantic view of human nature, especially that of men of action.'[26] There is subtlety and ambiguity in Buchan's novels, and in his view of Britain – it is not just a one-dimensional picture of manly imperial heroes chasing over moors and engaging with evil and scheming foreign powers. There is a wonderful sense of the many layers and dimensions of British society, not least of the diversity both within and between the Scots and the English. There is also a fascination with the largely invisible, submerged part of the population who exemplify older, more liminal values like the half-pagan Naked Men or Spoonbills in *Midwinter* who represent 'an old England, which has outlived Roman and Saxon and Dane and Norman and will outlast the Hanoverian. It has seen priest turn to presbyter and presbyter to parson and has only smiled. It is the land of the edge of moorlands and the rims of forests and the twilight before dawn, and strange knowledge still dwells in it.'[27] Buchan himself was particularly attached to the border country between England and Scotland and had an acute sense of the importance of borderlands, and of what C. S. Lewis called Shadowlands, in the shifting, slippery, perichoretic mixture that is British identity. He shared G. K. Chesterton's consciousness of and fascination with the forgotten people of England, with their visceral, almost pagan spirituality, and with their counterparts in Scotland who appear as shadowy figures in *WychWood*. Buchan leads us into strange and dark realms of primitive spirituality and mysticism as well as into the fresh open air of manly adventure, self-sacrifice and competence. In doing so, he opens up Britishness in all its picaresque richness and complex spiritual depth and diversity.

Just before we leave Buchan and move on to the second of the great twentieth-century exemplars and creators of Britishness, John Reith, it is worth pausing momentarily to note two later twentieth-century Scottish adventure novelists who created very British heroes. Alistair MacLean, another son of the manse, in his case of the established church, served in the Navy during the Second World War and went on to write highly successful and also highly patriotic British stories like *HMS Ulysses*, *The Guns of Navarone*, *Where Eagles Dare* and *Ice Station Zebra*. Like Buchan's shockers, they are packed with adventure and almost entirely devoid of sex and feminine characters. This latter imbalance was rectified in the character of James Bond, created by the Anglo-Scottish author, Ian Fleming. Bond's love life was certainly a great deal more colourful than that of Buchan's and MacLean's heroes but the Fettes-educated spy, played by both Scottish and English actors in his various cinematographic incarnations, does display the same impeccable manners and reckless courage, even if his manliness is not of an obviously Christian cast and his moral fibre occasionally frays a little.

John Reith (1889-1971) was certainly not lacking on the moral fibre front. An intensely driven man with extraordinary energy and a strenuous work ethic, he had an overwhelming sense of Providence and vocation, a strong religious faith and was, like Buchan, both a dreamer and a doer. Born in Scotland, where his father was a Free Church minister, he was educated at an English public school, spent most of his adult life south of the border but remained romantically committed to Scotland. Like Buchan, he gave allegiance to both the established churches of Britain, having his children christened by the Archbishop of Canterbury and rejoicing in his appointment towards the end of his life as Lord High Commissioner to the General Assembly of the Church of Scotland. His deeply romantic spirituality is summed up in his attachment to the metrical version of the 23rd Psalm sung to the tune Crimond, about which he wrote movingly in 1947 at the end of his autobiography *Into The Wind*. Hearing it coming from the wireless in his study as it is sung at the wedding of Princess Elizabeth and Prince Philip, he is led into an autobiographical reverie in which Scottish memories and an English present come together in a British state occasion:

> *That age-old song of Presbyterian Scotland, the national anthem of its faith. I see my mother trace its lines for me to read. I hear my father's voice: 'John, can you say the 23rd psalm yet? I hear it sung at family worship in the manse; in the College Church in Glasgow; in the little highland conventicle of halcyon summer holidays. The Abbey of Westminster dissolves into the Kirk of Rothiemurchus.*[28]

John Reith's abiding contribution to Britishness was, of course, his almost single-handed construction of what became one of its greatest institutional embodiments in the twentieth century, the British Broadcasting Corporation. He established at the heart of the BBC a commitment to high moral and intellectual standards, a distinction between news and propaganda, a detachment from the Government while remaining a public service free of commercial pressures and a mission to inform and educate the nation as much as to entertain it and to mould and improve rather than simply pander to or reflect public opinion and taste. This last mission was summed up in a characteristic diary entry about his fundamental difference of approach with Hugh Carleton Greene, the liberalizing Director General of the 1960s: 'I lead; he follows the crowd in all the disgusting manifestations of the age. I say I lead – all through my time in the BBC, and it all comes from the Manse. Without any reservation he gives the public what it wants; I would not, did not and said I wouldn't.'[29] In the words of Harold Laski, 'he seems to talk as though he was in charge of the national well-being.'[30] This autocratic approach could hardly be expected to last through the rebellious 1960s, yet much that Reith set in place did survive that iconoclastic decade. He effectively invented the concept of public service broadcasting, expressed in his aim 'to bring the best of everything into the greatest number of homes' and established the BBC as the voice of Britain, lofty, impartial and truly national yet independent from the Government.

For Reith, in the words of his biographer, Andrew Boyle, 'The rock on which the BBC stood was the rock of Christianity and the moral code that flowed from it.'[31] His determination to make the nation's broadcasting corporation a virtual arm of its national churches led to candidates for jobs at the BBC being grilled as to whether they 'could accept the fundamental teachings of our Lord Jesus Christ'. He also imposed a strict Sabbatarianism on the airwaves that made the Sunday schedule a mixture of lengthy religious services, long periods of silence and interludes of serious talks and serious music (Bach cantatas being much favoured), a combination that had many listeners switching their dials to Continental stations in search of dance music. Considerable airtime was given to religious broadcasting and especially to church services. Reith took particular pride in this aspect of the BBC's output, personally stage-managing the services held in the Concert Hall of Broadcasting House on great national occasions and insisting that all officiating clergy wore scarlet robes just as he insisted that announcers in these pre-television days always wore evening dress.

He had a tremendous sense of theatricality and national occasion. When the 1926 General Strike ended, Reith himself read the news bulletin. He then came on air in the evening to read messages from the King and the Prime Minister and finally to deliver his own homily which began with the words that 'Our first feeling on hearing of the termination of the General Strike must be one of profound thankfulness to Almighty God, who has led us through this supreme trial with national health unimpaired.' He concluded by calling on those going to work the following day 'to repair the gaps and build up the walls of a more enduring city' and launching into a reading of William Blake's 'Jerusalem'. 'I had an orchestra brought together and just as I began to read the poem, they played in the background. At the end they came in with full orchestra and chorus with the last verse and it was tremendously impressive.' Reith's use of this great anthem of the English radical and libertarian tradition to celebrate the crushing of militant trade unionism was warmly applauded by the Prime Minister and leading Anglican bishops. The Bishop of Winchester said it was precisely what the nation needed: 'It was a great opportunity for a Christian message and it was greatly used.'[32]

Reith's determination to invest national occasions and institutions with religious significance and to make the BBC the voice of Britain and Britishness both at home and to the world reached its fullest expression in his promotion of the monarchy as the unifying head of both the United Kingdom and the Empire. In 1923, he masterminded the first-ever radio outside broadcast, covering the Duke of York's wedding to Lady Elizabeth Bowes-Lyon. Microphones were positioned so that listeners could hear the sounds of the processional horses and carriages, the cheering crowds and the bells ringing as well as the church service itself. In this way an 'audible pageant' was created that did much to enhance the magic and spiritual aura of monarchy and its ability to draw the nation together. It established a pattern for future broadcasts of royal occasions, which did much to promote the ceremonial and the Christian aspects of British monarchy. It was Reith who first suggested, in 1927, that the monarch should make a Christmas broadcast to his subjects across the Empire. The first such broadcast took place in 1932. After it, he wrote characteristically in his diary:

> It was the most spectacular success in BBC history thus far. The King has been heard all over the world with surprising clarity; only in New Zealand were parts of the speech inaudible owing to atmospherics. It was sensationally starred in foreign countries; the New York Times in large type: 'Distant lands Thrill to His "God Bless You"'; two thousand leading articles were counted in Broadcasting House'.[33]

In 1937, Reith insisted that annual royal Christmas broadcasts should continue when the Prime Minister, Neville Chamberlain, proposed giving them up because of the impossibility of finding something new and interesting to say every year. 'How pathetic,' Reith noted in his diary. For the semi-jubilee of King George V's reign in 1932, he mounted a special service in the Concert Hall of Broadcasting House in which the Archbishop of Canterbury, the Moderator-designate of the General Assembly of the Church of Scotland and the Moderator of the Free Church Federal Council all took part, dressed on his specific instructions in scarlet cassocks. He noted with characteristic self-congratulation that it was generally judged to have been far more impressive than the official thanksgiving service held in St Paul's Cathedral the following day.

If Reith earned his sobriquet as Gold Microphone Pursuivant for the way in which he used the BBC to promote and celebrate the institution of monarchy, he also established a tradition of understated, restrained and dignified treatment of royal and national occasions which was to colour both Britain's self-image and the image of Britishness across the world. The BBC's coverage of the death of George V, which began with the announcement 'The King's life is moving peacefully to its close', earned newspaper headlines on 'The quiet dignity of the BBC'. Reith put the traditional British values of restraint, understatement, deference and respect for tradition at the heart of the nation's most powerful means of mass communication and in doing so almost certainly extended their shelf-lives through the latter part of the twentieth century. He also made sure that the BBC expressed Britain to itself and to the world in all its variety, establishing regional services for Scotland, Wales, Northern Ireland and the English regions, which both opted out of the national UK output and also contributed to it their own distinctive accents and cultures. Then there was the Empire Service and the services in foreign languages, regarded by Reith as 'the projection of England'. The BBC has remained the institution that perhaps best exemplifies Britishness in all its rich diversity and that lets different parts of the nation talk to one another.

At its best, it still wonderfully embodies the uniquely perichoretic nature of the United Kingdom and its overlapping identities. It also still has the ability to pull the nation together and unite it around significant national occasions. This last achievement is a legacy of Reith's single-handed identification of a number of state and sporting events that the BBC must cover. In the words of Richard Holt:

Reith was the true successor of the Victorian headmaster, rapidly establishing a range of sporting events which the BBC in its capacity as sole arbiter of airwaves deemed to be of national significance. A few big events joined the list of approved 'patriotic' moments like Remembrance Day – the Wembley crowd even sang 'Abide With Me' – and in Reith's words permitted the British people to be 'present equally at functions and ceremonials upon which national sentiment is consecrated'.[34]

So it was that Test cricket, Rugby Internationals, the Derby, the Cup Final, tennis at Wimbledon and the Boat Race all became seen as quintessentially British events, broadcast across the nation on Saturday afternoons, and taking their place alongside state occasions like Trooping the Colour, the Act of Remembrance at the Cenotaph, royal weddings and funerals. The commentators for these events, as much the sporting as the ceremonial, became in a real sense the voices of Britain – Richard Dimbleby, John Arlott, John Snagge, Dan Maskell and Brian Johnston. They were not just English voices – Bill McLaren and Cliff Morgan became the voices of rugby and the colonial strains of Richie Benaud came to be indelibly associated with test match cricket. More recently Tom Fleming has brought his stately and subtle Scottish tones and Huw Edwards his Welsh accent to commentaries on state occasions.

Reith deplored the collapse of moral standards at the BBC in his own lifetime, noting in 1958, when it started broadcasting betting prices, 'that is about the last trace of my management gone' and describing the programme *Juke Box Jury* as 'a manifestation of evil'. He was also appalled when the BBC lost its monopoly, which he had firmly defended, and commercial television began in 1955. Other changes since he died have left the BBC, and especially BBC television, looking less like the embodiment of Britishness and more like just another set of channels in a globalized, multi-choice, media industry. The rights to televise Test cricket and major football matches have gone to commercial broadcasters. The National Anthem is no longer played at the end of each night's transmissions and there is no longer a televised church service every Sunday morning. In its radio output, and especially in Radio 4 and the World Service, however, the BBC still clings to Reith's legacy and principles. Radio 4's morning flagship *Today* programme mixes the Home Counties vowels of newsreaders with the Scottish and Welsh accents of presenters James Naughtie and John Humphreys. It also includes in 'Thought for the Day' a brief spiritual reflection, preserved largely because of its popularity among listeners. There is still a live daily service every weekday morning and an act of Christian worship every Sunday, for which the audience is large and growing. The reassuring and authoritative chimes of Big Ben still introduce the six o' clock and ten o' clock evening news bulletins. In its radio stations at least traces persist of the understated restraint, the respect and reverence for British institutions and emphasis on their spiritual foundations and the high moral tone and seriousness that the tortured and troubled son of the Manse gave to the BBC. Its television channels may no longer so obviously embody and reflect his distinctively Scottish contribution to Britishness but it is still to the BBC that a majority of the population turns for great state events and at times of national crisis and celebration.

With George Macleod (1895-1991), the third great Scottish colossus of the twentieth century who made a significant contribution to Britishness, we return to several of the themes discussed in Chapter 3 of this book. His contribution lay more directly than the others in the area of spirituality and specifically in promoting and living out an engaged Christianity, at once rooted in Celtic tradition and deeply involved in contemporary needs and affairs, with a strongly communitarian and prophetic emphasis. Macleod was not a son of the Manse – his father was a Scottish Unionist MP - but his grandfather, great-grandfather and numerous other ancestors had been Church of Scotland ministers. His mother was of Yorkshire Unitarian stock and Macleod was, in the words of his entry in the *Dictionary of National Biography*, 'a thoroughly Anglicized Scottish aristocrat'. Like Reith, he was educated at an English public school, in his case Winchester, and like Buchan, he went on to Oxford. He won the Military Cross in the First World War and subsequently became a pacifist. A muscular Christian Socialist in the tradition of Thomas Hughes and Charles Kingsley, he committed himself whilst ministering at Govan in the heart of Glasgow's shipbuilding area at the height of the Depression to creating' a Christian Common Wealth'. He set out for Iona in 1938 with an all-male mixture of Divinity students and unemployed shipyard workers, who followed him down to the beach to take bracing dips in the sea early every morning before tackling the task of re-building the communal buildings around the Abbey.

Like Buchan and Reith, Macleod was a romantic and a realist, a dreamer and a doer. He also exemplified a very British way of working from within the establishment to change it, using his contacts with financiers and rich businessmen to obtain money to rebuild Iona and his seat in the House of Lords to campaign for nuclear disarmament. Unlike Buchan and Reith, he remained in Scotland but was in many ways a prophet without honour in his own country, being regarded by many in Church of Scotland as dangerously Romish, radical and socialistic, and found many of his strongest allies and supporters in England and Wales. The ecumenical Iona Community which he founded in 1938, and which now numbers over 250 members, 1,500 associates and 3,000 friends across the world, has been one of the most dynamic and influential movements in British Christianity over the last seventy years, promoting the social gospel, engagement with justice and peace issues and the reform and reinvigoration of worship. It is a very British community. While retaining strong Church of Scotland connections, there are many English and some Welsh members. The accents to be found among staff and volunteers working in the community's two island centres on Iona, the Abbey and the Macleod Centre, are preponderantly English, while those of the guests who come to experience life in community for a week are predominantly North American with a fair sprinkling from Scandinavia and Continental Europe. It is largely thanks to George Macleod and his legacy that Iona has become a magnet attracting those in search of spiritual nourishment and engagement and also that Celtic Christianity as a whole has undergone such a revival in the United Kingdom and beyond over the last forty years or so.

The strong commitment to the social gospel and to communitarianism championed by Macleod has informed the thinking and actions of the established churches of England and Scotland since the mid twentieth century. The groundwork was prepared during the Second World in an Anglican report produced under the direction of Archbishop William Temple, *Christianity and Social Order* (1942) and a commission set up under John Baillie, Moderator of the General Assembly of the Church of Scotland, in 1943. Both called for communal and state action in the field of health and social welfare and have been credited by historians with preparing the ground for the creation of the National Health Service and other welfare reforms introduced by the post-war Attlee Government. The two established churches, along with other churches like Methodists, the United Reformed Church and, increasingly the Roman Catholics, continued to commend the common good and the public service ethic and to stand for a comprehensive government-provided social welfare programme after the collapse of the cross-party Butskellite consensus which prevailed from the 1950s to the end of the 1970s. When Margaret Thatcher challenged the ideology of corporatism and state-provided welfare with a greater emphasis on competition and the free market, she found the churches providing some of the most sustained and carefully thought out opposition. The Church of England's *Faith in the City* report in 1985 was strongly critical of Government policy, laying the blame for the considerable urban deprivation existing in affluent Britain on the structure of the economy and complaining that public policy was 'inadequate and superficial'. The thrust of Thatcherite policy was called into serious question. 'To affirm the importance of wealth creation is not enough,' the report stated: 'economic policy should be as concerned with the distribution of income and wealth as with its creation ...We believe that at present too much emphasis is being given to individualism and not enough to collective obligation.'[35]

Margaret Thatcher had herself, of course, been schooled in the Protestant ethic of hard work, thrift and competitive individualism by her Methodist father. As such, she stood in a clear English Nonconformist tradition, which also had its echoes in Scottish Presbyterianism. The extent to which her combination of puritan individualism and free market economics was at odds with the communitarian and collectivist mentality of the established churches, however, was clear from the frosty relations she enjoyed with Robert Runcie, Archbishop of Canterbury through the 1980s and himself a Scot, and the cool reception which greeted her when she appealed to the tradition of Adam Smith when delivering her infamous 'Sermon on the Mound' at the General Assembly of the Church of Scotland in 1988. Much more in tune with the mood of the churches was the political philosophy of John Smith, leader of the Labour Party from 1992 until his sudden death in 1995, who did much to revive Christian Socialism in Britain and also to re-establish the Labour Party on the basis of fusing the English attachment to liberty and the more Scottish (and Welsh) emphasis on the common good. In his Tawney lecture of 1993 to the Christian Socialist Movement, he spoke of a democratic socialism which 'sought to enhance individual freedom in a framework of collective common purpose and opportunity, in which fellowship was the bond of a community of equality'.[36] Smith's emphasis on moral and ethical foundations paved the way for the more overtly Christian leadership of New Labour practised by Tony Blair, the Anglo-Scot whose own political philosophy owes much to the communitarianism of the early-twentieth-century Scots philosopher John MacMurray.

There is a striking preponderance of Scots in the Labour Governments that have run the United Kingdom since 1997. Not all of them conform to the admittedly somewhat stereotypical model of muscular Christianity and moral seriousness that has dominated this chapter, but some of them undoubtedly do, not least the Prime Minister Gordon Brown. Much was rightly made at the start of his premiership of the Presbyterian moral fibre of this son of the manse, as reflected in his reversal of Tony Blaire's plans for super casinos, his announcement of a review of the 24 hour drinking laws that have fuelled Britain's binge-drinking culture and the overall seriousness of his tone and approach. Perhaps we are seeing a new flourish of the distinctive Scottish contribution to Britishness. In other and deeper respects, however, the elements that have particularly distinguished the Scottish contribution to Britishness are in marked decline. The Protestant ethic, with its concomitant values of self-improvement, self-control, honesty, charity and respectability, is fast disappearing. Detailed research by Professor Christie Davies of the University of Reading in the mid 1990s suggests strongly that the decline of Protestantism has been a key factor in the growth of crime and antisocial behaviour in United Kingdom over the last fifty years. He sees the teaching of a personal moral responsibility derived from the British Protestant tradition being replaced by what he calls 'causalism', a way of thinking that seeks welfare and is not concerned with guilt or innocence, praise or blame. Attachment to the idea of the United Kingdom has weakened greatly in Scotland over the last three or four decades, with nationalist feeling steadily rising in the country which once saw itself as North Britain and arguably did more than any other to invent the idea of Britishness. The Church of Scotland, which until the middle of the twentieth century was largely Unionist in sympathy, is now much more inclined to adopt a nationalist position. Muscular Christianity and moral fibre have given way to mealy-mouthed political correctness and relativism in many quarters and find their main exemplars now either on the fringes of evangelical sectarianism or among the new black and Asian Britons from the Commonwealth who in this as in other respects are often more wedded to traditional British values than many within the longer-established white majority.

6 Carnival and Reserve

The Black and Asian Contribution

So far, this book has looked at the contributions made to constructions of Britishness by the Irish, Welsh, English and Scots. This chapter will focus on the contribution made by those who have come as immigrants to Britain in the last fifty years or so and their descendants. The majority of these new Britons hail from the old Empire, especially from Africa, the Caribbean and the Indian subcontinent. They form a diverse group that is very far from being homogeneous although they do generally display both a stronger sense of spiritual and religious identity and a greater feeling of being British than the longer-established white majority population in the United Kingdom.

This relatively recent immigration from the Commonwealth has hugely stimulated the debate about what Britishness means. Initially it provoked a reaction which framed British identity in defensive terms as essentially mono-cultural and white. Paul Gilroy, born in East London to Guyanese and English parents, has written of Britain's 'morbid fixation with the fluctuating substance of national culture and identity' with' the core of British particularity deemed to be under disastrous attack from three different directions: Americanization, Europeanization, and a non-specific subsumption by immigrants, settlers, and invaders of both colonial and post-colonial varieties'.[1] He sees a 'post-imperial melancholia' settling over the country since 1945, full of guilt-ridden self-loathing, depression and racism. Identifying race at the heart of such celebrated attempts to define Britishness as

Norman Tebbit's cricket test, Gilroy aggressively challenged what he took to be the prevailing consensus in his books *The Empire Strikes Back: Race and Racism in 1970s Britain* (1982) and *There Ain't No Black in the Union Jack* (1987).

If the 1970s and 1980s were characterized by a kind of white defensiveness and siege mentality matched by an increasingly assertive and confrontational black consciousness, the 1990s saw a significant change on both sides, with many black and Asian Britons giving up an oppositional identity in favour of one both more confident and more British, and the Government and other major institutions actively pursuing a commitment to pluralism and multiculturalism. Multiculturalism has, indeed, been the dominant ethic of the Labour Government first elected in 1997 and of the liberal intelligentsia and chattering classes who have generally championed a tolerant, secular vision of Britishness emphasizing cultural and ethnic diversity. This vision was well expressed in the 2000 report of the Commission on the Future of Multi-Ethnic Britain set up by the Runnymede Trust and chaired by Bhikhu Parekh, himself an immigrant from India. To some extent, the Commission confirmed Gilroy's view that the word 'British' carried racial connotations of 'white colonialism' and that many national symbols were exclusive and embodied a tacit racialism. It called on the Government to make a formal declaration of Britain's multicultural and multi-faith identity and suggested that the constituent nations of the United Kingdom were at a critical turning point in their history. The choice before them was either to become increasingly narrow, inward-looking countries unable to forge agreement between themselves or between the regions and communities from which they were composed, or to become a ' community of communities' both at the national level and also within every region, city, town or neighbourhood. Taking this latter course would involve rethinking both the 'national story and national identity', understanding the transitional nature of all identities, achieving a balance between cohesion, difference and equality, addressing and eliminating all kinds of racism, and building a state predicated on the principle of 'legitimate and irreducible plurality' rather than simply a liberal association of individuals. Britain, the Commission suggested, could become 'a confident and vibrant multicultural society at ease with its rich diversity'.

In many ways, the Parekh report constituted the high water mark of multiculturalism. Since 2000, the multiculturalist vision of Britain has come under attack from a number of quarters. Events have played a significant role in changing attitudes and perceptions. The serious riots in northern English cities in the summer of 2001 revealed the development of ghettoes and a dangerous level of segregation between different ethnic groups. The destruction of the World Trade Center on 11 September 2001 and subsequent terrorist attacks, not least the London bombings carried out in July 2005 by British-born Muslims, have exacerbated concerns about immigration and put the whole question of Muslim identity and its relationship to British and western values at the top of the political agenda and the forefront of national debate. There is no doubt at all that issues raised by the substantial Muslim presence in Britain and the pervasive Islamophobia that has gripped much of the West in the wake of recent terrorist attacks have contributed considerably to both the urgency and tone of the current debate about Britishness and the reaction against multiculturalism. In the words of Tariq Modood, 'it is clear that the behaviour of no other group in Britain – including groups defined by "race" – acts as a stimulant to debates about whether that group is "British" as do Muslims.'[2] But, quite apart from this specific spur, there has also been a more general questioning of the multicultural agenda of the late 1990s on the grounds that it was too predicated on diversity and separate development and did not emphasize community and cohesion enough. As early as 2000, Yasmin Alibhai-Brown, the *Independent* columnist who came to Britain from Uganda in 1972, declared her belief that it was time to kill off British multiculturalism and move on. In his *Prospect* article in 2004, David Goodhart raised concerns about maintaining a welfare state and respecting public spaces and institutions in a society without a common cultural identity. In the same year, Trevor Phillips, chair of the Commission for Racial Equality, criticized multiculturalism for failing to provide social glue and cohesion and creating an increasingly fragmented society.

What is striking about the debate over multiculturalism is that the new Britons who have been at the forefront on both sides of it have equally emphasized the importance of Britishness and called for a greater sense of common British culture and identity. This is as true among those still wedded to the multiculturalist agenda as to those like Yasmin Alibhai-Brown and Trevor Phillips who have criticized it. Alibhai-Brown's unease about the break-up of Britain encouraged by the rising narrow separatist mentality among Scots, Welsh and English and Phillips' emphasis on the need to assert 'a common core of Britishness' are shared by Tariq Modood and Bhikhu Parekh who remain committed multiculturalists. Modood, indeed, sees a renewed sense of Britishness as being the main solution to current problems of ethnic and religious identity. Parekh has recently argued that becoming a British citizen should involve not only rights and duties but also a moral and emotional commitment to the country. While remaining a multiculturalist, he now also wants to affirm Britain's 'self-understanding, history, values, constitutional principles and political institutions, as well as its symbols and images, such as the national anthem, national ceremonies and monuments to dead heroes' and believes that the best way to tackle the alienation of young British Muslims is to give them the opportunity 'to acquire a British identity that is strong and fulfilling'.[3]

In displaying a greater enthusiasm for Britishness than many within the long-established white population, these relatively recent immigrants from the Commonwealth stand in a clear tradition. An earlier wave of predominantly Jewish immigrants from central and Eastern Europe also included a number of notable Britophiles, among them George Mikes, who came to England from Hungary in 1931 and developed a love affair with the British sense of humour and satire, which he valiantly sought to analyse, explain and commend. George Fischer, another Hungarian, who became head of talks and features for BBC Radio, together with a trio of Viennese emigrés, Stephen Hearst, head of the Third Programme, Martin Esslin, head of radio drama, and Hans Keller, chief assistant, music, did much to sustain the Reithian agenda at the BBC through the 1970s and 1980s. The influence of this particular wave of immigration is very evident in the patriotism of Michael Howard, the Conservative party leader from 2003 to 2005, whose Romanian father fled to Britain in the 1930s to find sanctuary from the Nazis. Howard, who himself grew up in South Wales before going to Cambridge, and who lists Evelyn Waugh's *Brideshead Revisited* as his favourite novel, expressed his own personal and political credo in a series of statements which appeared in broadsheet newspapers in 2004. They began with the affirmation 'I believe the British people are only happy when they are free' and ended with the ringing declaration: 'I believe that by good fortune, hard work, natural talent and rich diversity, these islands are home to a great people with a noble past and exciting future.' Much of his own deep attachment to Britishness comes from his father's gratitude to the country that took him in as a refugee: 'My father was obviously extremely appreciative of the values of this country and grateful to the country. He always used to say to me, "This is the best country in the world." That is something I grew up with.' When pressed in a newspaper interview as to what these values were, he replied, 'The tolerance, the fairness, the anger at injustice, the great sense of moderation which is, I think, one of the great characteristics of the British people – all these things which we sometimes take for granted.'[4] Howard has written of his parents, 'They never thought their Britishness was inconsistent with their Jewishness. They would have recognized the difference between integration, which they supported, and assimilation, which they did not.' In an article following the London bombings of July 2005, he argued that more should be done to 'inculcate a sense of allegiance to the values that are the hallmark of Britain – decency, tolerance and a sense of fair play', to celebrate the merits of the national community and 'our virtues as a nation', and to promote 'the British dream', as well as to revoke the citizenship and right to remain in the country of those who make it clear they recognize no allegiance to Britain.'[5]

The Jewish community in the United Kingdom, which numbers around 270,000, has, indeed, played a significant role in defining and defending Britishness over the last hundred years or so. Yet for many centuries there was a strong vein of anti-Semitism in Britain, and Jews were seen as aliens and suffered considerable discrimination. It stands, along with the much bigger Roman Catholic population in the country, as an encouraging example of a faith group which has never lost its spiritual heart and soul and has come through a long period of prejudice and discrimination. There is still a disturbing amount of anti-Semitism in Britain – indeed there is some evidence that it is increasing. However, this has not prevented Jews from contributing a distinctive and significant spiritual element to British identity. Successive chief rabbis of Hebrew congregations of the United Kingdom have, like successive cardinal archbishops of Westminster, made a contribution to the nation's spiritual welfare and sense of values considerably greater than might be expected from their once marginal position. This is worth bearing in mind as we move now to considering in more detail the more recent and more visible immigrant communities in the United Kingdom.

As we have already noted (page 24), the proportion of the British population belonging to a non-white ethnic minority is still relatively small (eight per cent according to the 2001 census) but is growing considerably faster than the population as a whole. Nearly three-quarters of the ethnic minority population is accounted for by two ethnic groups who are overwhelmingly made up of post-1960 immigrants from the Commonwealth and their descendants – Asians (2.4 million) and African Caribbeans (1.14 million). Among the Asian population, which is increasingly defining itself in terms of religion rather than race or ethnicity, Muslims predominate (1.58 million, mostly of Pakistani and Bangladeshi origin). It is on the new black/African Caribbean and Muslim British that this chapter will largely focus, because they are particularly visible and have raised most issues in terms of the definition and redefinition of British identity. I am conscious that other significant ethnic and faith groups largely found within the Asian population, notably the 560,000 Hindus, 336,000 Sikhs and 15,000 Buddhists, receive much less treatment than they should. They, too, are contributing valuable spiritual identities to the emerging new Britishness. That they are doing so largely quietly and without fuss means, I fear, that they are unfairly neglected by academics and commentators. I am conscious that I am not doing anything very much to correct this imbalance. In their wonderfully (and characteristically British) understated way, Indians in particular are contributing hugely to the maintenance and reinvigoration of traditional British (and Indian) values of courtesy, reserve and respect for tradition and formality in the United Kingdom.

What can be said about all those who have come as immigrants from the Commonwealth, and indeed from elsewhere, and their descendants, is that they have made a disproportionate contribution to Britishness in terms of sustaining some of its defining institutions and values. The National Health Service, seen by over ninety per cent of the population as exemplifying Britishness (see page 52), is hugely dependent on recent immigrants for its workforce. Almost one-third of the doctors practising in the NHS come from the Indian subcontinent and a high proportion of nurses and auxiliary staff in British hospitals come from Africa, the Caribbean and the Philippines. They exemplify several of the values traditionally associated with Britishness – stoicism, cheerfulness and community spirit in the face of adversity. If Britain is still a nation of small shopkeepers then that is largely because of Asians who have saved comer shops from dying by being prepared to open long hours and resist the seemingly relentless progress of supermarkets and hypermarkets. Asian and African journalists like George Alagiah, Krishnan Guru-Murthy and Rageh Omaar, the BBC's voice from the Iraq War memorably described by the *Mail on Sunday* as possessing 'liquid chocolate eyes, long eyelashes and an impeccable British accent', are prominently involved in the news programmes which are at the heart of British broadcasting and its reputation for authority and impartiality. Trinidad-born Trevor MacDonald, almost a British institution in himself, the nation's favourite newscaster, long the face of Independent Television News and current affairs, commentator for state occasions and selector of classic British poems for the *Daily Telegraph*, cut his broadcasting teeth when he joined the Caribbean regional service of the BBC World Service in 1960.

Blacks and Asians are also disproportionately found among those who represent Britain in international sporting competitions. Since Frank Bruno was dubbed 'brawn of Britain' when he won the European heavyweight championship in 1985, British boxing has been black-dominated, as have many of the track and field events which play so a big a part in the Olympic games. One of the first great black British Olympic athletes, Daley Thompson, son of a Nigerian father and a Scottish mother, caused something of a sensation when he refused to carry the Union Jack in the Commonwealth Games in 1982. More recent Olympic gold medal winners, like Kelly Holmes, who has a Jamaican-born father and English mother and was the only mixed-race pupil at her school in Tonbridge, proudly carry the Union flag and stand for the National Anthem. Bhikhu Parekh has identified the laps of honour undertaken by medal-winning black British athletes draped in the Union Jack at the 2000 and 2004 Olympics as signalling the reclamation of the national flag from racist groups by ethnic minorities: 'They were saying that they belonged to Britain and were proud to do so. They were also saying that Britain belonged to them, and that its flag and national anthem were as much theirs as anyone else's and symbolized their presence as well'.[6] Kelly Holmes, with her early career in the army and commitment to training young athletes, displays something of the classic British sporting ethic which is also epitomized in Nasser Hussain, the Madras-born captain of the England cricket team from 1999 to 2003. Jason Robinson, who in November 2004 became the first black captain of the English rugby team, fits even more into the tradition of the clean-limbed sporting hero of the *Boy's Own Paper* and muscular Christianity. Born to a Jamaican father and Scottish mother, he grew up in considerable poverty in the Chapeltown area of Leeds, later becoming a born-again Christian, largely through the influence of a fellow rugby player for Wigan originally from Western Samoa, Va'aiga Tuigamala.

The qualities of reserve, reticence, modesty, self-effacement, understatement and gentility traditionally seen as distinguishing the British are now more likely to be displayed by recent immigrants than by longer-established white residents. As Robert Winder comments in *Bloody Foreigners: The Story of Immigration to Britain*:

When we dwell on the diligent and unpretentious good manners that once typified England – the much-satirised diffidence in the face of queues, courtesy in the face of mishaps, patience in the face of adversity – we need to realize that such traits may be more common now in migrant Britain, with its strong family loyalties and principles of obligation than in the brash, every-man-for-himself mainstream.

Reviewing Winder's book, Anthony Sampson, the famous 'anatomer' of Britain, observed that 'as an ageing Briton, travelling in a crowded bus or tube, I am more likely to be offered a seat by a young black or Asian than by anyone else'.[7] Female modesty and reserve is much more clearly exemplified by the hijab-wearing Muslim girl than the micro-skirted teenager vomiting into the gutter after a Saturday night binge-drinking session. In this and in other respects, indeed, British Muslims generally exemplify traditional British values more conspicuously than many in the white majority. On the whole, the relatively recent immigrant communities also live more communal and associational lives than the longer-established white population. They have a greater concern for family ties and are more likely to care for their elderly relatives and to be good neighbours.

They also lead lives which are much more likely to be influenced by religion and faith. This is especially true of the two groups of recent immigrants who are the main subject of this chapter. The black/African Caribbean population in the United Kingdom almost exactly mirrors the population as a whole in terms of its adherence to Christianity, with seventy-one per cent of blacks saying that they are Christians as against seventy-two per cent of the overall UK population and seventy-five per cent of whites. Yet blacks are far more likely to be active churchgoers than whites. While the overall figure for regular church attendance in the United Kingdom is less than ten per cent, among African Caribbeans it is over thirty per cent. Blacks make up just two per cent of the Christian population of the United Kingdom, and whites ninety-three per cent, yet in London there are now more black than white churchgoers on a Sunday morning. African Caribbean churches have doubled in size over the last fifteen years and account for most of the largest centres of worship in Britain, among them the Kingsway International Christian Centre, which claims to be the country's biggest single church, with over 10,000 regular worshippers. British Muslims are even more devout. There may be only a little over

1.5 million of them as against over 41 million Christians but we may not be far off the time when the number of regular worshippers in each faith group will be roughly the same. More than sixty-two per cent of British Muslims worship once a week or more, as against less than ten per cent of British Christians. In 2005, around 750,000 Muslims regularly attended mosques in England and around 950,000 Anglicans regularly attended Church of England churches. Christian Research, the organization that collates religious statistics, has calculated that, if present trends continue, the number of practising Muslims will outstrip the number of practising Anglicans by 2013 and that, by 2039, there will be more Muslims in mosques across the United Kingdom every Friday than Christians in churches of all denominations on Sunday mornings.[8]

The strong sense of spiritual identity felt by ethnic minority communities is confirmed by much recent research. The Fourth National Survey of Ethnic Minorities in Britain, published in 1997, revealed that while a third of Britons as a whole said they had no religion, virtually all South Asians claimed to have one and ninety per cent said that it was of personal importance to them, as against just thirteen per cent of whites. The survey also found that while a quarter of whites claimed to attend a place of worship once a month or more, the comparable figure for Hindus was more than fifty per cent and for Sikhs over seventy per cent, while among Muslims two-thirds attended at least twice a week. These high levels of religious commitment and identity extend to young people. Among those aged sixteen to thirty-four interviewed for the 1997 survey, two-thirds of Pakistanis and Bangladeshis, more than a third of Indians and African Asians and nearly a fifth of African Caribbeans said that religion was very important to how they led their lives compared to just five per cent of whites. An earlier survey into the lifestyles of young people aged between fourteen and twenty-five in England and Wales carried out for the Home Office in 1993 similarly found that attending religious services and meetings was very much more common among those from ethnic minorities. Young Indians, for example, were three times more likely to say they had gone to a religious service or meeting than white people of the same age group. It was a request from the Muslim community in Britain who wished to be classified by religion rather than ethnicity which led to a question about religious affiliation being inserted into the 2001 census. It confirmed that minority ethnic groups, with the notable exception of the Chinese, are markedly more religious than whites. The proportion of those saying that they had no religion was fifteen per cent among whites, fifty per cent among Chinese, 7.6 per cent among African Caribbeans, 1.4 per cent among Asians and less than 0.5 per cent among the overwhelmingly Muslim Pakistanis and Bangladeshis. More recently, the Home Office Citizenship Survey published in 2004 showed that faith is a key factor in how people from ethnic minority communities identify themselves, with Muslims, Hindus and Sikhs ranking their faith second only after family and Jewish people identifying themselves by their faith first.

Discussing the results of the 1997 survey, Tariq Modood comments:

Religion is particularly worth exploring in relation to British socialization. For, firstly it marks a significant dimension of cultural difference between the migrants and British society. Not only did most of the migrants have a different religion to that of the natives, but all the indications are that they, including the Christians among them, were more religious than the society they were joining. Not only was this likely to have been the case at the time of migration and in the early years of settlement but it is true today. Secondly, one of the major social changes that has taken place in Britain during the lifetime of most Asian settlers has been the decline of indigenous religious observance and faith, and so religion among ethnic minorities is an important test case of the effect of British socialization. Thirdly, generally speaking, most of the cultural practices of migrants and their descendants usually decline with the length of their stay in the society to which they have migrated. This is usually so with language, dress, arranged marriages and so on. It is also the case with religion, though perhaps descendants of migrants are more likely to keep alive a distinctive religion rather than a distinctive language.[9]

In fact, what the Fourth National Survey of Ethnic Minorities found was that there is a weakening of the hold of religion the longer that immigrants have been in Britain and exposed to its secular culture, although this is counteracted by the tendency for religious belief to be stronger the older a person is.

As well as having a markedly more religious identity and lifestyle, those from ethnic minorities, as we have already noted, also feel more 'British' than the majority white population. In 2002, the Government's General Household Survey included for the first time questions on perceived national identity. These revealed that while most white people living in Britain do not regard themselves primarily as British and prefer to state their identity as English, Scottish, Welsh or Irish, a clear majority of those from ethnic minorities living in Britain confidently assert their Britishness and do not feel that they belong to any other national grouping. In the population as a whole, only thirty-one per cent said they were British and gave no other answer, as against fifty per cent who described themselves as solely English, Scottish, Welsh and Irish and thirteen per cent who opted for a hybrid identity. Among those from ethnic minorities, however, fifty-seven per cent described their national identity as solely British. The Fourth National Survey of Ethnic Minorities found that more than two-thirds of Asians and nearly three-quarters of African Caribbeans felt themselves to be British, with the proportions rising among younger people and those who had been born in Britain. In a Guardian poll of ethnic minorities in March 2005, seventy per cent identified themselves as either mainly or fully British and only thirteen per cent as not at all British. Among Asians, the proportions were seventy-eight and ten per cent, and among African Caribbeans, sixty and twenty-two per cent respectively.[10]

Is there a link between these high levels of religious and British identity? It is tempting to suggest that there is, and that the factors which promote strong faith among the new Britons also contribute to their feelings of Britishness. I suspect that the imperial connection, so often overlooked or treated largely in terms of embarrassment and guilt, has played a significant role in the identification with Britishness on the part of immigrants from the Commonwealth. It is true that, among younger second- or third-generation migrants, there is evidence of growing identification, as in the white population, with Englishness and Scottishness, although not necessarily at the expense of identification with Britain as a whole but rather in the form of hyphenated identity. The hugely important development of hyphenated identity, about which we shall have more to say shortly, often brackets religious and British allegiance, as in such increasingly popular self-definitions as Muslim British or Sikh British. It provides one of the most hopeful and fruitful ways of constructing a new Britishness which combines respect for diversity and plurality with a common loyalty and coherence.

Let us turn now to look more closely and specifically at the two groups of new Britons who have been singled out for special attention in this chapter, the black African Caribbeans and the Muslims. There are clear differences as well as similarities between them. African Caribbeans are more likely to identify themselves by ethnicity or colour rather than by religion than are Asians, and especially Muslims. They also appear in many ways more integrated into mainstream British culture, or at least are taken to be by sociologists and cultural commentators. Henry Louis Gates noted in 1997 that 'a culture that is distinctively black and British can be said to be in full flower.'11 Stuart Hall has argued that 'black British culture could be described as confident beyond measure in its own identity' and, indeed, that young black people have made themselves '*the* defining force in street-oriented British youth culture'.[12] Paul Gilroy argues in his latest book, *After Empire*, that the prevailing melancholia of post-1945 white Britain is being challenged by a new black-led convivial urban culture.

It may well be that the urban youth culture of reggae, rap and hip-hop has entered the cultural mainstream and provides a distinctive black-led and black-inspired British identity. But there are other aspects of black identity in contemporary Britain which are very much at odds with the prevailing culture of hedonistic secular materialism. Gilroy has, indeed, been criticized for 'essentializing' black people, defining them as having certain characteristics regardless of their actual diversity and writing as if they only consisted of hip-hoppers and intellectuals. Religion is still a very important focus for many African Caribbeans in the United Kingdom, as can be gauged from the statistics of church attendance noted earlier. This is the theme of Nicole Toulis' fascinating study *Believing Identity*, which focuses on the way in which first-generation Jamaican migrants to Britain constructed their identity through participation in Pentecostalism, in response partly to the racism that they encountered and also to what they perceived to be the extreme secularism of British society. Her key finding is that 'religious participation remains a central feature in the lives of many African-Caribbean people in Britain.'[13] In the New Testament Church of God in Birmingham, the specific focus for her study, she finds an all-black community based, not on kinship, race, nationality or ethnicity, but rather on shared religious dispositions where the only significant distinction recognized was that between Christians and non-Christians. Members describe themselves as 'children of God' and 'people of God' and this heritage and identity is reaffirmed by the use of such fictional kinship terms as 'Brother' and 'Sister'. In Toulis' words, 'Secular citizenship in the nation of Britain is replaced by spiritual citizenship in the imagined community of God's nation.' This spiritual concept of citizenship:

neatly side-steps debates about how, and on what terms, African–Caribbeans may be included in the British nation, for this inclusive spiritual nation is not premised upon racial differentiation … It is their identity as Christians which serves as the basis for their interaction with others in British society.

To some extent, this emphasis is profoundly counter-cultural, in this case challenging the dominance of secularism rather than of whiteness, but Toulis points out that it also plugs into a distinctive and traditional British value system, born out of Protestant Christianity:

> *The continuing appeal of African–Caribbean Pentecostalism for both young and old, economically advantaged and disadvantaged African–Caribbean people in Britain is not only that it offers a framework for the explanation and transcendence of questions of suffering, status and identity but that it also privileges values like thrift, discipline and individual conscience which are compatible with the wider value system and with life in Britain.*[14]

There are, indeed, further interactions between African-Caribbean Pentecostalism and Britishness. I was fascinated that when Wilton Powell, the national organiser of the New Testament Church of Prophecy, came to preach in the chapel of St Andrews University in 2004, he began with a moving disquisition about what the ancient chapel said to him of the British (not the Scottish) spiritual and Christian tradition. Much of the rest of his sermon was devoted to a call to restore the nation to these spiritual roots. Black Christians do, indeed, have much to offer in the spiritual revival of Britain and it is highly appropriate that they are increasingly occupying key positions well beyond the confines of African Caribbean and Pentecostal churches. The move of the Jamaican-born Joel Edwards from being General Secretary of the African Caribbean Evangelical Alliance to General Director of the Evangelical Alliance UK and of the Ugandan-born John Sentamu from being Bishop of Stepney to Bishop of Birmingham and then in 2005 to being Archbishop of York testify to a recognition of the extent to which the future of Christianity in Britain depends on the dynamism and commitment of the black population.

Black Christianity may also have a role to play in the reconfiguration of British patriotism and pageantry. What it can offer was demonstrated very vividly in the

5,000-strong Gospel choir led by Patti Boulaye, the Nigerian-born singer, which danced and sang its way down the Mall as part of the parade for the Queen's Golden Jubilee celebrations on 4 June 2002. The choir, predominantly black and drawn from Pentecostal, Apostolic, Methodist and Catholic churches with members of the Metropolitan Police Gospel Choir in the front row, sang Patti Boulaye's own specially written jubilee anthem, 'Celebrate Good News', with its message 'It's been so long since we felt so strong', along with Gospel standards like 'Michael Row the Boat Ashore', 'He's Got the Whole World in His Hands', 'Oh Happy Day' and 'This Little Light of Mine'. These upbeat Gospel numbers and the West Indian steel bands that also paraded down the Mall appeared to catch the mood of the day and the imagination of the crowds more than the traditional national airs played by military bands. One of my most abiding memories of the Jubilee celebrations is of seeing Pearlie kings and queens dancing in front of Buckingham Palace to the black Gospel songs being belted out by the Kingdom Choir with members of the Treorchy Male Voice Choir enthusiastically joining in. Here was a Britishness which enthused and embraced cockneys, Welshmen and many others, a black-led Britishness not quite of Paul Gilroy's urban, streetwise, convivial culture but rather of carnival, revivalist Christianity and fervent monarchism – colourful, happy and exuberant. The other striking musical contribution to the Jubilee celebrations came later in the day when the crowds in the Mall waiting for the Queen struck up 'You'll Never Walk Alone', the deeply spiritual anthem from Rodgers and Hammerstein's *Carousel* which has crossed over from the stage to the sanctuary and found its way into many hymn books on both sides of the Atlantic. Thanks partly to its particular associations with Liverpool Football Club and the Hillsborough disaster, it has taken on something of the status of a national hymn for many Britons and is hugely popular at weddings and funerals. But it was the Gospel songs that really expressed the exuberant patriotism of the crowds celebrating the long reign of their beloved monarch.

The whole emphasis of the Jubilee celebrations was, indeed, on carnival and heavily tilted towards ethnic minorities. The first parade down the Mall was the Notting Hill Carnival and the last was a Commonwealth Parade with four rainbow arches containing 1,900 wishes sent in by children from every country in the Commonwealth. Both these parades were almost entirely made up of recent Commonwealth immigrants to the United Kingdom. Indeed, the Commonwealth, so often underplayed in constructions of Britishness, played a very significant role in this celebration of a monarch who has done so much to promote it and its values. So also more generally did black and Asian Britons. Another potent image caught by the television cameras during the closing moments of the day when the Queen stood alone on the balcony of Buckingham Palace was that of an Asian woman vigorously waving the Union Jack and pouring her heart and soul into a rendering of 'Land of Hope and Glory'. As she sang 'Wider still and wider shall the bounds be set', it seemed to presage not so much nostalgic longing for an imperialistic past as the dawning of a new carnival and rainbow Britishness, diverse and pluralistic yet focused on traditional symbols of unity like the Union flag and the monarchy.

This aspect of the Jubilee celebrations has been little picked up and commented on, although it was referred to by Matthew d' Ancona in his contribution to the 2002 Foreign Policy Booklet, *Reclaiming Britishness*:

> *The parade on the Mall was a sparkling celebration of British pluralism,*
> *a pageant which paid tribute to the profound role that immigration from*
> *the Commonwealth has played in the evolution of patriotism in this*
> *country over the past half century. The gospel choir, Bollywood performers*
> *and Notting Hill Carnival dancers were all vibrant proof that those who*
> *would pit traditional Britishness against its modern variant miss the point*
> *completely. The Jubilee revealed a sense of nationhood which is not embattled*
> *and defensive but porous, adaptable and confident.*[15]

If black Britons are helping white Britons to celebrate the monarchy with more enthusiasm, they are also encouraging them to affirm other traditional aspects of their heritage. Trevor Phillips, chair of the Commission for Racial Equality, feels that one of the unfortunate consequences of the multicultural agenda has been a neglect of the English language and English literature, of Shakespeare and Dickens, as well as of traditional British values like parliamentary democracy. These, he argues, should be celebrated and taught as much to white children as to black and Asian immigrants.

> *We need to assert there is a core of Britishness. For instance, I hate the way*
> *this country has lost Shakespeare. That sort of thing is bad for immigrants*
> *too. They want to come here not just because of jobs but because they like*

this country – its tolerance, its eccentricity, its Parliamentary democracy, its energy in the big cities. They don't want that to change. We have to remember that migrants have become British in an incredibly short space of time. Lombardy bankers, Jewish tailors, Afro-Caribbean bus drivers and German kings are as British as you and me.[16]

Phillips is keen to emphasize both what immigrants like himself have gained from Britishness and also how they are changing it: 'I get emotional about this country because my community came from a long way away and, while it was not always perfect, by and large we have been embraced, we have become British and changed what being British means.' One senses that he is almost willing the majority white population into having more pride in themselves and their tolerance: 'People talk about ordinary British folk as if they are terribly afraid or bigots. We have forgotten how good we are at handling diversity, we have been good at it for a thousand years.' This is why he wants to turn from multiculturalism, which for him suggests separateness, towards a much greater honouring of British values and cultures. Indeed, he sees the positive assertion of Britishness as the best way to address the whole vexed question of Muslim identity and alienation, the threat of terrorism and the rise of militant Islam. 'To be a British Muslim,' he insists, 'is not the same as being a Muslim in Riyadh or Islamabad … The best way to help young Muslims is to tell them they are British again and again and again until they know they are accepted.'[17]

It is time to turn to that faith group about whom Phillips and others are so concerned in respect of their loyalty or otherwise to Britain and Britishness. Even more than African Caribbeans, Muslims in Britain define their identity overwhelmingly in religious and spiritual terms. This, indeed, is a characteristic of British Asians as a whole who are increasingly rejecting the label 'Asian' in favour of a religious identity. The term 'Asian' is, in fact, British in origin, having been corned in 1948 by British administrators working in colonial Kenya to describe citizens of the newly independent India and Pakistan. What began as an administrative classification was later taken up by Pakistanis, Indians and Bangladeshis living in Britain. But for some time now, and especially post 9/11, they have moved away from using the ethnic/ racial label and taken to calling themselves British Muslims, British Hindus and British Sikhs rather than British Asians. The question as to whether this new emphasis on religious identity is more exclusive and overrides national identity was addressed in a BBC Radio 4 programme, *Don't Call Me Asian*, in January 2005. The presenter, Sarfraz Manzoor, concluded that, in fact, the new assertion of religious identity might actually open the way to a greater sense of Britishness:

> *Britain's Hindus, Sikhs and Muslims were long defined by others in terms of what they were not: not white, not black, not British. Now, for the first time, identities are being forged from inside the communities and with confidence. These identities emphasize religion but do not necessarily imply disloyalty to being British.*[18]

Among Muslims, religious identity is especially marked. A survey carried out by the Policy Studies Institute in 1997 found that ninety-six per cent of people of Pakistani origin in Britain and ninety-five per cent of those of Bengali origin said they were Muslims, compared to sixty-eight per cent of the white population who said they were Christians. Among those of Pakistani origin, eighty-three per cent mentioned religion as an important self-attribute. A *Guardian*/ICM Poll of British Muslims in 2004 found a high level of personal devotion, with just over half of respondents saying that they prayed five times every day and eighty per cent that they prayed at least once a day. In many ways, indeed, one of the key defining characteristics of British Muslims is not so much the particular character or nature of their faith as that they have a strong faith at all. This was the overall impression left on the *Guardian* journalist, Madeline Bunting, after talking to a hundred young British Muslims:

> *This generation is being called on to explain their faith to a secular society which has long since lost all interest in God, angels, prophets and holy books. What does it mean to 'put God first in everything' as one participant described British Muslims' distinctive contribution to British society? ... You could put a devout Muslim and a devout Christian together and, while they might not agree, they could understand much of what the other had to say, but to the broad swath of the secular British, the gulf of incomprehension is gaping – and the onus is upon the faithful to explain themselves.*[19]

For Bunting, the young Muslims she encountered 'open a new chapter in Britain's complex history of race and multiculturalism: how we negotiate a faith-based political identity. On this, there are no inspirations we can borrow from.'

The fact is, however, that there are precedents in British history in terms of negotiating faith-based identities. Two have already been alluded to in terms of the integration of Jews and Roman Catholics, both initially greeted with prejudice and discrimination but ultimately brought into full political and civil society while being allowed to maintain their distinctive faith and religious beliefs and practices. The example of Roman Catholics in particular, long seen as a potentially treacherous and un-British fifth column with loyalties to foreign rulers but ultimately fully integrated into the British state, is often cited in contemporary discussions of the question of Muslim integration into Britain. One of the key demands made by British Muslims of the British Government, the provision of publicly funded faith schools, was conceded to Roman Catholics and has arguably played a major part in giving them a sense of being accepted as British. Other Muslim demands, like the passing of laws against blasphemy and incitement to religious hatred, chime with the agenda of evangelical Christians, on which most Muslims also have similar views on a broad range of moral issues, especially in respect of adultery and homosexuality. As yet, as far as I am aware, no coalitions have been formed between more conservative Muslims and evangelical Christians on these or other issues, and it is perhaps unrealistic to expect them given the strong perceived theological differences between the two groups. Yet they do point to one way in which Muslims are not, in fact, isolated in many of their values and in which they might form common cause with others in contemporary Britain.

In the eyes of many older and more traditional Muslims, there is, in fact, a remarkable correspondence between the values of Islam and those often associated with Britishness. For Khalil Martin, treasurer of the Shah Jehan Mosque in Woking, the first purpose-built mosque in northern Europe when it was opened in 1889, 'The British character is naturally in harmony with Islamic values if you define it as modest, polite and broad-minded.'[20] Whether the British are any longer modest and polite is, as we have already noted, a matter of some debate and it may be that an important part of the Muslim contribution to Britishness will be to restore those lost values. On the other side, it is difficult to find a broad-mindedness in the narrow judgementalism and fundamentalism found in some Muslim teaching and interpretation of the Qur'an and maybe there can be a reciprocal British contribution to Islam in making it more open and tolerant.

If this sounds hopelessly Utopian in the wake of terrorist attacks and in the climate of Islamophobia that hangs over so much of the western world just now, it is worth reminding ourselves that the surveys conducted in the aftermath of the 2001 riots in northern English cities, the 9/11 attacks in the USA and the London bombings in 2005 all suggest that most Muslims in Britain see themselves as British – the proportion is fairly consistently between seventy-five and eighty per cent – and that they see no conflict between both aspects of their identity. Indeed, for many, there is a triple identity – Navid Ahkter, a television producer interviewed for *The Guardian*'s in-depth look at 100 young Muslims, announced, 'I am absolutely British. I am absolutely Pakistani. I am absolutely Muslim. I am all of these.' He then went on to say encouragingly, ' "British Muslim" is a title with an empty page, we have a good opportunity to start defining it.' There was, indeed, a general optimism about creating a British Muslim identity in this admittedly articulate and educated group, summed up by Sarah Joseph, editor of the Muslim lifestyle magazine *Emel*: 'Islam is about ethos and morals. It's not about a particular place. So you can have an Islam that draws on British culture and heritage. It's about creating an Islam that is authentically British.'[21]

The complexity of British Muslims' attitudes towards their British identity, and the extent to which they feel that they are not accepted and respected is clearly revealed in the first survey of its kind examining the relationship between British citizenship and adherence to Islam which was conducted among 1,125 practising Muslims across England, Scotland and Wales by the Islamic Human Rights Commission in connection with Islam Awareness Week in November 2004. While eighty per cent of respondents saw no contradiction between being a good British citizen and being a practising Muslim, only eight per cent agreed with the proposition that British society respects British Muslims and just thirty per cent said that they were satisfied with life in Britain. Far from being an obstacle to Muslim identification with Britishness, the survey suggests that faith is a major element in promoting it. In the words of Arzu Merali, one of the survey's authors: 'Based on the response of Muslims themselves, it finds that religion is one of the main factors that has influenced a high level of loyalty amongst the United Kingdom's Muslims despite clear feelings of discrimination and hatred being levelled against them.' Chief among the reasons cited for the high level of loyalty to the United Kingdom was the relatively greater religious freedom found there than in many countries, while prominent among the factors which led to negative responses was 'the British aversion to religion'.[22]

It is clear that the secularism of modern Britain is a major reason for Muslim feelings of alienation. Others include the low economic status, educational underachievement and victimization that have made Muslims an underclass in the urban areas in which they are particularly concentrated. The inquiries that followed the riots in Bradford, Burnley and Oldham in the summer of 2001 also found a fundamental lack of civic identity and a 'them-and-us' attitude rather than a sense of belonging among the overwhelmingly Muslim Asian communities that make up over twenty per cent of the population in these towns. A similar sense of alienation characterized many in the white population. Fuad Nahdi, editor-in-chief of *Q-News*, the British Muslim magazine, has argued that, while poverty, exclusion and discrimination lie at the root of the alienation and marginalization felt by many Muslims, they do not explain the radicalism and extremism found within the Muslim community. This, he believes, 'is not the result of only political, social and economic alienation and marginalization. It is also about how a great faith has been hijacked and debased by forces obsessed with power and its abuse'. He fears that certain Muslim communities and mosques are breeding grounds for terrorism and that this can only be countered by British support for traditional Islam and a revival of the faith:

Our young people need a vision to inspire and uplift them, charismatic leadership and a society that not only tolerates and respects them but also values and appreciates their chosen identity. Britain must wake up to the reality that the Islam it invests in today is going to produce the kind of Muslim it will get tomorrow. The authorities need to go on being serious in their dialogues with leaders of the community from as varied a background as possible. But the priority should be to seek those who represent and are well-versed about traditional Islamic scholarship and understanding – not accountants; retired GPs, failed activists and dangerous sloganeers.

At the moment there is no hope that British Muslims – ostracized from their faith, consumed by anger, marginalized and alienated from society – will make the ideal partners we need to fight terrorism. So we need Islam – that great faith of reason, peace, truth and love – to make a comeback to our shores. Without it the future is scary, very scary. [23]

Other British Muslim commentators agree that, properly taught and understood, Islam has the capacity to make its adherents feel more rather than less British. Dilwar Hussain, a research fellow at the Islamic Foundation in Leicester, believes that 'Islam lends itself easily to a reading which inspires Muslims living in Britain to set down roots and to live their values in a British context.' He also points out that several Muslim scholars argue that the objectives of Islamic law, or shariah (protection of life, faith, intellect, family/lineage and property), are actually better achieved in a country like Britain than under the despotic rule found in several countries in the Muslim world. [24]

There is a long British tradition of respect and admiration for Arabic and Islamic culture and character which stretches back to Charles Doughty, Richard Burton and T. E. Lawrence and perhaps finds its leading representative today in Prince Charles, who has shown considerable interest in Islamic art and praised its spiritual emphasis. There has also been a small but steady stream of British converts to Islam, particularly women attracted by its clear moral values, strong emphasis on community values and sense of modesty and reserve. When so many in the West seem to feel that it is at war with Islam, a sentiment encouraged by Christian conservatives in the United States and secular liberals in Europe, it would be good to have this particular British tradition reasserted and revived. This might encourage more Muslims in Britain to come out of their ghettos and embrace Britishness more enthusiastically. As yet, there is a distinct ambivalence in Muslim attitudes, as exemplified by two of the contributors to the book, *Islam, Race and Being British*, published in the aftermath of the 2005 London bombings. Berating non-Muslims for offering only tolerance and not acceptance or space to be part of a shared vision of the future, Ajmaal Masoor, who leads Friday prayers in several London mosques, writes: 'I feel alienated from your history, from your values, and from your experience. There is no shared paradigm, no shared heritage and certainly there is no room for developing a new narrative.' Yet just thirty pages on, Dilwar Hussain berates his fellow-Muslims for largely shunning Britishness:

> *How many Muslims have a deep understanding of the history, literature and traditions of Britain? How many actively interact and engage with*

their non-Muslim co-citizens? How many lead lives that involve almost no interaction with non-Muslims in their day-to-day affairs? Unless Muslims are able to feel the pulse of society, they will not talk to people, but talk at them, and their words will have very little effect. Muslims need to be in tune with their Britishness. Islam can make us British but for this to happen we have to live Islam and not just talk about it.[25]

As yet, it is too early to see which of these perspectives will predominate. There is clearly room for more respect and less suspicion on both sides of the Muslim/non-Muslim divide in Britain as elsewhere. Much will depend on the way that Islam is interpreted and taught in British mosques and how far it is allowed to have an indigenous British feel. Striking an optimistic note, Tariq Ramadan, the distinguished Muslim academic now based in Oxford and the grandson of Hassan al-Banna, founder of the Muslim Brotherhood in Egypt, argues that Islam has, in fact, contributed to the building up of a European as well as a British consciousness since the Middle Ages, in a similar way to Judaism and Christianity. Insisting that Islam is not a culture but a body of principles and universal values, he says that it is important that these principles should not be mixed up with a Pakistani, Turkish or Arabic way of living them:

Islam allows Muslims to adopt aspects of the culture they find themselves in, as long as it does not oppose any clear prohibition specified by their religion. While practicing their religion, they can preserve features of their own culture of origin – in the form of richness, not dogma – at the same time as integrating themselves into British culture, which in turn becomes a new dimension of their own identity. No one asks that they remain Pakistani or Arabic Muslims, but simply Muslims; with time, they become Muslims of British culture. This is a process that is not only normal but desirable.

Western Muslims need to find again this intellectual, social and political creativity that has been missing in the Islamic world. British legislation recognizes and protects the fundamental rights of all citizens and residents. This common legal framework allows equality within diversity. The presence of Muslims has forced British culture to experience a greater diversity of cultures. A British identity has evolved that is open, plural and

constantly in motion, thanks to the cross-fertilisation between reclaimed
cultures of origin and the British culture that now includes its new citizens.[26]

Perhaps one of the most positive and concrete signs of hope is the increasing emergence of a sense of overlapping or hyphenated identity among many Muslims living in Britain. When Ismailis living in London were asked in 2003 how they would define their national identity, fifty-nine per cent gave a hybrid answer in which Britishness was combined with another geographical or ethnic identity: forty-one per cent said they were British-Asian, ten per cent Indo-British, four per cent British East African Asian and four per cent British Indian. Thirty-one per cent answered in terms that suggested that they felt no British identity, describing themselves simply as Asian, East African Asian or Indian, and ten per cent described themselves simply as British. Religion was, however, the single most important aspect of their identity and that which gave them a sense of belonging and daily routine, although even here there was an interesting and encouraging example of overlap – while eighty-five per cent of those interviewed celebrated Muslim festivals, forty-two per cent also celebrated Christmas.[27] It may be that we should now be talking about post-British identities among ethnic minority communities, as Amir Saeed, Neil Blain and Douglas Forbes do in an article in *Ethnic and Racial Studies*. They argue that 'if it is increasingly difficult to use the term "British" of indigenous white English and Scottish majorities, then we must likewise re-define the field of inquiry into what might now be argued as the post-British identity of Afro-Caribbeans, Pakistani Muslims and other minorities'. Their interviews with Pakistani teenagers in Glasgow in the late 1990s revealed a bewildering variety of ethnic identities, although a virtual uniformity in terms of religious identity, with ninety-seven per cent describing themselves as Muslims, easily the clearest and strongest expression of identity. In answer to a general question about national identity, forty-six per cent described themselves as Pakistanis, twenty-two per cent as Scottish, nine per cent as British and eight per cent as Asian. When asked more specifically what ethnic group they considered themselves as belonging to, however, more than three-quarters opted for a hyphenated or hybrid identity, with thirty-three per cent replying Scottish-Pakistani, nineteen per cent Scottish Muslim, eight per cent Pakistani-Muslim, five per cent Asian-Muslim, five per cent British Pakistani, five per cent Scottish Asian and three per cent British Muslim.[28]

The increasing trend for people to describe their identity in hyphenated, hybrid or overlapping terms – as a both-and rather than as an either-or – is, of course, not confined to Muslims, nor indeed to ethnic minorities and immigrants. It is perhaps an aspect of postmodernism and of the tendency for all of us to affirm multiple loyalties and affiliations. What is particularly significant from the point of view of this book and its thesis is the growing tendency of Asians living in Britain in particular to describe themselves in terms of an overlapping identity which embraces their religion, their ethnic origin and their Britishness.

There are few people more enthusiastic about the growth of this overlapping or hyphenated identity, and its importance in emphasizing Britishness in a way that promotes both social pluralism and coherence, than Tariq Modood, Professor of Sociology, Politics and Public Policy at the University of Bristol. His own life story has strongly informed both these passions. He recalls that, when he came over to Britain as a young boy from Pakistan in 1961, his father, a devout Muslim, was 'full of admiration for the British' having 'long been of the view that the idea of an English gentleman comes very close to what the Qur'an requires from the individual'.[29] His father was particularly impressed by British institutions, such as schools, universities, the BBC and the British Museum, but the emergent 1960s morality of 'Swinging London' bewildered and perplexed him, especially the way it seemed to be welcomed and led by the élite British institutions he so much admired:

> *For him Britain was materially brilliant but becoming a morally decadent culture. People like us had to assimilate the former and reject the latter. In his later years he came to think that we had to follow this strategy not just to stay on the 'straight and narrow' ourselves but to be an example to the white British in the hope that they might one day learn from us. Among the features of Britain that he continued to respect the most were the sense of honesty and service that informed its institutions and professions and which he thought were more Islamic than their counterparts in the contemporary Muslim world.[30]*

In his book *Not Easy Being British*, Modood relates how he recently went back to his old school in the London Borough of Brent, where now only ten per cent of the pupils are white, and confronted an 'A' Level English Literature class with Chaucer's ideal of 'The Parfit Gentil Knyght' from the prologue of *The Canterbury Tales*. The class found the medieval idolization of chivalry and militaristic Christianity archaic, sexist, classist and Christian-centric. Yet, when he went on to ask them to list their own values, these included telling the truth, respect for elders, courtesy, consideration for others, self-control and being true to oneself. The pupils went on to blame television for too much sex, violence and swearing. 'For a moment,' he writes, 'I closed my eyes and could hear my father talking.'[31]

Modood attributes his enthusiasm for hyphenated identity and for Britishness more generally both to the influence of his father and to his own involvement in race and community relations. He was appalled in the late 1980s by the rise of a political blackness movement, expressed most prominently in the demand for a separate black section in the Labour Party, which he felt would reduce the plurality of ethnic and racial identities to just two, black and white. He is also wary of the tendency towards English, Scottish and Welsh nationalism and particularism. Writing about moves to make more of St George's Day, he says:

> *It is essential that English celebrations should be inclusive and embrace multi-ethnicity and strengthen our sense of belonging to a common country, not create obstacles. Moreover, it should include civic values and be supportive of British political institutions – 'English' should not be an exclusionary or a separatist identity. Britain is a nest of identities and none should be too big for the nest, or worse, threaten the nest itself.*[32]

A committed and unrepentant believer in multiculturalism, he believes that it is, in fact, a very British concept, pointing out that

> *multiculturalists have emphasized internal differentiation (relatively easy in the case of Britain which encompasses up to four national or semi-national components, England, Scotland, Wales and Northern Ireland) and fluidity, with definitions of national belonging being historical constructs and changing over time.*[33]

He is adamant that 'multiculturalism and Britishness are not exclusive concepts.'

For Modood, hyphenated identity is at the heart of the new Britishness that is now emerging and which combines a plurality and diversity in matters of religious belief, culture and behaviour with an all-inclusive, overarching sense of nationality and belonging. It is in the creation of this 'complex Britishness' rather than in the breaking up of Britain that he sees hope as lying for the future: 'This is particularly worth emphasizing because in Britain there are people who want not just to be black or Indian in Britain but positively want to be black British or British Indians.'[34] Unlike many multiculturalists, Modood sees religion as a more important component than race in ethnic minority identity and points to the way that it is bracketed with a strong sense of Britishness in hyphenated expressions of identity such as Muslim British or British Hindu. While he concedes that many younger members of ethnic minority communities are-increasingly feeling the pull of what he calls 'sub-state nationalities' and describing themselves, like whites, as English, Scottish, Welsh or Irish rather than British, he wants to hold on very strongly to the Britishness which, as he rightly says, is still felt more strongly by the ethnic minorities than the white majority. He sees it as a 'nested identity' which can hold all other identities together much better than a sense of being English or Scottish. He also feels that there is a crucial difference between the ethnic hybridity he is championing in his vision of a new complex and mixed Britishness and the sub-state nationalism of Scottishness or Catalan:

> *The contrast between ethnicity and nationality is politically important. Right-wing commentators used to worry about the threat that Commonwealth migrants and their descendants posed to Britishness. It is clear now that many in these ethnic minority groups think of Britain, appropriately reimagined and restructured, as a unifying identity. It is in fact those groups that have a national-territorial base in the British Isles and a historical grievance with the British state who today most shrink from the label 'British'. While Pakistanis in Bradford have been coming to an understanding of themselves as British, it is the Scots and the Irish – both within and outside their territorial nations – that are in denial about being British, who see one national identity as incompatible with another.*[35]

Modood believes that Britain is better placed than many other countries in Europe to embrace a multicultural and pluralist society:

There is a kind of openness in Britain not found in continental Northern Europe ... A characteristic of British culture, despite its self-image of insularity, is the readiness to borrow and mix ideas and influences, as supremely exemplified in the English language. It is perhaps more accurate to say that Britons and mainland Europeans are open to outsiders in different ways. Europeans have sought to put the excesses of nationalism behind them by seeking rapprochement with their neighbours but saw no inconsistency in requiring cultural assimilation from migrants of non-European origin. The British, especially the English, are less open to their European neighbours, but less hostile than most Europeans to multiculturalism and to international exchange.[36]

This engaging faith in the British value of openness is combined with an optimistic assessment of the prospects of a new form of Britishness emerging which will include rather than exclude even some of the more alienated members of minority communities. Modood argues that ethnicity and colour are increasingly experienced less as an oppositional identity to Britishness than as a way of being British. He also feels that the existence of established churches and religious rituals like the coronation of the monarch provide a public space for and acknowledgement of religion and faith which chimes in with the increasing emphasis on religion as a key determinant of identity. Like Dilwar Hussain, Trevor Phillips and Bhikhu Parekh, he sees a greater confidence in and bolder affirmation of Britishness as the way to address the problem of Muslim alienation and the threat of terrorism and extremism:

We need to fill the public space with alternative ideas and help people feel that they belong to Britain. British people in the second half of the twentieth century have had the sense that national identity shouldn't be stressed very much and that it should be more apologized for than stated. That makes it very hard for large groups of immigrants coming in. If you don't have an idea of what we have in common as opposed to what differentiates us, then you get into the situation where it is very clear what it is to be a Muslim, but what on earth is it to be British? We have gone too far in the direction of hollowing out and disparaging the British identity that holds us together.[37]

I have dwelt at some length on Tariq Modood's thoughts, partly because I agree with them and they echo in many ways the central thesis of this book, but also because they articulate particularly clearly what seems to me to be a definite and very significant tide of opinion among the 'new Britons' who have come here predominantly from the Commonwealth in the last fifty or so years. While they insist that the concept of Britishness needs to move on and be refreshed to be less white, less mono-cultural and more pluralistic, they are also adamant that the baby should not be thrown out with the bath water. On the whole, they take Britishness more seriously and hold it in higher regard than do many of the more cynical commentators drawn from the ranks of the longer-established white population. Maybe it is the zeal of the new convert, or in this case the new Briton, maybe, too, the legacy of empire or perhaps it is just the fresh eye which appreciates what others have long taken for granted.

There are two aspects of Britishness which are particularly often commended by the new Britons and which are not always appreciated as much as they might be. The first is the liberal tradition of tolerance and freedom of expression discussed in Chapter 4. This is particularly prized by Muslims. The most common comment made in the *Guardian* survey by those Muslims who do feel happy in Britain was that this was because 'Britain provides a tolerant and democratic environment for religious practice.' It is put in rather more folksy terms by Nazir Ahmed, Labour life peer:

> *I am a Muslim Kashmiri but also a Yorkshire lad who loves his fish and chips and his curry and chapatti. One of the most important parts of my identity is the values I share with my fellow Britons: I would put the freedom to express our views as one of the most important. Britain is one of the countries in Europe where we Muslims have the greatest number of rights.*[38]

Britain's particular traditions of freedom of expression and belief have always been valued by immigrants who have come as asylum seekers and political or religious refugees, fleeing persecution in their own countries. Many of the Muslims who now value them came to this country primarily for economic reasons. In the context of the current debate on immigration and Britishness, some have argued, like the journalist Sarfraz Manzoor, that economic migrants are likely to have less commitment to British values than those fleeing religious or political persecution: 'The most urgent question to ask about any fresh immigrants is how can we expect them to have a deep sense of loyalty to any idea of Britain if their sole reason for being here is economic.'[39] The Muslim experience would appear to suggest that this does not always follow. In their case, it is the freedom to practise their religion without interference from the Government or society which they most value about living in Britain and which plays a major part in making them feel British. This makes it all the more important that in the current climate of fear about extremism and terrorism, Britain continues its historic attachment to religious freedom, respecting such expressions of faith as the hijab and not demonizing Muslims as terrorists or disloyal citizens.

The other aspect of Britishness which has won support from many in the ethnic and religious minorities is the public space for and acknowledgement of spirituality and religion provided by the existence of established churches. It is ironic that while the call for church disestablishment has come largely from the Christian or secular majority, the principle of church establishment has found some of its staunchest defenders from among religious and ethnic minorities. The most eloquent proponent of establishment has almost certainly been Jonathan Sacks, Chief Rabbi of the United Hebrew congregations of the Commonwealth. In his 1990 Reith Lectures, he argued that established churches provide a 'sacred canopy' or overarching framework of shared meanings and moral landscape, create a sense of belonging and 'put faith at the centre of our national symbols'. Disestablishment, he suggested, would further erode the significance of faith in national identity, weaken the sense of common good necessary 'if our communities are to cohere as a society' and mark a retreat from the notion that there are some values that all can share.[40] More recently, a report on institutionalized religious discrimination in the United Kingdom commissioned by the Home Office from the University of Derby and published in 2000 found, somewhat to the compilers' surprise, that far from being a major grievance among those from the minority faiths, the principle of church establishment was generally supported along with such rituals as the Christian coronation of the monarch for putting religion at the heart of the state and national identity and affirming the sacred and spiritual.[41]

The extent of minority faith support for the existence of established churches was demonstrated in a fascinating conference on 'Church, State and Religious minorities' convened by the Policy Studies Institute in 1995. Here it was the Christian and humanist speakers, along with the sole representative of Buddhism, who opposed establishment and the representatives of Judaism, Sikhism, Hinduism and Islam who supported it, albeit in a form which allowed the Church of England and the Church of Scotland to speak on behalf of other faiths. The Jewish contributor, Rabbi Sylvia Rothschild, expressed the fear that disestablishment would bring about less rather than more pluralism by removing religion from the core structure of society and ushering in a purportedly neutral secularism that would in fact marginalize all religion and religious expression:

> *It is interesting to note that religious communities themselves have not pressed for the disestablishment of the Church of England, and indeed where they have commented on the issue have done so in a way which makes clear their respect for other religious communities, and their lack of desire to do anything to diminish them. That is because religious communities are well aware that the secular crusade against the Anglican church is an attack on all forms of religious expression and thus indirectly harmful to us too.*
>
> *Religious communities know too that whatever the problems for a minority religious group – and there are real and painful problems for us all – they will not be addressed by denying the mechanism which allows for the voice of religion to be heard in the public arena, but will only be dealt with when our difference and diversity is acknowledged and celebrated there. The way to tackle the disabilities of all minority groups is to create the climate where it is not only possible but actively accepted that those groups are valued for who they are and what they represent. To push formal religious identity out of the public domain and into individual private ' morality is to deny the value to society of groups whose identity and particularity is based on religious expression.*[42]

Ramindar Singh suggested that the view of most British Sikhs was that 'as long as the Church of England can preside over the multifaith situation with sensitivity, tolerance, respect and non-interference there should be no resentment of its special relationship with the British state.'[43] The most enthusiastic endorsement of establishment at the conference, and indeed of keeping the Christian coronation service and the position of the monarch as Supreme Governor of the Church came from the main Muslim contributor, Daoud Rosser-Owen, Amir of the Association for British Muslims. Echoing Jonathan Sacks' argument for a sacred canopy of overarching values, and also uniquely acknowledging the role and position of the Church of Scotland as well as the Church of England, he commended the Coronation Oath taken by the monarch for acknowledging the ultimate sovereignty of the spiritual and moral order in human affairs. In it, indeed, he found something very close to the Muslim position: 'For us there must be a church-state link, or rather a religion-state link, in order to keep in touch with Reality (*Al Haqq*, which is one of the Appellations of God Almighty) and the Ultimate Sovereign (*Al Malik*, which is another).'[44] He argued that the existence and role of established churches in the United Kingdom provide public acknowledgement of the fact that 'Governments exist so to order matters at home and abroad that God may be worshipped and human beings be enabled freely to conduct their lives in ways pleasing to the Almighty' and went on to say that 'most of us believe that the removal of establishment from the Church of England would be followed by out-and-out (or fundamentalist) secularism, which, in its late twentieth century manifestation, is a climate inimical to any religion.[45] Like several other speakers, Rosser-Owen strongly applauded Prince Charles's statement that he would like, when King, to act as 'Defender of Faith' rather than just 'Defender of the Faith'. In Rosser-Owen's view:

> *Muslims would hope that he will continue to lead the Church, and to have himself crowned according to the Anglican rites and taking the solemn Coronation Oath in the process. As the eventual Supreme Governor of the Church of England, he clearly sees a future role for the established church in speaking out for other religions and looking after their interests in the councils of state through its unique position.*[46]

It is significant that two of the leading advocates of multiculturalism in contemporary Britain are also broadly in favour of church establishment. Tariq Modood argues for 'pluralizing' the state-religion link rather than severing it and suggests that an established church, far from being archaic and an obstacle to multiculturalism, could actually broker greater recognition of and respect for religious minorities and the importance of faith in their identities. He commends the presence of bishops in the House of Lords and the coronation of the monarch by the Archbishop of

Canterbury as aspects of what he calls Britain's 'moderate secularism'. This piece of nomenclature, I may say, is about the only point on which he and I disagree - it seems to me to be the antithesis of secularism and betoken rather a moderate religiosity or spirituality at the heart of the state – but we are agreed that, whatever we call it, it is a good thing. Bhikhu Parekh also favours the principle of church establishment, seeing Christianity as 'woven into the very structure of British national identity' and being happy for it to continue to be given a privileged status as long as public recognition is given to other religions: 'Christianity may rightly remain the central part of British collective identity, provided that other religions receive adequate, though not necessarily equal, recognition in the institutions, rituals and ceremonies of the state.[46]

Overall, the new Britons who have been the subject of this chapter have made three major contributions to the ever-evolving and ever-elusive entity of Britishness. First, they have reasserted and reaffirmed the importance of religion and faith in a nation and society that is often categorized as secular. In their different ways, the black Gospel songs that captivated the crowds in London during the Queen's jubilee celebrations and the faithful lives of prayer and worship of so many Muslims restore a spiritual heart to Britain that was in danger of disappearing in a blanket of cynical secular materialism. Black Christianity may well prove to be a key agent in the re-evangelization of Christian Britain and to that extent it stands as heir and companion to the Celtic tradition explored in Chapter 3. It is no coincidence that if you go to a service in Iona Abbey, a place at the very heart of the Celtic Christian revival, you are likely to go out singing an African 'Hallelujah', a Korean Kyrie or a Mexican hymn. The songs of the world church, and especially of the church in Africa, Southeast Asia and Latin America, are heard increasingly often in the services of churches of all denominations across the United Kingdom, thanks in part to their championship and promotion by the Iona Community's Wild Goose Group, and are reinvigorating worship. African pastors and priests are coming to serve Protestant and Catholic congregations in Britain as part of a bigger movement whereby the old missionary flow from Europe to the Third World is being reversed.

In a different but related way, British Muslims are challenging the prevailing secularism of western society by their readiness to pray five times a day, to talk openly and respectfully about God and to lead lives governed by strict rules in accordance with their faith. They are also, perhaps, more radically redefining Britishness in terms of a more spiritual and faith-based identity as against the shallow consumerism that is so prevalent at all levels of our society. This challenge is summed up in the question posed by a Muslim woman who was among the fifty people assembled by *The Guardian* early in 2005 to discuss the consequences of an increasingly assertive Muslim identity in Britain and what might replace a discredited multiculturalism: 'Am I only British when I get my suit from Next?'[48] I have already quoted and commented on Madeline Bunting's observation following this intensive exercise: 'It brought right out into the open the issue of how does secular Britain deal with the reassertion of religion in political life.' Perhaps even more pertinent is her comment:

> *Multiculturalism has, to some extent, succeeded in dismantling the definition of British as white. Now another chapter has to be written in which British identity is no longer synonymous with a Christian/secular accommodation. 'I believe in God' one participant prefaced her remarks, and you could hear in the quality of silence in the room the shock that religious belief is unapologetically trespassing into mainstream debate for the first time in a generation.*[49]

What Madeline Bunting calls the trespass of religious belief into mainstream debate in Britain has, in fact, been happening for some time. It was there in the Muslim outrage over Salman Rushdie's *Satanic Verses* and more recently in the Sikh community's reaction to the play *Behtzi* and evangelical Christians' objections to the BBC screening of *Jerry Springer – The Opera*. These and other calls for censorship need to be seen not just as an assault on the British tradition of tolerance and free speech but also as a reminder of the importance of the sacred and the taboo, that there are boundaries of respect and propriety. The British liberal tradition, as we have seen, is predicated on moral and religious precepts and is not just an easy, anything goes, laissez-faire indifference. One of the most important contributions which Muslims in particular may be making is in putting a brake on the permissive society and putting a premium on respect, something that is more demanding than mere tolerance, and yet which is crucial in the creation of a new British identity which is both pluralistic and cohesive.

Secondly, as well as recalling us to the importance of religion, and a sense of the holy and the sacred, the new Britons are also reasserting some core British values which have been neglected by many old Britons. Both African Caribbean and Asian Britons are generally more community-minded and more respectful of their elders than most white Britons. Asians, in particular, also often display those qualities of reserve, modesty and understated reticence than were long associated with the British character. Shortly after the Salman Rushdie affair, the *Daily Mail*, not a paper noted for its enthusiasm for immigrants, carried a series of articles celebrating the hard work and family values of British Asians under the title 'The New Victorians'. As Home Secretary, Jack Straw made a speech suggesting that fellow Britons had much to learn from Asians about respect and care for the elderly. Writing in the aftermath of the London bombings of July 2005, *The Times* columnist, Libby Purves, argued that one of the reasons for Muslim alienation was the moral vacuum which fills contemporary Britain: 'Our public institutions are too shy of our religious heritage to defend Christmas and Easter, the Cross and the Bible, even as cultural symbols. Our media would rather torment the monarchy than enjoy it. Clever dicks mock anything traditional'. She went on to suggest that Muslims might prove to be the best allies of those seeking to restore traditional British values:

> *For what Muslims want and respect is not so very unlike what the despised 'Middle Britain' wants. Islam – like Christianity – sets great store on family, self-control, support of the weak and respect for tradition. And in many parts of Britain they do not see those things … Many Muslim values are eerily similar to the lost social consensus that made Britain the open, generous, free country that it basically is. Bombast is not the answer. But nor is shrugging self-disgust. Muslims and Middle Britain should fight some good fights, hand in hand.*[50]

It is clearly Utopian to suggest that Muslims can single-handedly, or even together with other new Britons, steer the nation towards more spiritual values and respect for others. But Libby Purves' call for a coalition with Middle Britain has much to commend it, not least because it locates Muslims where they and many other new Britons belong – in the middle of Britain rather than on the edge of it. This brings us to the third important contribution which the new Britons are making to the idea of Britishness, which is to emphasize not just its pluralistic and diverse quality but also its essentially perichoretic, interpenetrating nature. They are bringing new overlapping layers to the rich and complex construction and imagined community that is Britain as well as giving a welcome vote of confidence to some of the core values embodied in older layers that have perhaps gone unappreciated and unsung for too long. Let the last word be with the Muslim scholar and critic, Ziauddin Sardar:

> *What we need is to recover our confidence in the notion of Britishness as the product of various and diverse traditions. Before Muslims can feel that they belong, we need to recognize that any identity is the means to synthesize similarity through difference as a discrete means of expressing basic similarity.*[51]

7 Wider Still and Wider

Overlapping Spiritual Identities

This book has suggested that Britishness can be conceived of and explored as a series of overlapping spiritual identities, constantly changing, adapting and expanding. It has also pointed to the way that Britishness has long been framed in terms of hyphenated identity, with people often happily assuming and embracing two or more identities, sometimes ethnic, sometimes national, sometimes religious. In this hyphenated identity, the British element has often been softer and less definite than the others. Yet it has also often been the glue that has held diversity together and connected those from very different backgrounds.

The whole concept of Britishness is the subject of intense scrutiny and attention now for a variety of reasons. Significant immigration, the threat of terrorism, the development of ethnic ghettoes in major cities and widespread evidence of alienation and lack of a sense of belonging have pushed national identity and the challenge of creating a greater sense of community and social cohesion up the political agenda. As we have seen, the multicultural agenda which broadly guided social policy through the 1980s and 1990s has come under strong attack from those, including many themselves from immigrant backgrounds, who feel that it has not sufficiently emphasized Britishness and left an identity vacuum which has been filled by religious and ethnic extremism. The reassertion of religious identity, especially although not exclusively among Muslims, has raised particular questions for a society that is generally perceived as liberal and secular.

211

More broadly, the cultural climate associated with postmodernism has produced a much greater focus on where people feel they belong and with whom or what they identify. There is also a growing emphasis on diversity, individual choice and self-fulfilment, often, it seems, at the expense of social cohesion, duty and responsible citizenship. Community, authority and tradition are giving way to individualism, freedom and change.

Does a reassertion or even a reworking of such an old-fashioned, pre-modern idea as Britishness really offer any help in tackling these huge contemporary problems? It is the clear argument of this book that it does, especially if Britishness is understood as a series of constantly changing and overlapping spiritual identities, embodying the realized paradox of holding diversity in unity and exemplifying the Trinitarian principles of perichoresis, mutual indwelling and interpenetration. British identity, I have argued, is emphatically not secular but rather an essentially spiritual and religious compound, constantly refreshed and reinvigorated by new influences and contributions. Britain is, indeed, better placed than many other western countries and societies to meet the challenge of the twenty-first century and to link the great spiritual traditions and legacies from the past with the complex multi-faith present. As we seemingly hurtle towards ever-greater confusion, suspicion and fear and ever-narrower autonomy, separatism and selfish individualism, there are counter-resources that we can summon up to help us from the four specific elements of British identity that have been identified and described in this book.

The Celtic contribution to and understanding of Britishness emphasizes the importance of myth, memory, imagination, passion and faith. It links the primal and the Christian, the deeply spiritual with the simple and practical. Its revival over recent decades has greatly enhanced the profile of the cradle places of British spirituality like Iona and Lindisfarne. It is noticeable that much of the renewal of Christian worship and witness and much of the new thinking about the future spiritual landscape of Britain is coming from these places. The Iona Community has focused on peace, justice, spirituality, sexuality and the integrity of creation and reinvigorated worship through the work of the Wild Goose Resource Group and the writing of new liturgies and hymns in a recognizably Celtic idiom. On Lindisfarne, the Community of Aidan and Hilda, drawing on British and Celtic traditions, has pioneered a new model of the church which is at once monastic, communal, inclusive and hospitable, resourcing the local community, based around stillness and prayer and having a simple and uncluttered lifestyle.

In his important book *Church of the Isles*, Ray Simpson, guardian of the Community of Iona and Hilda, argues that the future of churches is national rather than denominational. His book is an extended tribute to Britishness, its Celticity, spirituality, diversity and inclusivity, and calls for a new 'Rainbow Church of the Isles' which will form inter-denominational and inter-faith villages of God:

> *A village of God may include places of prayer, education, counsel, art, silence and leisure. In these, churches will not compete, they will complete. A Catholic home for lone mothers, a Salvation Army soup kitchen, an Anglican meditation centre and a New Church arts and youth centre can each be true to themselves and yet be part of one village. There could even be a synagogue, mosque or temple which, though independent, share a common eating place with the Christians. Over the year different ethnic groups would host distinctive seasonal celebrations to which all are invited.*
>
> *There is a place in this Rainbow Church of the Isles for people of every ethnic and ecclesial background, for new Christians who have not joined a local church and for non-believing neighbours who want to be friends. There is room for every kind of creative impulse to be explored, for styles of worship and prayer that fit every temperament.*[1]

If the Celtic strain in Britishness provides a vision of new religious and spiritual communities connecting with the people, the Anglo-Saxon strain reminds us of the importance of the pursuit of freedom, tolerance and openness. These values are much needed now in the face of growing indifference, narrow-mindedness and conformist authoritarianism. Those British institutions which have traditionally exemplified them, such as Parliament, the BBC and the established churches, may need reforming but they also need cherishing and supporting. The English tradition of satire, irony and not taking anything too seriously has much to commend it but it needs to be balanced by the Scottish strain of moral seriousness, common purpose and ethical integrity if it is not to become over-iconoclastic and destructive of the very institutions and climate that have sustained it. It is arguable that Britishness has moved too far away from its muscular Christian Scottish roots in the direction of hedonism, as exemplified in the culture of binge drinking and loutish behaviour. There is a clear tension if not an actual incompatibility in the new British identity championed by Tony Blair's Government. At one level it harks back to the swinging sixties, with Britain the world leader in fashion, pop music and nightclubs and the home of all-night drinking and gambling. On the other it hand it seeks to renew the ethical springs of community and put duty and responsibility back into the idea of citizenship.

This tension is also reflected in the contribution of the new Britons who have come to the United Kingdom over the last fifty years predominantly from the Commonwealth countries of Asia, Africa and the Caribbean. While African-Caribbeans have brought to Britishness a convivial, carnival culture of urban tribes and rapping, Asian immigrants have brought a greater sense of reserve and modesty. Maybe both these elements can be held together and blended with those other ingredients that have fed into the ever-fluid and ever-expanding mixture that is Britishness. One of the glories and wonders of British identity is the way in which it has incorporated much that once seemed incompatible. It has done so because there has always been sufficient certainty and clarity about the core identity, even as it was being subtly changed and adapted. The need for that certainty and clarity remains very important today, when, as we have seen, we are faced with the fascinating but frustrating paradox that those who feel most British, the 'new British' Asians and African-Caribbeans, are not being given enough pride in Britishness, or enough sense of what it is, by the indigenous white majority. As David Goodhart says, 'Immigrants should be encouraged to become part of the British "we", even while bringing their own very different perspectives on its formation'.[2]

But what is the British 'we'? Is British identity now so fuzzy and muddled that it is impossible to promote it or, indeed, believe in it? Is it possible to have an identity that embraces diversity and pluralism but yet provides some overarching framework and some common points of loyalty, that maintains a modem, broadly secular, liberal emphasis on tolerance and yet also allows for the public expression of deeply felt religious and faith positions? I have argued in this book that Britain does manage to square these circles and that an important aspect of modem Britishness is its distinctive stance on these crucial and difficult issues. This is particularly evident in the attitude towards national identity taken in the United Kingdom compared to that of our neighbours both across the Atlantic and across the Channel.

The USA prides itself on its diversity as a nation of immigrants and on separating church and state. Its national identity is based in large part around worship of the flag, which is to be found unfurled in the sanctuaries of churches of many different denominations and to which schoolchildren regularly pledge allegiance. This heavy patriotism is reinforced by a growing Christian fundamentalism which is increasingly interpreting the nation's mottos, '*E Pluribus Unum*' (Out of Many, One) and 'One Nation Under God' to suggest that those who are not of a conservative, evangelical Christian (or possibly Jewish) faith and disposition are somehow un-American and un-patriotic. At the same time, there is a pervading atmosphere of insecurity, fear and foreboding at the heart of American national identity, exemplified in the huge success enjoyed by apocalyptic novels predicting imminent Armageddon and brilliantly analysed by the writer and film-maker, Michael Moore. France currently cultivates a rather different but equally narrow and authoritarian identity through its official obeisance to the shrine of secular republicanism. The policy of *laïcité* imposed in 1905 to undercut the power of the Catholic Church, and rooted in nineteenth-century anti-clericalism, aims to ensure equality in the public sphere by shutting out all religions. It has resulted in policies such as the 2004 ban on the hijab or Muslim headscarf and other 'conspicuous religious symbols' including Jewish skullcaps and large Christian crosses in state-run and approved schools which run wholly counter to the principle of multiculturalism and diversity and are stirring up antagonism and feelings of alienation among faith communities, especially Muslims.

The United Kingdom has never conceived of itself as a secular state in the way that France has. Nor has it rigidly separated church and state, allowing the privatization of religion and the consequent growth of fundamentalism, as has happened in the USA. In its two biggest nations, England and Scotland, there are established churches built into the constitution that have a close relationship with the monarch and a looser, but still significant, relationship with other public institutions. This arrangement, which is increasingly being extended to other denominational and faith groups, keeps religion in the civic and public sphere rather than relegating it to a privatized ghetto where extremism is more likely to breed. As we have seen, the principle of church establishment is supported by many within the minority faiths in the United Kingdom who recognize that it provides public space for religion and puts spiritual symbols and values at the heart of the nation. A growing and influential lobby, made up of secularists and drawn from the ranks of the politically correct, is, however, seeking to limit this space and destroy these symbols in the mistaken belief that they constitute an obstacle to creating a truly multicultural and multi-faith society. This misguided thinking, which is becoming increasingly prevalent in official circles, manifests itself in such ill¬conceived actions as the removal of the Cross from the municipal crematorium chapel in Torquay by Torbay Council, the objection by Islington Council to a new Church of England secondary school in the borough including the word 'Saint' in its name and various much-publicized moves by local councils and education authorities to downplay the Christian aspects of Christmas in public celebrations and school activities. Such curbs on the overt expression of Christianity in public places are seldom if ever asked for or, indeed, supported by members of minority faiths. Rather they are prompted by an official ideology which seeks to secularize the public sphere and has little feeling for the overlapping spiritual identities and traditions of coexistence and respect that stand at the heart of Britishness. They often have the opposite effect to that intended by their perpetrators, fanning popular resentment against religious and ethnic minorities who are wrongly seen as campaigning to de-Christianize Britain and destroy its historic traditions.

These and other moves in the direction of making Britain more like France would remove religion from public and civic life and create a secular nation very alien to the whole tradition of Britishness as it has been explored and described in this book. Equally alien to the British tradition would be the espousal of an aggressive US-style flag-waving patriotism and conservative Christian fundamentalism. Both these options, tempting though they may be to liberals and conservatives respectively in the current climate of uncertainty, fly in the face of the contemporary resurgence of religious identity and of the British tradition of open tolerance and respect for diversity linked to loyalty to venerable institutions like the monarchy and the established churches. A much better – and much more British – way forward is to wrestle with achieving the difficult task of holding together diversity and unity. One way of approaching this task is through the theme of overlapping spiritual identities that has dominated this book and which, I have suggested, is at the heart of British identity. This was the way that David Blunkett chose to approach the particularly sensitive question of divided loyalties among British Muslims in his Heslington Lecture at the University of York in 2003 which was entitled 'One nation – many faiths':

*It is a worrying trend that young, second-generation British Muslims are
more likely than their parents to feel they have chosen between feeling part*

of the UK and feeling part of their faith – when in fact as citizens of the United Kingdom and adherents of a major faith they should feel part of wider, overlapping communities.[3]

The specific question of Muslim identity has come up frequently in this book, just as it comes up frequently in general discussions about the nature of modern Britishness, the right balance between secularism and religion in the modern state and the limits to tolerance and pluralism. It is important not to let the particular demands of Muslims dominate the discussion or dictate the agenda but they do highlight in a very definite way many of the issues around this whole area which are currently the subject of so much attention and debate and which often seem so intractable. They also highlight the very considerable space that Britain still allows for the expression of different faiths and the respect which it accords them, certainly more than secularist republican France or the fundamentalist and fearful USA. I have already quoted the positive views of British Muslims about the freedom accorded to them compared with that granted in most other countries (see page 195). Reviewing the position of Muslims across Europe as a whole in a recent academic study, Philip Lewis concludes:

> *The UK allows more spaces for Muslim self-expression than most other European countries: a state which comprises four nations, which has gradually made institutional space for denominational diversity since the Reformation, and which enjoys the relatively plastic category 'British' allowing some measure of multiple identities has gradually extended to Muslims the same rights enjoyed by other faiths.*[4]

He goes on specifically to commend this model of making space as the way forward for the mixed communities in the Balkans. Tariq Modood equally sees this British quality of openness with regard to other faiths and cultures as offering a model and message for other European countries:

> *The British, especially the English, are less open to their European neighbours but are less hostile than most Europeans to multiculturalism and to international exchange. This I think gives Britain and especially British*

*multiculturalists a 'mission' in Europe, that is to make Europe more open to
the world and to multicultural situations, perhaps to be a bridge between
Europeans and non-Europeans.*[5]

A clear recent example of the application of this distinctively British approach
is to be found in the United Kingdom's enthusiasm for Turkish membership of
the European Union. More strongly than any other member state, Britain has
championed Turkey's cause, extolling the benefits of having a largely Muslim country
in the largely Christian (or post-Christian) European Union and the possibility of
exorcizing the 'clash of civilizations' ghost by embracing a democratic, economically
successful and relatively secular Muslim state and so demonstrating that Islam is not
incompatible with human rights and modernity.

This book has emphasized the spiritual dimension of Britishness as being
central both to British identity and to the resolution of some of the difficult issues
lying around the areas of reconciling pluralism with social cohesion and a broad
open-minded tolerance with the rise of increasingly strong religious feelings. I am
glad to say that I am not alone in this emphasis. It is a perspective which I share
with Tariq Modood, who has perhaps thought and written more on these topics
than anyone else. I strongly agree with his conviction that the British tradition of
tolerance and respect for diversity, combined with the provision of a public space for
religion which derives from the principle of established churches, provides a working
model for the future. I share his commitment to 'a multicultural Britishness that is
sensitive to ethnic difference and incorporates a respect for persons as individuals
and for the collectivities that people have a sense of belonging to. That means a
multiculturalism that is happy with hybridity but has space for religious identities.'[6]
I also share his conviction that 'multi-culturalism must rest on an affirmation of
shared moral certainties: it cannot just be about differences. We have a lot in common
and must work to bring this out. Some of the moral certainties would be to do with
family, community, religious or quasi-religious ethics' and that 'to extend and enrich
our understanding of our Britishness, a sense of belonging capable of embracing a
number of hyphenated nationalities; we will need the assistance of the moral and
religious traditions that at least partly constitute what we mean by ethnicity.'[6]

A similar emphasis on the spiritual element in the public space underlies an
important recent lecture by the Archbishop of Canterbury. Speaking in Oxford in

2004 about 'Convictions, Loyalties and the Secular State', Rowan Williams referred to the rise of the idea that the state is threatened by religious loyalties and the concomitant notion that the public space is necessarily secular. He noted:

> *Increasingly what we see is a presumption that the rational, secular state is menaced by the public or communal expression of religious loyalty. It is not a matter of one sacred order facing a rival, but of a sense that the public space of society is necessarily secular - that is, necessarily a place in which no local or sectional symbolic activity is permissible.*

He saw this view supremely represented in a secular state like France, but also increasingly championed in Britain, being reinforced not just by the general consensus of liberal secularism, but also by the 'aspect of modern Christian rhetoric which has come to speak of religious conviction as essentially a matter of individual option'. The desired aim in this view is a non-confessional state in which private conviction is free but public loyalty exclusively claimed by the state itself. Williams looked at the challenge posed to this increasingly pervasive view by Islam with its loyalty both to divine law and to the state and commended such overlapping loyalties, emphasizing the public character of religious belonging which, even in the secular state, 'cannot just be reduced to the level of private voluntary associations of the like minded'.[8]

So how can we best promote Britishness as a network of overlapping spiritual identities, which allows diversity to flourish while also providing social cohesion and an overarching sense of loyalty and commonality? There is a general consensus that while Britain is good at creating hybrid and hyphenated identity from disparate ingredients, it is currently less successful in finding symbols and expressions of shared loyalty and common focus. The official report on the riots in northern English cities in 2001 painted a picture of different ethnic and faith communities living together in close proximity but leading separate and parallel lives with little overlap. A national survey in 2003 found that seventy-seven per cent of respondents said that cultures co-exist rather than connect in Britain. There is also, as we have seen, a growing call, not least from the Asian and African-Caribbean 'new Britons', for a more definite and confident assertion of Britishness. Here, to conclude this book, are twelve proposals for creating a more focused and coherent British identity in the twenty-first century.

1. New Patron Saints

The United Kingdom's four patron saints reflect Britain's religious roots and provide the spiritual symbols that make up the national flag. In other respects, as we have already noted, they are not particularly suitable or appropriate figures for the nation to rally round. Andrew was foisted on Scotland thanks to a sharp piece of public relations work by the Picts, who realized that the only way that they could trump the patron saint of their Gaelic rivals, Columba, was by fabricating the wildly improbable story that the relics of one of the apostles had been brought from Constantinople to the coast of north-east Fife. The Palestinian George supplanted the two native English patron saints, Edward the Confessor and Edmund, King of East Anglia, after the Crusades and his invocation by Henry V at the battle of Agincourt. A patron saint who owes his position to militant medieval Islamophobia and anti-French sentiment looks increasingly anomalous as we move towards a more multi-faith and European future. Patrick is also a slightly curious choice for Ireland given that he was a Briton who rather disliked the Irish (not surprisingly, given that they had captured him to be a slave). I suppose there is something to be said for three of the four UK patron saints being aliens from other lands in terms of the message that they give about embracing the stranger, but otherwise they seem rather poor representatives of Britain's spiritual identity and heritage.

Given their association with the national flag and the rising interest in celebrating them, with considerable pressure now being exerted to give both St George's Day and St Andrew's Day some of the prominence that St Patrick's Day has long had, it is almost certainly not feasible to pension off the current quartet of patron saints. David, indeed, has no need of replacement, standing as a true Welshman and a fine exemplar of the Welsh values of concern for the marginalized and the little things. There is, however, a strong case for promoting a new trinity of indigenous saints for the rest of the United Kingdom who would at the very least stand alongside the existing ones and better reflect Britain's Celtic and Anglo-Saxon heritage. The Scots should regain Columba, who uniquely manages to appeal to Presbyterians, Episcopalians and Catholics (and who as an Irishman would nicely balance the British Patrick as patron saint of the Irish). The English could return to the gentle Edward the Confessor who founded Westminster Abbey. The Irish might strike a blow for gender equality and pagan-Christian dialogue by adopting Bridget.

What is even more important is to find a patron saint for the United Kingdom as a whole. In his song 'Take Down the Union Jack', Billy Bragg observes of Britain, 'It's not a proper country, it doesn't even have a patron saint.' This is a very reasonable point. I can think of few better candidates for the role than Aidan, who almost certainly came originally from Ireland, spent many years as a monk in Scotland and did his greatest work in England. Summoned from Iona in 635 by King Oswald of Northumbria to evangelize the northern part of his huge kingdom, Aidan established his base at Lindisfarne and served there as both abbot and bishop. He had several characteristics which make him an ideal patron saint for Britain in the twenty-first century. He was famous for reproving those with money and authority who abused their power and wealth and he was also a model of Christian humility and gentleness. When King Oswald's successor, Oswy, gave Aidan a fine horse on which to ride round his diocese, he promptly gave it away to the first poor man he met, saying that he preferred to walk and meet people at their own level. As well as having these new overlapping national patron saints, to reflect the perichoretic nature of British identity, it would also be good to have more local and regional saints. After becoming officially recognized as a city, Sunderland adopted St Benedict Biscop as its patron saint and held a splendid ceremony to install him in 2005. There is much to be said for honouring local saints and heroes. They do not all have to be long-dead figures from early medieval times although such people provide a touch of romantic myth and legend as well as providing role models.

2. Redesign the Union Flag

With its superimposed representations of the crosses of George, Andrew and Patrick, the Union flag is a dramatic symbol of some of the overlapping spiritual identities that make up Britishness. This is not, however, how it is generally perceived. It has come to be associated with the xenophobia and racism of the far right. The Government is right to be seeking to reclaim it, to encourage its flying on public buildings and to attempt to link it with core British values like tolerance and the rule of law. The veteran *Guardian* columnist, Polly Toynbee, is also right to suggest that it should be cherished as much by those on the left as by those on the right of the political spectrum:

> *The left, with its infinite ironising, recoils from national symbolism, vacating valuable ground necessary for any collective social democratic identity. The*

union flag that we mocked in the 1960s, worn as Carnaby Street bell-
bottoms, does symbolize laws and values. So the sight of Muslim fanatics
burning it outside the Regent's Park mosque is just as outrageous as the sight
of BNP football hooligans waving it as they charge at Turkish football fans.
It is our collective symbol.[9]

The Union flag has been an evolving rather than a static symbol of British identity. It has been changed twice in its four-hundred-year history, most recently in 1801 to incorporate St Patrick's Cross. Is there a case for further change now to make it more inclusive and representative of contemporary British identity? At the very least, there is a very strong case for incorporating the cross of St David, which is represented either as a gold cross on a black background or a black cross on a gold/yellow background. This symbol is of relatively recent origin, having been devised in 1939 by the Church in Wales on the basis of the armorial banner of the See of St David's. As well as acknowledging Wales' place in the United Kingdom, the incorporation of St David's cross in either of its forms (the gold cross on a black background is perhaps to be preferred) would also address Paul Gilroy's complaint that 'there ain't no black in the Union Jack.'

On its four hundredth birthday, there is a strong case for a national debate and discussion on the design and use of the Union flag and the extent to which it can still act as a symbol of unity in diversity and overlapping spiritual identities in a relevant and meaningful way. It may well be that the flag as it stands has become so iconic, and also such a well-recognized brand, that it would be difficult and ill advised to change its design now. It is, however, at least worth floating the idea of redesigning or at least re-branding it to make it more inclusive and representative of contemporary British identity. If, as I suspect may well be the case, the result of such a debate is a vote of confidence in the present design by ethnic and religious minorities as well as by the white Christian majority, then that in itself will be a positive step towards a greater and wider sense of Britishness.

3. More Focus on the Monarchy
John Habgood, Archbishop of York from 1983 to 1995, has wisely observed:

There is not a single free nation in the world which has managed to hold a pluralist society together without some very powerful unifying factor. In Britain, we used to have a whole network of such factors mostly linked in some way to the Church and Crown. One of the effects of the decline of the national role of the Church has been to isolate the Crown as almost the only effective symbol of national unity.[10]

Sadly, the ability of the Crown to provide this symbolic unity has been eroded in recent decades both by a relentless campaign of degradation in the media led by the Murdoch press and by some spectacular own goals on the part of certain members of the royal family and their advisers. Yet the monarchy is still seen by many people as the single most visible symbol of Britain (see page 53) and it has the potential to provide a focus of unity. This was demonstrated over the period of the Queen's Golden Jubilee celebrations in 2002. The institution of monarchy is particularly important in the spiritual identity of Britishness. As the Victorian constitutionalist, Walter Bagehot, noted, 'It strengthens our government with the strength of religion ... constitutes the solitary transcendent element in the body politic ... and consecrates our whole state.'[11] This is particularly true at the time of a coronation. The last coronation in 1953 was described by two academic sociologists, Edward Shils and Michael Young, as 'the ceremonial occasion for the affirmation of the moral values by which the society lives. It was an act of national communion.'[12] They based this assertion on observation of the coronation's impact on 'ordinary' people, who frequently spoke of it as 'an inspiration' and a 're-dedication of the nation'. It is not too early to begin to think about the shape and form of the next coronation and to make sure that it provides a similarly transcendent experience which speaks eloquently of the consecration of the nation as well as of the monarch and underlines the spiritual values at the heart of Britishness. There has already been some constructive thinking and writing about this and specifically about the way in which different faith groups might be involved in the inauguration rite of the next British monarch.[13]

I have recently written a book about the spiritual dimension of monarchy which argues that it still has the potential both to act as an important symbol of unity and a common focus of loyalty in Britain and also to re-sacralize the nation.[14] Like so much else in British life and tradition, the monarchy is valued more now by many of the new Britons who have come as immigrants in recent decades than by many in the long-standing native population. We could do with cherishing the institution more and sniping less at those who represent it today. We would also do well to heed the words of that old Etonian socialist, George Orwell, describing his ideal post-revolutionary England (by which he essentially meant Britain):

> It will not be doctrinaire, nor even logical. It will abolish the House of Lords, but quite probably will not abolish the monarchy. It will leave anachronisms and loose ends everywhere, the judge in his ridiculous horse hair wig and the lion and the unicorn on the soldier's cap buttons.[15]

These 'anachronisms and loose ends', the monarchy chief among them, are embedded deep in the soul of Britain and are at the very heart of that quirky but precious mixture of dignity and self-deprecation, pomp, pageantry, tolerance and openness that is Britishness.

It is worth noting the extent to which the two senior members of the Royal Family have themselves emphasized and extended the spiritual and unifying dimensions of their roles in recent years. Prince Charles's statement in a television documentary in 1994 that he would rather be known as Defender of Faith than Defender of the Faith, subsequently amplified on various occasions, has been enthusiastically taken up by leading members of minority faith communities in Britain as signalling a commitment by the heir to the throne to religious diversity and pluralism and to the defence of the spiritual and sacred against the rising tide of secular materialism. The Queen has increasingly used her Christmas broadcasts to the nation both to speak intimately and movingly about her own strong Christian faith and to commend the British tradition of tolerance. She has also specifically underlined the importance of the churches and of other faith groups in fostering national identity and unity. In his book *Chosen People*, Clifford Longley contrasts Rudi Giuliani's farewell speech as mayor of New York in December 2001 with the Queen's Christmas broadcast two days later. Giuliani explicitly invoked America, saying that the test of Americanism is how much you believe in America 'because we are like a religion really. A secular religion. We believe in ideas and ideals.' The Queen invoked neither Britain nor Britishness, but rather spoke of looking to the church 'to bring us together as a nation or as a community'. She went on to say that 'It is to the church we turn to give meaning to these moments of intense human experience through prayer, symbol and ceremony' and to talk about the need for everyone, whatever their religion, to have faith.[16] This understated and reserved approach, emphasizing the importance of religious faith, and of the established churches, rather than banging the patriotic drum, epitomizes the very British qualities of the sovereign who has ruled over the United Kingdom so wisely for the last half century.

4. A New Role for Established Churches

As we have seen, both the concept and the practice of established churches have been significant and distinctive features of British identity. They help bind monarch and people together, they stage-manage significant national rituals like coronations, state funerals, services of Remembrance and important commemorations and anniversaries and they also provide a public space for religion and faith. They tend to promote a broad, liberal, eirenic, open Christianity, being fuzzy round the edges rather than sharply defined, and are, at their best, especially welcoming to the great unchurched majority of half-believers. Their ministry is national and territorial rather than just to the committed 'holy huddle' found in the pews every Sunday morning. There is now considerable pressure from a number of sources, including from within the church itself, to disestablish the Church of England. There may well be a case for reforming establishment and making the Church of England more like the Church of Scotland. There is certainly a case for widening it and working towards the kind of ecumenical united Church of the British Isles that James Cooper strove for a hundred years ago (see page 161). But it would be a retrograde step to move towards total disestablishment as secularists, many Evangelicals and not a few Anglo-Catholics are now demanding. Rather we should be resisting the creeping congregationalism and sectarianism that is gripping both the Church of England and the Church of Scotland and threatening to turn these great national institutions from being concerned with all their parishioners and connecting with the widespread latent Christianity in the United Kingdom.

It is striking that support for the principle of establishment tends to be strongest among the minority faiths in Britain (see pages 204-7). It has also been championed by Nonconformists who have perceived the benefits of having national churches and beseeched the Church of England to make more of its role in this regard and not look on it as an unfortunate encumbrance. In his book on the identity and religion of the British, Daniel Jenkins ventured to suggest that the Church of England:

may miss many of the opportunities of effective influence which are open to her in the common life of England and of Britain as a whole unless she resists her present tendency to regard being established as a burden to be shrugged off rather than an inescapable responsibility which she has inherited, and which has been a major factor in making her what she is.[17]

It has taken the first black Archbishop of York, John Sentamu, to state that 'The Church of England has to reconnect with England.'[18]

There is a very influential current of contemporary Christian thought that sees Christians as being on the margins of society rather than at its heart. It is expressed in Stanley Hauerwas' phrase 'resident aliens' and emphasizes the churches' uncomfortable, anti-establishment, prophetic role, arguing for a complete separation of church and state. It is, of course, true that churches can be too cosy in their relationship with the powers that be and must always maintain their uneasy, costly and sacrificial prophetic role. However, this can be exercised on the basis of engagement with rather than withdrawal from the public sphere. Instead of disestablishment, it would be much better to see a broader version of establishment whereby the established churches, in close alliance with other denominations and faith groups, act as protectors of religion and the spiritual dimension in more general terms. This role was well articulated by George Carey, when Archbishop of Canterbury, in a St George's Day Lecture in 2002. He called for the national church to serve the entire community and underlined the importance of a spiritual underpinning of the state so that religion is not a purely private matter. Carey specifically advocated what he called a 'hospitable establishment' in which the established church acts on behalf of faith generally, providing 'the opportunity and the right atmosphere for the many dealings and interactions between faith communities and the wider society'.[19] Ray Simpson has made the specific suggestion that Westminster Abbey, the symbolic mother church of the established Church of England and a 'royal peculiar' with particularly strong links with the monarch and the nation, should incorporate a chapel or place of prayer for Muslims and also establish a chapel 'to celebrate the roots that are common to Ireland, the devolved parts of the United Kingdom, the Isle of Man and the Channel Isles' and to display the eight flags represented in the recently created Council of the Isles.

There may, indeed, be a more pro-active role for the established churches to take in terms of engaging with other faiths. This has been spelled out in an interesting and challenging way by Dr Jeevan Singh Deol, a Sikh lecturer at the School of Oriental and African Studies at the University of London.

He urges them to be less mealy mouthed in their dealings with other faith communities, which, he suggests, are often poorly educated by teachers who have come from outside and unable to ask questions:

> *One way for Anglicans to encourage the rest of us to grow into the roles and values that our presence requires of us could be to challenge us. As the established Church, the Church of England has an almost overpowering presence in the national religious life, and a voice at the heart of power. The Church has been shy of that position in recent years. In this, it short-changes both itself and other faiths.*
>
> *It must feel virtuous to ally with other faiths over the latest social issue – be it Islamic dress in the schools or inflammatory plays – but the Church should be looking at the bigger picture. The real virtue in engaging with other faiths lies in bringing them to a position where they are more able to participate in national life and to challenge themselves – in the same way that the Church does. This is the Church's real national duty: it's high time that it abandoned political correctness and set about engaging with us as equals.*[20]

Perhaps this critique has a wider application, not just to the established church but to the British as a whole, in reminding us that our openness and readiness to see others' point of view should not mean that we ourselves go completely empty or devoid of conviction and belief in ourselves.

5. More Emphasis on the Commonwealth

There is a wonderful prayer, used insufficiently in both the Church of England and the Church of Scotland, which begins 'God, grant to the living grace, to the departed rest' and continues 'to the Church, the Queen and the Commonwealth, peace and concord'. The third element in this particular trinity has been sadly neglected and underrated in recent years. The British Commonwealth of nations deserves much more emphasis and celebration than it currently receives as a model of multiculturalism and diversity in unity. Here is a multi-faith and multicultural global family of fifty-three nations united by loyalty to the British Crown and by a set of values long associated with and largely learned from the United Kingdom. Sadly, the Commonwealth is too often the forgotten player among international groupings and organizations. It has played a key role in fighting apartheid, promoting democratic elections, combating poverty and promoting racial harmony. Many of its inhabitants are still distinguished by a 'British' outlook and character which is not always found now in the United Kingdom itself (see pages 180-83). A recent academic study has pointed to the extent to which the Commonwealth was often represented in twentieth-century British political thought as an example to the world in its 'spiritual' unity of otherwise distinct nations, linked by their common loyalty to the Crown, history and tradition.[21] It still surely has a very significant role to play in the world as an example of the marriage of diversity and unity through essentially spiritual bonds.

A greater emphasis on the Commonwealth and its role in shaping and fashioning British identity need not be at the expense of acknowledging the increasing importance of the European dimension. It would have the effect of generally broadening Britain's horizons and making them less focused simply on the ' special relationship' with the United States of America. Teaching more Commonwealth history in schools, including a rounded history of the British Empire, would also help to address the weakness noted in the current narrow school history syllabus by the Government's Qualifications and Curriculum Authority, which has pointed to 'the under-valuing of the contribution of black and other minority ethnic peoples to Britain's past'. A greater emphasis on the history of both the Empire and the Commonwealth would, indeed, affirm the role of African-Caribbeans and Asians especially in the evolving story of British identity and their key place within both past and present constructions of Britishness. There is also an urgent need to offer more scholarships for Commonwealth students to come to British universities.

6. More Public Space and Support for Religion

Britain has long offered a considerable amount of public space for religion. This has in part been bound up with the spiritual role of the monarchy and the existence of established churches. From bishops sitting in the House of Lords to prayers opening every day's business in the House of Commons, from Remembrance Day rituals to state-funded church schools, from the 'Thought for the Day' slot and daily worship on BBC Radio 4 to parish clergy having right of entry into schools and hospitals, there has been a considerable public acknowledgement of religion and a strong religious element in the frame-work of the state and in public institutions. With other faiths claiming a share of the action, there is now considerable debate about the future of these and other arrangements which privilege Christians and especially the established churches. One option is to move towards a French-style secular state, another to separate church and state and effectively privatize religion and encourage fundamentalism as in the USA. There is also a very British third way, which adapts the existing arrangements to provide public space and support for all major faith communities, not just those of the Christian establishment.

A good example of this adaptation is provided by the new Scottish Parliament. The first-ever motion tabled in the parliament called for prayers to open its proceedings. After debate, this was widened first to inter-denominational prayers and then to inter-faith reflections. As a result, a four-minute 'Time for Reflection' opens business every week. Of the 127 reflections in the first session of the parliament, 103 were given by Christians, five by Jews, four by Muslims, two by Buddhists, two by representatives of charities and one each by Hindus, Sikhs, Humanists, Mormons, Bahais and Christian Scientists. There were also five 'inter-faith' reflections. An analysis of the reflections presented between 2003 and 2005 shows that sixty-nine per cent were given by Christians, and forty per cent by ministers or members of the Church of Scotland – figures which almost exactly mirror the proportions of the population of Scotland as a whole describing themselves as Christians and claiming affiliation with the Church of Scotland in the 2001 census. The reflections, which follow closely the model of 'Thought for the Day' on the BBC's early morning news magazine programmes, stand in contrast to the Anglican prayers delivered at ·the start of House of Commons business every day by the Speaker's Chaplain. They show a Presbyterian preference for the sermon over prayer and ritual, although they have included Hindu meditations. No other parliament in Europe has gone down this interesting road of providing an officially endorsed and structured religious reflection to open its proceedings. But then no other parliament has had an opening ceremony which featured the singing of a Psalm (in English for the initial opening of the Parliament and in Gaelic for the opening of the new Holyrood building). In its imaginative use of singing, as in other ways, the Scottish Parliament is developing new rituals and expressions of civic and national spirituality which could perhaps be taken up on the wider British stage.[22]

Perhaps the most contentious issue around the area of public support for religion is that of faith schools. Britain has long had church-governed schools within the public education system, upholding a distinctively Christian ethos while being fully funded by the state. They currently provide education for over twenty per cent of the nation's primary and secondary school pupils. It is often argued that the existence of Roman Catholic state schools has been a major factor in integrating Roman Catholics into British society. There has been a marked growth of independent faith-based schools, predominantly evangelical Christian and Muslim, in recent years and a rising demand for more state-supported Muslim schools. There are those who argue that such schools, whether publicly or privately funded, constitute a challenge and even a threat to the coherence of British society. This is an aspect of the wider criticism levelled against the multicultural agenda. In a speech to the Hansard Society in 2005, David Bell, the chief inspector of schools, suggested that too often those educated in faith-based schools learn little of their wider responsibilities and obligations to British society:

> *The growth in faith schools needs to be carefully but sensitively monitored by government to ensure that pupils at all schools receive an understanding of not only their own faith but of other faiths and the wider tenets of British society. We must not allow our recognition of diversity to become apathy in the face of any challenge to our coherence as a nation ... I would go further and say that an awareness of our common heritage as British citizens, equal under the law, should enable us to assert with confidence that we are intolerant of intolerance, illiberalism and attitudes and values that demean the place of certain sections of our community, be they women or people living in non-traditional relationships.*[22]

This is a very important point, not just for faith schools but for all schools to take on board if the central and common tenets of British identity and citizenship are to be made more clear to young people. Perhaps one of the best ways that faith schools, and those who go to them, can be made more British and develop both aspects of their hyphenated identity as British Catholics, British Muslims or British Jews, is for the state to support these schools and make sure that they are fully accountable, properly inspected and teaching the full national curriculum including citizenship,

English language and literature and the basic outlines of British history.

There is, indeed, a wider argument that public support for faith groups will promote a greater sense of integration, coherence and Britishness. This is, perhaps, especially true in the case of Muslims who are particularly concerned with securing public space for the expression of their beliefs. Philip Lewis rightly observes that 'because public and civil life in Britain is permeated with Christian influence it is proving increasingly hospitable to the religious concerns of Muslims.'[24] The state is already paying for Muslim hospital and prison chaplains, who are often collaborating with Christian clergy. This is helping the professionalization and clericalization of imams and their education in the English language and in British ways. There needs to be a corresponding willingness on the part of the leaders of faith communities to adopt a more public role and exercise a responsible discipline over their own preachers such as is exercised in the mainstream churches. One of the measures introduced as a result of working groups set up by Charles Clarke, the then Home Secretary, in the wake of the London bombings of 2005, was the creation of a national council of imams and mosques to nurture home-grown preachers and reduce reliance on foreign clerics. Introducing it, the Muslim Labour peer, Lord Ahmed, specifically linked the initiative to the wider drive to show Muslim youth how to be both British and Muslim:

> As British Muslims, we need to be prepared to modernize the way we operate, encouraging integration and helping our children feel proud to be British. We are no longer Pakistani Muslims or north African Muslims but British Muslims. We need to attract young suitable candidates who will be home-grown imams rather than asking for imams from outside.[25]

7. Promotion of Inter-Faith Forums and Exchanges

The extent to which minority communities in Britain, as elsewhere, are increasingly defining themselves in terms of their faith rather than according to ethnic or other identities, underlines the importance of providing places and forums where people can meet, talk and act together on the basis of their faith commitments as well as on the basis of shared political beliefs, hobbies or leisure interests. In terms of promoting social cohesion and a sense of common 'Britishness', there is also much to be said for these being publicly rather than privately provided spaces and forums.

I am a founder member of the recently established Fife Inter-Faith Forum, which was set up on the initiative of the Fife Fire and Rescue Service. It came about partly as a result of a Government directive requiring local fire services to consult with faith communities in their areas and be aware of their concerns and partly through the more personal commitment of two senior officers, both themselves Roman Catholics. At the inaugural meeting of the Forum, they spoke openly about their own faith and about the belief in some transcendent dimension and being and the element of faith that united all those gathered from the different faith communities in the region. This model of a public body, in this case an emergency service, taking the initiative in setting up an inter-faith forum seems to me very fruitful and encouraging.

Other public bodies, including some of those widely taken to exemplify the best of Britishness, are also taking a lead in promoting inter-faith dialogue, cooperation and partnership. Chaplaincy services in the Health Service, higher and further education, the armed forces and the prison service are being reorganized along multi-faith lines. At the very least, this is leading to more overlapping in spiritual identities and in many cases it is fostering closer cooperation and greater mutual respect. Since 2002, Markfield Institute of Higher Education near Leicester has been running a course to prepare Muslim chaplains for work in higher and further education, prisons and hospitals. Half the advisory board overseeing the course are Christians, trainee Muslim chaplains are often paired with more experienced Christian practitioners and there is a strong emphasis on preparing and training chaplains who can work collaboratively with colleagues of other faiths.

Within the university where I teach and serve as an honorary chaplain, the chaplaincy building is a multi-faith centre where Christians, Muslims and Jews worship under the same roof. A play in the 2005 Edinburgh Festival by the Glasgow dramatist Shan Khan, entitled 'The Prayer Room', featured the tensions and rivalries between Christian, Muslim and Jewish students sharing a multi-faith prayer room in a British university. These eventually spilled over into violence, with a black student being shot by a Muslim. I have to say that my own experience is completely different. Among the different student faith groups who share our chaplaincy building for worship (and significantly both the Islamic and Jewish society prefer to call it the Chaplaincy rather than use the neutral secular name 'Mansfield' which the university gave it when it ceased to be for Christians only) there is a good deal of give and take as well as respect for each other's beliefs. Uncertainty over the precise start of Ramadan produced a flurry of mobile phone calls between the presidents of the Islamic Society and the Christian Union to negotiate the sharing-out of rooms at the last minute. Jews, Muslims and Christian groups share a small kitchen and sometimes cook together, taking their food from their own designated fridges and freezers. Members of each of the main faith groups are clear in their own identity but respectful of others in theirs. They overlap in their concern that the university should respect holy days and festivals, in looking to the university chaplain to represent their needs and concerns and in seeing the university not as a secular institution but as a religious foundation with a commitment to diversity.

There may be a case for having a national Council of Faiths on the model of the all-party Privy Council and with a similarly close relationship to the monarch. Another way of integrating the major faith communities into a broader British identity would be by inviting their leaders or representatives to sit with bishops of the Church of England and representatives of other Christian churches in a reformed House of Lords. As conducive to promoting greater social coherence as these constitutional changes at national level are local grassroots encounters and initiatives. Quite the most moving inter-faith activity that I have been involved in has been a joint project involving Christians and Muslims in St Andrews and Dundee based around the our shared interest in recovering and exploring the theme of pilgrimage that is so central in both religious traditions. Our patron saints have played an important role here – not least, I am compelled to say, St Andrew of Scotland about whom I should perhaps be more positive!

8. Recognizing the Importance of Faith Communities in British Public Life

There is a growing recognition of the importance of faith groups in providing social cohesion in Britain, especially in deprived areas where other social infrastructures may be absent. The setting up of a Faith Unit attached to the Home Office is an indication of the Government's acknowledgement of and interest in the role that faith communities can and do play in generating and supporting 'social capital'. Faith groups are involved both in the provision of services and in community consultation and engagement. The extent of their activities in the former area is revealed in the recent report 'Faith in Action' based on interviews with members of twelve religious groups based in Luton and Peterborough. Among the projects which it highlighted was an advice centre run from the Islamic Centre in Peterborough, a book club, library and bereavement visiting service run by the Reform synagogue in Cambridge and a clean-up of a children's playground and other public areas on a deprived housing estate over a bank holiday weekend by a group of 100 volunteers from St Mary's Parish Church in Luton. Significantly, it was the church-run project which reached out to the whole community and not just to adherents of one particular faith.

It may well be that it is in the area of campaigning, consultation and community engagement that the involvement of faith groups is going to lead to a greater sense of overlapping identity and common cause. Opposition to the war in Iraq has brought together many Christians and Muslims. It is his experience in protest marches over this issue that has caused David Partridge, a retired Anglican parish priest, to become involved in inter-faith projects and specifically to pray regularly in his local mosque as well as in his own parish church: 'It came home to me that Muslims and Christians were not only protesting together: they were also praying (and crying) about the same questions of peace and justice.' He was struck by the fact that, whereas a Good Friday service organized by six churches and led by the diocesan bishop drew a congregation of around sixty, the Friday prayers that he went on to at the mosque down the road drew more than 600 worshippers despite the fact that for Muslims this was not a special day. He is adamant, however, that it is not just 'the congregational counts' that make him want to worship with Muslims as well as his fellow-Christians but rather the recognition of a common if differently experienced sense of spiritual poverty: 'For both Christians and Muslims in security-anxious Britain, the poverty we share is the struggle with a prevailing culture that regards the members of any faith community as either mad or missing out on the pleasures of plush modernity – probably both.' [26]

The extent to which local community engagement and organizing is creating overlapping interests and identities between different faith groups in Britain is identified in a recent academic study entitled 'Faith Communities in Public Action'. It looks particularly at the work of The East London Communities Organisation (TELCO), a broad-based community group in which Christian and Muslim congregations are particularly active and which has achieved considerable success in obtaining affordable housing, cleaner and safer streets and other environmental improvements in a deprived area of the capital. The study points to the way that community organizing offers Muslims, with their considerable concerns about the character of consumerist capitalism, 'a way of being a "contrast society" that is at once peaceable and in alliance with other faith groups in Britain, including Christianity' and also provides a way for Anglicans to retain their historic commitment to ministry for all, and not just the minority who attend church, and so continue to be a church for the whole nation and not become an inward-looking sect. It concludes that 'the faith communities involved in organizing are both distinct from the dominant culture and committed to working for the common good'.[27]

It may be that such fusions of the Islamic pursuit of social justice, Stanley Hauerwas' concept of Christians as 'resident aliens' and the established churches' concern for the good of the community as a whole offer one of the best and most practical hopes for promoting social cohesion and regeneration in some of the most divided and deprived parts of Britain.

9. More Support for the BBC

The BBC is one of the great bastions of Britishness, in its commitment to public service, its open, tolerant, fair-mindedness and the way it reflects Britain to itself in all its diversity, richness and eccentricity. It is extremely important that it is given adequate financial and other support by the Government in an era where broadcasting is becoming more and more commercial and also where narrowcasting and niche marketing is increasingly replacing the breadth and mixed programming traditionally associated with the BBC. There is a strong argument for giving the BBC exclusive rights to televise major national sporting events such as Test cricket, the FA Cup, Wimbledon and the Boat Race. It is also extremely important that in future financial settlements, its UK-wide radio networks, and Radio 4 in particular, the jewel in the BBC's crown in terms of its projection of British identity and values, are not just protected but promoted and given additional resources.

The BBC has recently been engaged in looking at how it might reflect the diversity and promote the coherence of Britain even more effectively. Its 'commitment to building public value' exercise, launched in 2005, was inspired by the belief expressed by the Chairman of the Governors, Michael Grade, that 'in an age of globalisation and social fragmentation, the BBC has a special role to play in bringing communities together, exploring and celebrating the cultures, languages and diversity which so characterize life in the United Kingdom.'[28] It has already led to more devolving of programme-making out of London, notably to Manchester.

What is important is that this process does not simply lead to more specifically local programmes and opting-out. What the BBC must continue to do is report and reflect on the whole of Britain to itself.

There is a particular role for the BBC in reflecting the strength of faith communities in Britain and their ability to provide the social glue which is so badly needed in an age of increasing fragmentation and isolation. Reference has already been made to *Songs of Praise*, BBC One's flagship religious programme, which at its best provides one of the very few opportunities on national television for 'ordinary' people to talk about and demonstrate their faith and the very extraordinary things that they are doing in and for their local communities. The 'Thought for the Day' slot in the *Today* programme on Radio 4 has been rightly described by Jonathan Sacks, the Chief Rabbi, as

> the most extraordinary agent of good community relations that Britain has ever had. You are allowed to speak to people who are not members of your own faith community – that's broadcasting as distinct from narrow casting …While television news and panel discussion tend to emphasize conflict and are structured in an adversarial mode, this radio slot is very healing.[29]

These and other programmes that reflect the diversity and vitality of the faith communities in Britain, and their contribution to social coherence and community, deserve to be protected and extended.

10. More Emphasis on Citizenship

The Government is right to be putting more emphasis on the concept of citizenship, teaching it as a core subject at school and making more of it through ceremonies. It may be sad, and seem somehow very un-British, that we are having to teach citizenship and emulate the USA in introducing initiation ceremonies for immigrants which involve taking an oath of allegiance and singing the National Anthem. However, the huge contemporary pressures pushing us towards being more selfish and less altruistic, quite apart from any other considerations arising from globalization and mass migration, make it highly expedient that the duties and responsibilities of citizenship are spelled out more clearly, as much to those who have lived in the country all their lives as to those more recently arrived. In an age where we are encouraged to be consumers above all else, and where choice is the great god, it is important that we are also reminded of the competing and contrasting role of being good citizens.

In fact, imaginatively conconceived and presented, the new citizenship ceremonies can enhance the sense of Britishness as a nest of shared identities and values embracing both diversity and coherence. Oxfordshire County Council has taken a lead in this area, devising a three-stage ceremony which begins with speeches from the Superintendent Registrar and the Lord Lieutenant, proceeds with the oath of allegiance to the sovereign and the pledge of loyalty and concludes with the presentation of certificates of British citizenship by the Lord Lieutenant and the singing of the National Anthem. The council has produced an excellent short explanatory DVD which explains the nature and purpose of the ceremony and contains some moving interviews with new British citizens about what it means to them.

The concept of citizenship has become very closely associated with the current debate about Britishness in the context of the Government's proposals for classes and tests both in the English language and in core British institutions and values for those seeking United Kingdom nationality. While there is considerable concern that these proposals, like the citizenship ceremonies which they are seen as leading up to, have been somewhat half-baked and inadequately funded, they have involved for the first time a serious attempt to define what is meant by British citizenship, and so, by implication, what it means to be British. One of the most concise formulations came from David Blunkett when Home Secretary:

> *To be British seems to us to mean that we respect the laws, the elected parliamentary and democratic political structures, traditional values of mutual tolerance, respect for equal rights and mutual concern; and that we give our allegiance to the state (as commonly symbolized in the Crown) in return for its protection. To be British is to respect those over-arching specific institutions, values, beliefs and traditions that bind us all, the different nations and cultures, together in peace and in a legal order.*[30]

This definition was fleshed out in the report of the Life in the United Kingdom advisory group chaired by Sir Bernard Crick, which reported to the Government in 2002. It recommended six broad categories in a programme of studies for those seeking British citizenship: British national institutions in recent historical context (which would include 'concepts of British political life including adherence to human rights, the values of toleration, fair play, freedom of speech and of the press and open government'); Britain as a multicultural society; knowing the law; employment; sources of help and information; and everyday needs. The emphasis here is solidly pragmatic and utilitarian, perhaps excessively so. The group considered the view, for example, that 'the required test should be in British history to create a sense of Britishness'. However, while accepting that 'some opening of a door to understanding the presuppositions and common allusions among the four historic nations of these islands is indeed needed,' it felt that 'history only becomes meaningful from the sense of obligation, of duties as well as rights, which should be the consequence of the pride and security of becoming a citizen.'[31]

In fact, it would be good to see those anxious to become British citizens being taught some British history, just as it would be good to see much more British (and Commonwealth) history taught in schools. It also seems quite reasonable that they should be taught and tested in the English language, as does the Government's requirement that imams and priests coming into Britain to preach be required to pass a language and citizenship test after they have been in the country for a year to demonstrate that they have engaged with British civic life and understood other faiths. Given the growing importance of faith as a key determinant of identity among minority groups, it is especially important that faith leaders are made aware of the central British values of toleration, fair play, freedom of speech, open government and the rule of law.

It is sometimes argued that Britain has a weak tradition of citizenship because the existence of a hereditary monarchy has promoted a political culture where the emphasis is on being subjects rather than citizens. In fact, it seems to me that the fact of being subjects of the Queen and owing loyalty to the Crown may well create a more tangible sense of belonging and a stronger concomitant set of rights and responsibilities than the more abstract and less personal status of citizenship. Rather unfashionably I would, indeed, want to argue that we should be emphasizing the status of Britons as subjects as well as citizens and that a dual approach, based on the personal, traditional and mystical ties of loyalty to the monarch in addition to the legal rights and responsibilities that go with citizenship is more likely to promote a greater sense of shared Britishness and common identity than simply concentrating on the fashionable idea of the citizen.

11. New Rituals

Ritual, like myth, is important in establishing, confirming and reinforcing national identity. It has been undervalued in modem Britain. Traditional rituals like the state opening of Parliament, Trooping the Colour and changing the guard at Buckingham Palace testify to the British love of pageantry, although it is probably fair to say that they engage more with overseas tourists than with the British themselves. Other more occasional rituals, particularly those associated with royalty, like coronations, state funerals and jubilee celebrations establish deeper connections, as was shown with the Queen's Jubilee celebrations and the funerals of both Diana, Princess of Wales and Queen Elizabeth, the Queen Mother. The annual Remembrance Day rituals which link the Queen, the established church, national political leaders, Commonwealth representatives and ex-servicemen at the Cenotaph with local church services and acts of remembrance at war memorials across the land still provide a powerful sense of national bonding and it is significant that key elements within them, like the two-minute silence, seem to be growing rather than diminishing in popularity, not least among young people. For some, they remain too militaristic and backward looking, but there have been creative attempts to produce new Remembrance liturgies which look forward and emphasize peace and reconciliation. We should not belittle the impact still made by these and other generally solemn and dignified church-run ceremonies, which evoke what has been disparagingly referred to as 'the transcendent God of the state occasion'. There are moments that call for transcendence, perhaps more now in our ever-more frenetic and fearful times than in more stable and secure days.

Other national rituals have recently been subjected to 'makeovers' aimed at diminishing their lofty transcendence and giving them a greater sense of populist imminence. Perhaps the most obvious example is the Last Night of the Proms, where the focus for television viewers at least is no longer simply on the Albert Hall but also on nearby Hyde Park, where a less high-brow diet of music is concocted by BBC Radio 2 under the title of *Proms in the Park*, and on the live offerings from Scotland, Wales and Northern Ireland. Whether these innovations have made the event more truly British and more inclusive and representative is a moot point but they signify a general trend, hugely encouraged by television's ability to bring together a series of live links and its unwillingness to dwell on any one image or subject for very long, to dethrone national institutions and events from their lofty London bases and make them more regionalized, participatory and interactive.

We need new national rituals. The Scottish Parliament's imaginative use of song, music and poetry for its inauguration ceremony and the opening of its new building and the hugely impressive and moving carnival parades down the Mall with the Gospel Choirs at their centrepiece to celebrate the Queen's Golden Jubilee provide hopeful pointers. Perhaps one significant new national event to which serious consideration should be given is the establishment of an annual UK Day. Britain is very unusual in not having a national day – it is not just more self-consciously jingoistic and patriotic nations like France, with Bastille Day, and the USA, with both Independence Day and Thanksgiving Day, that have a day to celebrate the nation: so do most other countries in the world. They often bring together people of different ethnic backgrounds who otherwise might never meet or speak for the rest of the year. This is certainly the recent experience of Australia Day for Australians with whom I have recently spoken. Australia Day, celebrated annually on 26 January, began as a way of bridging isolated communities separated by the country's vast geographical extent. With increasing immigration into the country, it has become important as a simultaneous celebration of national unity and cultural diversity. In 1979, a national Australia Day council was set up to promote local grassroots involvement and ensure that the day was not Simply hijacked by politicians. Jeremy Paxman has rightly observed that the 'Orange parades in Northern Ireland, those booming swaggering marches every 12 July are almost the only popular rituals to celebrate Britishness in the British Isles'. [32]

There is much to be said for setting aside a day to celebrate the United Kingdom in its wonderful perichoretic, overlapping diversity and unity. Gordon Brown's call for the institution of a 'British Day' in his 2006 Fabian lecture provoked considerable media interest and led to several suggestions as to when it might best be celebrated. A poll conducted by the BBC found that the most popular date was June 15, the day of the signing of Magna Carta in 1215, an encouraging vote of confidence in the continuing identification of Britishness with the principles of freedom and liberty. Other popular suggestions were May 8 (VE Day), 6 June (D-Day), 21 October (Trafalgar Day) and 11 November (Remembrance Day, suggested by Brown himself as the best occasion for a celebration of Britishness) but they are perhaps rather too militaristic anniversaries for this purpose. Adopting Aidan as the UK's patron saint would allow a British national day to be celebrated on his feast day of 31 August, coinciding with the late summer Bank Holiday, as well as providing a reminder of the nation's spiritual foundations. More discussion on this would be good.

Whether we need, as David Goodhart suggested in his *Prospect* article, a British State of the Union address is more debatable. If something along these lines were to be introduced, it would be better for it to come from the monarch and follow the example of the Queen's Christmas broadcast rather than the model of a Prime Ministerial broadcast. Indeed, in many ways the Queen's annual speech to the United Kingdom and the Commonwealth on Christmas Day does serve the purpose of a state of the union address and this is another reason for cherishing and promoting this inspired Reithian initiative.

12. A Museum or Institute of Britishness?

Gordon Brown has proposed the establishment of an Institute of Britishness. It does seem bizarre in many ways that while there are departments of Scottish, Welsh, Irish and English studies in UK universities, the discipline of British studies seems largely to be confined to North American and other overseas universities. Perhaps we also need a museum of Britishness. The British Museum hardly fills that role, being filled with Egyptian and Greek antiquities rather than chronicling and celebrating the overlapping and changing identities of Britain. There is no museum devoted to Englishness either, although the splendid newly extended National Museum of Scotland in Edinburgh shows how the history and character of a nation can be put across imaginatively and attractively.

Another model for a museum expressing the distinctive values and ethos of a nation is the National Constitution Center in Philadelphia which is dedicated to exploring and explaining the principles of the United States constitution in a way that is both friendly and challenging. A visit there begins with 'Freedom Rising', a live dramatic presentation in which an actor darts around a multi-media set telling the story of the drafting of the US Constitution and ends with the challenge 'Now it is our decision – what will we do with our freedom?' The galleries in the main exhibit hall devoted to 'The American Experience' have numerous interactive features, which allow visitors to be sworn in as president, serve on a jury, try on a judge's robe, vote for their favourite president and add a name to the National Tree which celebrates distinguished Americans. Visitors are encouraged to express their own thoughts by writing and putting up stickers answering such questions as 'Tell us, what does it mean to be an American?' and contacting their elected representatives through Internet terminals. The whole tone is more evangelical and self-congratulatory than one could ever imagine in Britain, with themed areas given such titles as 'Perfect Union', 'Domestic Tranquility', 'Common Defense' and 'Blessings of Liberty'. Even the impeachment of Bill Clinton and the close result of the 2000 presidential election are hailed as great triumphs for democracy. At the end of the exhibition, there are three large debate boards on which comments are invited to topical questions. When I visited the Center, these were 'Should the Ten Commandments be posted on public buildings?' (to which the response was overwhelmingly affirmative), 'Should individuals continue to have the right to carry guns?' (which drew an overwhelmingly negative response) and 'Is the balance of security and freedom right in the Patriot Act introduced in the wake of 9/11?' (no clear view).

Given the drive to focus more on the duties and responsibilities of British citizenship, there is something to be said for having a similar museum devoted to the nature of the United Kingdom constitution and way of life. Indeed, a visit there could be an important component of the citizenship classes being undertaken by those seeking UK nationality. An existing museum which might also feature on their itinerary is the St Mungo Museum of Religious Life in Glasgow, dedicated to the local Celtic saint but pluralistic in its objectives and outlook, exploring how different themes and rites of passage are tackled in the world's major faiths. Other nations have chosen more dramatic ways to explore and express their national identity. Canada emphasizes its openness and multiculturalism in a *son et lumiere* presentation which plays out against the backdrop of the Parliament buildings in Ottawa every evening in the summer months. The nation's identity is expressed as a story told by the wind blowing over the landscape which gives it a primal, spiritual feel and also emphasizes the themes of youth, movement, generosity and tolerance. This acknowledgement of spiritual and physical forces in forming the country's character is balanced by the solid Victorian Gothic of the buildings on which the images are projected. During the day, a very British element of pomp, pageantry and heritage is added by the changing of the guard by young volunteers in bearskins and redcoats on the lawns outside and official tours of the Parliament buildings are enlivened by the appearance of actors impersonating key figures from the country's past. Even the rather smelly collection of wooden huts behind the Parliament buildings built in the 1970s as a refuge for the numerous stray cats in the capital is enlisted as a symbol of the nation's character. The official guide to the Parliament Hill points out that 'The juxtaposition of the formality, pomp and ceremony of the Parliament Buildings and the modest cat sanctuary reflects the important Canadian values of tolerance and compassion.'

It is hard to imagine Britain indulging in anything quite like this but in an age where image, icon and symbol are increasingly important, we do need to think creatively about ways in which we can engage young people to visualize, connect with and believe in Britishness. We should not be afraid of appealing to their imaginations and their romantic and spiritual yearnings. In our image-led, postmodern culture, we need to be re-presenting myths and stories that give shape to our national identity and developing new icons of diversity. This book has surveyed some of the different streams that have fed into and are feeding into Britishness and their essentially spiritual nature. They are diverse and they encourage a sense of hybrid or hyphenated identity but they also overlap and speak of a sum that is greater than its parts and of a unity which transcends the diversity. There is a growing consensus on both left and right of the political spectrum, among liberals as much as among conservatives, that we do need a greater assertion of Britishness. As Jonathan Freedland, the *Guardian* columnist, wrote in the wake of the July 2005 London bombings, after quoting the complaints of Muslim commentators that Britishness is so downplayed and denigrated by the British themselves that it is hardly surprising if young Muslims brought up here look elsewhere for their identity:

> *In Britain, liberals especially have striven so hard to accept that people are Scottish or Jewish or Asian, they may have forgotten that they are also British. For bothness to work, you have to have both. In other words, we let the British part of the equation lapse. We were frightened of it, fearing that it reeked of compulsion or white-only exclusivity. But Britishness need not be like that ... The challenge is to forge a Britishness which welcomes difference – but which is not so loose, so nebulous that it leaves a hole where national identity should be.*[33]

This book has sought to work out and present one possible understanding of Britishness – as a set of shifting and overlapping spiritual identities. In a sense this is quite a minimalist vision – it does not go for assimilation, perhaps just for limited integration. But nor does it pose or predicate separate development and parallel lives. I believe it is realistic. It looks for overlap rather than coherence around great principles, including the principle of multiculturalism as it has been set forth by some of its more naive proponents. I strongly agree with Jock Young, Visiting Professor of Sociology at the University of Kent:

> *Conventional multiculturalism encourages differences which often do not exist; and insists on ethnic, nationalist and religious pigeon-holing which ignores the multi-faceted experience and identities of people living in the real world. It occludes the actual overlaps, blurring and hybridization of cultures, as well as of the common cross-cutting interests which people share.*
>
> *A genuine culture of diversity would not engage in binaries (Muslim/ Christian or black/white) but would encourage a pluralism of cultures which borrow and bricolage from each other. It would celebrate diversity and seek to achieve common values.*[34]

The overlapping identities that are already contributing to remoulding and reshaping that infinitely malleable and expandable entity that is Britishness take many forms, by no means all of them spiritual. Nor do they necessarily involve communities or groups – they can be highly individualistic and to that extent very postmodern. They are forged in queues at Tesco's, in doctors' waiting rooms and on trains and buses as well as through more conscious expressions of solidarity like inter-faith campaigns against the Iraq war, Make Poverty History rallies or Countryside Alliance marches. I think of the trio of students, one Scottish, one English and one from Northern Ireland, respectively a Jew, a Muslim and a Christian, who were washing up together after an inter-faith gathering at the University Chaplaincy where I work and cheerfully complaining together about the inadequate size of the sink. Somehow their communal grouse summed up for me what it is to believe in Britain, that understated, un-selfconscious identity which so strangely and yet so wonderfully embodies the Trinitarian principle of perichoresis and unity through diversity.

Notes

Chapter 1. Believing in Britain

1. A MORI poll for *The Economist* in 1999 revealed that only 18 per cent of Scots and 27 per cent of Welsh respondents identified themselves as British. Among English respondents, the proportion was 43 per cent but 41 per cent described themselves as English. Surveys analysed by Ross Bond and Michael Rosie ('National Identities in Post-Devolution Scotland', Institute of Governance, Edinburgh University, June 20(02), show that whereas, in 1979, 38 per cent of Scots said that 'British' best described their nationality while 56 per cent opted for 'Scottish', by 2001 the proportions were respectively 16 per cent and 77 per cent. Young people seem to feel noticeably less British than their elders. A citizenship poll carried out by ICM Polls among 14 to 16 year olds and their teachers at the end of 2004 found that 64 per cent of the students and 81 per cent of the teachers considered themselves to be British, while the proportions considering themselves to be English were 34 per cent and 12 per cent.

2. P. Ward, *Britishness since 1870* (London: Routledge, 2004), p. 1.

3. *The Times*, 19 July 2004.

4. BBC News online, 11 October 2000.

5. See also Blunkett's article 'For far too long we have left patriotism to the extremists', *The Guardian*, 19 March 2005.

6. G. Brown, speech to British Council, 7 July 2004.

7. H. Goulbourne, *Ethnicity and Nationalism in Post-Imperial Britain* (Cambridge: Cambridge University Press, 1991), p. 70.

8. A. Smith, Chosen Peoples: Sacred Sources of National Identity (Oxford: Oxford University Press, 2003), p. 25.

9. C. Longley, *Chosen People: Anglo-American Myth and Reality* (London: Hodder and Stoughton, 2002), p. 10.

10. Quoted in Ward, *Britishness since 1870*, p. 156.

11. M. Wills, 'What Defines British Values', in P. Griffin and M. Leonard (eds.), *Reclaiming Britishness* (London: Foreign Policy Centre, 2002), p. 17.

12. G. Brown, speech to British Council, 7 July 2004.

13. J. Paxman, *The English* (London: Penguin Books, 1999), p. 240.

14. 'Britishness in the 21st Century', lecture at the London School of Economics, 8 December 1999, p. 7.

15. Y. Alibhai-Brown, 'The Excluded Majority: What about the English?', in Griffin and Leonard (eds.), *Reclaiming Britishness*, p. 45.

16. Y. Alibhai-Brown, *The Independent*, 12 September 2005.

17. Y. Alibhai-Brown, *After Multiculturalism* (London: Foreign Policy Centre, 2000), p. 5.

18. *The Guardian*, 21 January 2005.

19. H. Goulbourne, *Ethnicity and Nationalism*, pp. 236-37.

20. Interview with Ted Cantle, *Society Guardian*, 21 September 2005.

21. D. Goodhart, 'Discomfort of Strangers', *The Guardian*, 24 February 2004.

22. *The Guardian*, 26 February 2004.

23. *The Guardian*, 23 September 2005.

24. *The Guardian*, 3 August 2005.

25. T. Modood, talk at Edinburgh Book Festival, 23 August 2005.

26. Qur'an, Surah 11:117, 49:13. This somewhat neglected aspect of Islam is usefully highlighted and explored in Dilwar Hussain, 'Can Islam make us British?', in M. Bunting (ed.), *Islam, Race and Being British* (London: The Guardian/Barrow Cadbury Trust, 2005), p. 40.

27. J. Moltmann, *The Trinity and the Kingdom of God* (London: SCM Press, 1981), pp. 198, 202, 216. Moltmann's doctrine of the Trinity is quoted and applied to Northern Ireland in J. Dunlop, 'A Turning Point in Ireland and Scotland? The Challenge to the Churches and Theology' (Lecture to Centre for Theology and Public Issues, New College, Edinburgh, 27 February 1998). It is also picked up by Murdoch Mackenzie in 'Integrity and Identity', The Maitland Memorial Lecture 2004, also at New College, Edinburgh.

28. Translation by Noel Dermot O'Donoghue in J. Mackey (ed.), *An Introduction to Celtic Christianity* (Edinburgh: T and T Clark, 1989), p. 47.

29. Translation by Tom Clancy in T. Clancy and G. Markus, *Iona: The Earliest Poetry of a Celtic Monastery* (Edinburgh: Edinburgh University Press, 1995), p. 45.

30. M. Kenny, in *The Times*, 9 November 2004.

31. B. Maddox, 'I'm glad to be here', *The Guardian*, 28 September 2001.

32. Press release for 'Take Down the Union Jack' (Mediamorphosis.co.uk).

33. D. Jenkins, *The British: Their Identity and Their Religion* (London: SCM Press, 1975), p.8.

34. Ibid. pp. 157, 136.

35. Ibid. pp. 8-9.

36. Ibid. p. xi.

37. A. Smith, *Chosen Peoples*, pp. 122-23.

38. F. Bacon, *Life and Letters* (London: Longman, Green and Roberts, 1857) Vol. 10: 3, p. 228

39. D. Hume, *The British Union* (Aldershot: Ashgate, 2002).

40. A. Nicolson, *Power and Glory* (London: Harper Perennial, 2003), pp. 63, 77.

41. B. Crick, in *The Guardian*, 12 April 2004.

Chapter 2. Red, White and Blue – What Does It Mean to You?

1. B. Crick in *The Guardian*, 12 April 2004.

2. L. Colley, 'Britishness in the 21" Century', lecture at London School of Economics, 8 December 1999, pp. 4-5.

3. Report of 'Life in the UK' Working Party, Home Office Website, 2003, p. 3.

4. M. Howard in *The Guardian*, 17 August 2005.

5. G. Brown, speech to British Council, 7 July 2004, p. 3.

6. B. Bradshaw and P. Roberts, *British Consciousness and Identity* (Cambridge: Cambridge University Press, 1998), p. 3.

7. Quoted in C. Kidd, *British Identities before Nationalism* (Cambridge: Cambridge University Press, 1999), p. 77.

8. T. Phillips in *The Guardian*, 4 September 2003.

9. In 'What is Britishness anyway?', BBC News online, 10 September 2002.

10. D. Lammy, 'Rediscovering Internationalism', in *Reclaiming Britishness*, p. 6.

11. M. Wills, 'What Defines British Values?', in *Reclaiming Britishness*, p. 16.

12. W. C. Sellar and R. J. Yeatman, *1066 and All That* (Harmondsworth: Penguin Books, 1960), p. 13.

13. Speech to British Council, 7 July 2004, p. 3.

14. M. Leonard, in *Reclaiming Britishness*, p. xv.

15. J. Paxman, *The English*, p. 240.

16. Student Room Forum website.

17. Billy Bragg and the Blokes, *England, Half English* (2002).

18. R. Holt, *Sport and the British* (Oxford: Oxford University Press, 1989), pp. 6, 11.

19. M. McLaren in *The Guardian*, 20 March 2004.

20. G. Brown, speech to British Council, 7 July 2004, p. 4.

21. M. Porter, 'Don't ever lose your Britishness', *Daily Mail*, 25 July 1995.

22. In *The Guardian*, 23 March 2005 .

23. G. Davie, *Religion in Britain Since 1945* (Oxford: Blackwell, 1994); S. Bruce and T. Glendinning, 'Shock Report', *Life and Work*, June 2002.

24. J. Major, speech to Conservative Group for Europe, 22 April 1993.

25. E. Jacobs and R. Worcester, *We British: Britain Under the MORIscope* (London: Weidenfeld and Nicolson, 1990).

26. L. Woodhead and P. Heelas, *The Spiritual Rvolution* (Oxford: Blackwell, 2005).

27. In *The Times*, 22 July 2004, p. 34.

Chapter 3. The Celtic Spirit

1. J. F. Dimmock (ed.), *Expugnatio Hibernca*, Vol. V (Rolls Series, 1867), p. 351; J. Boswell (ed.), *Journal of a Tour of the Hebrides* (London: Heinemann, 1963), p. 3.

2. M. Pittock, *Celtic Identity and the British Image* (Manchester: Manchester University Press, 1999), p. 11.

3. *Ibid.* p. 104.

4. J. Adamson, 'The Queen of British Hearts', *Sunday Telegraph*, 6 March 2005, p. 5. On Boudicca, see R. Hingley and C. Unwin, *Boudica: Iron Age Warrior Queen* (Hambledon and London, 2005).

5. P. Thomas, *Candle in the Darkness: Celtic Spirituality in Wales* (Lladysul: Gomer, 1993), p.19.

6. D. Jenkins, *The British*, pp. 56, 156.

7. See M. Dresser, 'Britannia', in R. Samuel (ed.), *Patriotism: The Making and Unmaking of British Identity*, Vol. III (London: Routledge, 1989).

8. J. A. Giles (ed.), *Six Old English Chronicles* (London: Henry G. Bohn, 1848), pp. 300, 307.

9. J. McClure and R. Collins (eds.), *Bede's Ecclesiastical History of the English People* (Oxford: World's Classics, 1969), p. 290.

10. I have developed this theme and much else in this chapter in my book *Celtic Christianity: Making Myths and Dreaming Dreams* (Edinburgh: Edinburgh University Press, 1999).

11. R. Van de Weyer, *Celtic Fire* (London: Darton, Longman and Todd, 1990), pp. 11-12.

12. Geoffrey of Monmouth, *The History of the Kings of Britain* (Harmondsworth: Penguin Classics, 1966), p. 53.

13. *Ibid.* p. 54.

14. A. Smith, *Chosen Peoples*, p. 182.

15. J. Richards, 'Robin Hood, Arthur and Cold War Chivalry' (draft paper from the author), f.32. On the cult of Arthur, see A. MacColl, *History Today*, March 1999, pp. 7-13.

16. G. Ashe, *King Arthur's Avalon: The Story of Glastonbury* (London: Fontana, 1990), p. 241.

17. J. Perkins, *The Crowning of the Sovereign* (London: Methuen, 1937), p. 60.

18. P. Roberts, 'Wales and the British Inheritance', in B. Bradshaw and P. Roberts (eds.), *British Consciousness and Identity: The Making of Britain, 1533-1707* (Cambridge: Cambridge University Press, 1998), p. 8. For the Britishness of Wales in this period, see also G. Williams, *Recovery, Reorientation and Reformation: Wales c.1415-1642* (Oxford: Oxford University Press, 1987).

19. P. Roberts, 'Wales and the British Inheritance', p. 20.

20. *Ibid.* p. 39; M. Pittock, *Celtic Identity*, p. 17.

21. On this, see M. Caball, 'Irish nationality, 1558-1625', in Bradshaw and Roberts, *British Consciousness*.

22. S. Piggott, The Druids (London: Thames and Hudson, 1968), p. 171; E. Davies, *Mythology of the British Druids* (privately printed for author, 1809), pp. 479, 497.

23. M. Arnold, *The Study of Celtic Literature* (London: Smith, Elder and Co., 1891), pp. 11, 7, 177-78.

24. T. Burgess, *Tracts on the Origin and Independence of the Ancient British Church* (London: F. C. and J. Rivington, 1815), p. 143.

25. G. T. Stokes, *Ireland and the Celtic Church* (London: Hodder and Stoughton, 1886).

26. S. J. Stone, *Lays of Iona and Other Poems* (London: Longmans, Green, 1897), P: xix.

27. *Ibid.* p. 6.

28. R. B. Foster, *W B. Yeats: A Life*, Vol. I (Oxford: Oxford University Press, 1997), p. 129.

29. C. Davis, *The Art of Celtia* (London: Blandford, 1994), p. 8.

30. On this, see D. Lorimer, *Radical Prince* (Edinburgh: Floris Books, 2003).

31. R. Simpson, *Church of the Isles: A Prophetic Strategy for Renewal* (Stowmarket: Kevin Mayhew, 2003), p. 160.

Chapter 4. Liberty, Tolerance and Indifference

1. G. Brown, British Council lecture, 7 July 2004.

2. Z. Nadjer, *Conrad's Political Background* (London: 1964), p. 232.

3. E. Dodds and E. Reiss, *The Logic of Liberty* (Unservile State Papers, no date), p. 3.

4. G. Watson, *The English Ideology* (London: Allen Lane, 1973), P: 10.

5. *Ibid.* p. 48.

6. L. Colley, *Britons: Forging the Nations, 1707-1837* (New Haven: Yale University Press, 1992), pp. 357-58.

7. J. Clark, 'Protestantism, Nationalism and National Identity, 1660-1832' (*Historical Journal*, 2000), p. 262.

8. P. Wormald, 'The Venerable Bede and the Church of England', in D. G. Rowell (ed.), *The English Religious Tradition* (Wantage: Ikon, 1992).

9. Quoted in A. Hastings, *The Constitution of Nationhood* (Cambridge: Cambridge

University Press, 1997), p. 50.

10. A. D. Smith, *Chosen Peoples: Sacred Sources of National Identity* (Oxford: Oxford University Press, 2003), p. 125.

11. *Ibid.* p. 126.

12. J. Clark, 'Protestantism', p. 67.

13. See especially A. MacColl, 'Legendary History and the Construction of "British" Protestantism in Sixteenth Century England'.

14. C. Longley, *Chosen Peoples*, p. 65.

15. Introduction, *The First English Prayer Book* (Alresford: Arthur James, 1999), p. xi.

16. J. Bennett, *Reviving Liberty: Radical Christian Humanism in Milton's Great Poems* (Harvard University Press, 1989).

17. S. Jeffries, 'If only we were more like the French', *The Guardian*, 31 January 2005.

18. M. Kettle, 'Socialism is dead. Long live liberalism and social justice', *The Guardian*, 26 October 2004.

19. Quoted in C. Kidd, 'Protestantism and British Identity', in Bradshaw and Roberts, *British Consciousness*, p. 338.

20. *Ibid.* pp. 336, 338.

21. *Ibid.* p. 341.

22. C. Kidd, *British Identity Before Nationalism* (Cambridge: Cambridge University Press, 1999), p. 75.

23. *Ibid.* pp. 93, 105.

24. *Ibid.* p. 283.

25. J. Clark, 'Protestantism', p. 275.

26. J. C. D. Clark, *The Language of Liberty, 1660-1832* (Cambridge: Cambridge University Press, 1994), p. 18.

27. C. Kidd, 'Protestantism and British Identity', p. 339.

28. W. Blake, *A Selection of Poems* (Harmondsworth: Penguin Books, 1958), pp. 176, 199.

29. *The Times*, 2 March 1916.

30. W. Wordsworth, *Poems Dedicated to National Independence and Liberty, XVI* (1807).

31. E. Burke, *The Works* (Oxford: World's Classics, 1906-1907), pp. iv, 34-35.

32. Quoted in Watson, *The English Ideology*, p. 12.

33. L. Lipson, 'The two party system in British polities', *American Political Science Review*, Vol. 47 (1953), p. 353.

34. Quoted in W. H. Greenleaf, *The British Political Tradition*, Vol. 2: The Ideological Heritage (London: Methuen, 1983), p. 26.

35. Quoted in I. Bradley, *The Optimists: Themes and Personalities in Victorian Liberalism* (London: Faber, 1980), p. 104.

36. Quoted in V. Bogdanor (ed.), *Liberal Party Politics* (Oxford: Oxford University Press, 1983), p. 16.

37. In *The Guardian*, 9 February 2005.

38. Quoted in I. Bradley, *Marching to the Promised Land: Has the Church a Future?* (London: John Murray, 1992), p. 220-21.

39. W. Rees-Mogg, 'proud to be English', *The Times*, 14 October 1993.

40. A. Hastings, 'The Case for Retaining the Establishment', in T. Modood (ed.), *Church, State and Religious Minorities* (London: Policy Studies Institute, 1997), P: 42.

41. R. Page, 'Divine Grace and Church Establishment', in *Theology*, Vol. XCI (July 1988), p. 284.

42. A. Suggate, *William Temple and Christian Social Ethics Today* (Edinburgh: T and T Clark, 1987), pp. 4-5.

43. J. Morley, *On Compromise* (1913 edition), p. 127.

44. S. Jeffries, *The Guardian*, 3 October 2005.

45. M. Kettle, 'New Labour must find its way back to liberal England', *The Guardian*, 22 March 2005.

46. M. Kinsley, 'Constitution can't match British reverence for rights', *Philadelphia Sun*, 11 November 2005.

47. S. Chakrabarti, 'Freedom Fighter', *The Guardian*, 10 December 2005.

Chapter 5. Moral Fibre and Muscular Christianity

1. S. Howe, 'Loyalism's rage against the fading light of Britishness', *The Guardian*, 10 October 2005.

2. D. Jenkins, *The British*, p. 135.

3. G. Brown, British Council speech, 7 July 2004. See also his speech reported in *The Guardian*, 19 March 2005.

4. R. Crawford, *Devolving English Literature* (2nd edition, Edinburgh: Edinburgh

University Press, 2000), pp. 18, 24.

5. *Ibid.* p. 46.

6. J. Thomson, *Complete Poetical Works* (Oxford: Oxford University Press, 1908), p. 394.

7. *Ibid.* p. 395.

8. *Saturday Review*, 21 February 1857.

9. D. Hall, *Muscular Christianity: Embodying the Victorian Age* (Cambridge: Cambridge University Press, 1994), pp. 67, 72.

10. J. Pennington, 'Muscular Spirituality in George MacDonald's Curdie Books', in Hall, *Muscular Christianity*.

11. N. MacLeod, *Reminiscences of a Highland Parish* (Alex Strahan, 1867), p. 42.

12. Quoted in M. Girouard, *The Return to Camelot* (New Haven: Yale University Press, 1981), p. 64.

13. *Ibid.*

14. R. Holt, *Sport and the British*, p. 81.

15. *Ibid.* p. 220.

16. J. Cooper, *A United Church for the British Empire* (Forres, 1902), pp. 11-12; *Reunion: A Voice from Scotland* (London: Robert Scott, 1918), pp. 69, 71.

17. A. Lownie, *John Buchan: A Presbyterian Cavalier* (Edinburgh: Canongate, 1987), p. 227.

18. A. Buchan, *Unforgettable, Unforgotten* (London: Hodder and Stoughton, 1945), p. 14.

19. J. Buchan, *The Half-Hearted* (London: Hodder' and Stoughton, 1900).

20. A. Lownie, *John Buchan*, p. 228.

21. *The Spectator*, 30 August 1975.

22. J. Buchan, 'Men and Deeds: Montrose', quoted in *The Clearing House: A Survey of One Man's Mind. A Selection from the Writings of John Buchan* (London: Hodder and Stoughton, 1946), p. 182.

23. J. Buchan, *The Half-Hearted*, p. 175.

24. A. Lownie, *John Buchan*, p. 170.

25. J. Buchan, *The Half-Hearted*, pp. 175-76.

26. A. Lownie, *John Buchan*, p. 175.

27. J. Buchan, *Midwinter*, Chapter 1.

28. J. C. W. Reith, *Into The Wind* (London: Hodder and Stoughton, 1949), p. 531.

29. J. C. W. Reith, *The Reith Diaries*, ed. C. Stuart (London: Collins, 1975), diary entry,

10 January 1964, p. 510.

30. I. McIntyre, *The Expense of Glory. A Life of John Reith* (London: HarperCollins, 1993), p. 187.

31. A. Boyle, *Only the Wind Will Listen: Reith of the BBC* (London: Hutchison, 1972), p. 174.

32. I. McIntyre, *The Expense of Glory*, pp. 145-46.

33. J. C. W. Reith, *Into the Wind*, p. 169.

34. R. Holt, *Sport and the British*, pp. 311-12.

35. Quoted in I. Bradley; *Marching to the Promised Land: Has the Church a Future?* (London: John Murray, 1990), p. 128.

36. Quoted in C. Bryant (ed.), *Reclaiming the Ground* (London: Spire, 1993), p. 127.

Chapter 6. Carnival and Reserve

1. P. Gilroy, After Empire (London: Routledge, 2004), p. 13.

2. T. Modood, 'Muslims and the Politics of Multiculturalism in Britain', in E. Hershberg and K. W. Moore (eds.), *Critical Views of September 11* (New York: New Press, 2002), p. 206.

3. B. Parekh, 'British Commitments', *Prospect* (September 2005), p. 40.

4. *The Times*, 2 January 2004.

5. *The Guardian*, 17 August 2005.

6. *Prospect*, September 2005, p. 40.

7. *The Guardian*, 12 June 2004.

8. Figures extrapolated from The Fourth National Survey of Ethnic Minorities in Britain (1997) and Religious Trends (2002). See 'Muslims will soon outnumber Anglicans', *Sunday Telegraph*, 28 October 2001.

9. T. Modood, 'New Forms of Britishness: Post Immigration Ethnicity and Hybridity in Britain', in R. Lentin (ed.), *The Expanding Nation: Towards a Multi-Ethnic Ireland* (Dublin: Trinity College, 1999), p. 4.

10. *The Guardian*, 21 March 2005.

11. *New Yorker*, 28 April 1997.

12. S. Hall, 'Aspiration and Attitude: Reflections on Black Britain in the Nineties', *New Formations*, 33 (Spring 1998), p. 39.

13. N. Toulis, *Believing Identity: Pentecostalism and the Mediation of Jamaican Ethnicity and*

Gender in England (Oxford: Berg, 1997), p. 25.

14. *Ibid.* pp. 180, 210, 121.

15. Griffin and Leonard (eds.), *Reclaiming Britishness*, p. 9.

16. *The Times*, 3 April 2004.

17. *Ibid.*

18. *The Guardian*, 11 January 2005.

19. 'Young, Muslim and British', *The Guardian*, 30 November 2004.

20. *The Times*, 16 November 2002.

21. *The Guardian*, 30 November 2004.

22. IHRC Website, press release posted 22 November 2004.

23. *The Guardian*, 7 April 2004.

24. D. Hussain, 'Can Islam Make Us British?' in M. Bunting (ed.), *Islam, Race and Being British* (London: Barrow Cadbury Trust, 2005), p. 37. See also Hussain's paper on British Muslim Identity, f. 23.

25. *Ibid.* pp. 10, 40-41.

26. *The Guardian*, 21 January 2005.

27. Research by Anjoom Mukadam and Sharmina Mawani, presented at Spiritual Identities conference, Lancaster University, November 2004.

28. A. Saeed, N. Blain and D. Forbes, 'New ethnic and national questions in Scotland: Post British identities among Glasgow Pakistani teenagers', *Ethnic and Racial Studies*, Vol. 22 (1999), p. 824.

29. T. Modood, *Not Easy Being British* (London: Runnymede Trust and Trentham Books, 1992), p. 3.

30. T. Modood, *Multicultural Politics* (Edinburgh: Edinburgh University Press, 2005), p. 211.

31. T. Modood, *Not Easy Being British*, p. 4.

32. T. Modood, 'The Rise of St. George', *Western Mail* (n.d.), sent by the author.

33. T. Modood, 'Anti-Essentialism, Multiculturalism and the "Recognition" of Religious Groups', *Journal of Political Philosophy*, Vol. 6, No.4 (December 1998), p. 378.

34. *Ibid.* p. 389.

35. T. Modood, 'New Forms of Britishness', p. 10.

36. T. Modood, *Multicultural Politics*, p. 193.

37. T. Modood, talk at Edinburgh Book Festival, 23 August 2005.

38. *The Guardian*, 21 March 2003.

39. *The Guardian*, 27 April 2005.

40. J. Sacks, *The Persistence of Faith* (London: Wiedenfeld and Nicolson, 1991). The quotations from Sacks' lectures used here can also be found in my book, *Marching to the Promised Land*, pp. 214-15.

41. Religious Resource and Research Centre, Religious Discrimination Project: Interim Report (Derby: University of Derby; 2000).

42. T. Modood (ed.), *Church, State and Religious Minorities* (Policy Studies Institute, 1997), pp.56-57.

43. *Ibid.* p. 67.

44. *Ibid.* p. 83.

45. *Ibid.* p. 84.

46. *Ibid.* p. 87.

47. B. Parekh, *Rethinking Multiculturalism: Cultural Diversity and Political Theory* (Basingstoke: Palgrave, 2000), p. 260.

48. *The Guardian*, 21 January 2005.

49. In M. Bunting (ed.), *Islam, Race and Being British*, p. 11.

50. *The Times*, 26 July 2005.

51. In Griffin and Leonard (eds.), *Reclaiming Britishness*, p. 52.

Chapter 7. Wider Still and Wider

1. R. Simpson, *Church of the Isles* (Stowmarket: Kevin Mayhew, 2003), pp. 173, 175.

2. D. Goodhart, 'Discomfort of Strangers', *The Guardian*, 24 February 2004.

3. D. Blunkett, 'One Nation – Many Faiths. Unity and Diversity in a Multi-Faith Britain' (Heslington Lecture, University of York, 30 October 2003), typescript, p. 4.

4. P. Lewis, 'Muslims in Europe: Managing Multiple Identities and Learning Shared Citizenship', Political Theology, Vol. 6, No.3 (July 2005), p. 350.

5. T. Modood, 'New Forms of Britishness', p. 9.

6. *Ibid.* p. 10.

7. T. Modood, *Not Easy Being British*, pp. 4, 9.

8. R. Williams, 'Convictions, Loyalty and the Secular State' (Chatham Lecture, Trinity College, Oxford, 29 October 2004). Text

from the *Church Times* website.

9. P. Toynbee, *The Guardian*, 15 August 2003.

10. J. Habgood, *Church and Nation in a Secular Age* (London: Darton, Longman and Todd, 1983), p. 30.

11. W. Bagehot, *The English Constitution* (Oxford: World's Classics Edition, Oxford University Press, 1928), pp. 35, 39, 40.

12. E. Shils and M. Young, 'The Meaning of the Coronation', *Sociological Review*, New Series, Vol. I (1953), p. 67.

13. See, for example, the first four articles in *Political Theology*, Vol. 4, No.1 (November 2002).

14. I. Bradley, *God Save the Queen: The Spiritual Dimension of Monarchy* (London: Darton, Longman and Todd, 2002).

15. G. Orwell, *The Lion and the Unicorn*, quoted in Bunting (ed.), *Islam, Race and Being British*, p. 47.

16. C. Longley, *Chosen People*, pp. 20-21.

17. D. Jenkins, *The British: Their Identity and Their Religion*, p. 95.

18. *The Guardian*, 6 October 2005.

19. G. Carey; St George's Day Lecture (23 April 2002). Text on *Church Times* website.

20. J. S. Deol, 'Join Your Partners As Equals', *Church Times*, 31 December 2004, p. 7.

21. P. Coupland, 'Britain, Europe and Christendom in mid-Twentieth Century British Christian Thought', *Political Theology*, Vol. 6, No.3 (July 2005), p. 384.

22. Research carried out by Steven Sutcliffe of the Religious Studies Department, Edinburgh University and presented to a seminar of the Centre for the Study of Religion and Politics in St Andrews University, 27 October 2005.

23. Reported in *The Guardian*, 18 January 2005.

24. P. Lewis, 'Muslims in Europe', p. 351.

25. Reported in *The Guardian*, 23 September 2005.

26. D. Partridge, 'Why I pray at the mosque', *Church Times*, 25 November 2005.

27. S. Deneulin, D. Hussain and A. Ritchie, 'Faith Communities in Public Action: Community Organizing as a British Case Study', paper presented at the Von Hugel Institute conference on 'Faith's Public Role: Politics and Theology', St Edmund's College, Cambridge, April 2005.

28. Building Public Value (BBC, 2005), p. 3.

29. Interview in *Life and Work* (magazine of the Church of Scotland), November 2005, p.14.

30. Speech by David Blunkett, 9 September 2002.

31. Home Office Immigration and Nationality Directorate website.

32. J. Paxman, *The English*, p. 30.

33. J. Freedland, 'The identity vacuum', *The Guardian*, 3 August 2005.

34. J. Young, in *The Guardian*, 10 November 2005.

Index

256